JANE FOSTER

VALKYRIE

the Sacred and the Profane

FOR YEARS, DR. JANE FOSTER WAS A FRIEND AND CONFIDANTE TO THE MIGHTY THOR. FOR A TIME, SHE EVEN WIELDED THOR'S HAMMER AS THE GODDESS OF THUNDER. AND WHEN MALEKITH'S WAR OF THE REALMS FINALLY CAME TO MIDGARD, ASGARD CALLED ON JANE ONCE MORE. SHE PICKED UP THE HAMMER OF THE WAR THOR, THE THOR OF A DIFFERENT UNIVERSE, AND ONCE AGAIN COMMANDED THE THUNDER.

MALEKITH'S WAR REACHED NOT ONLY THE REALMS OF THE LIVING BUT ALSO THE DEAD: HIS ARMIES KILLED THE VALKYRIES, THE WARRIOR GODDESSES WHO ONCE FERRIED THE HONORABLE FALLEN TO THEIR ETERNAL REWARD IN VALHALLA.

WHEN THE WAR FINALLY DID END, JANE'S HAMMER SHATTERED — AND RE-FORMED INTO THE ALL-WEAPON. FATE HAD A NEW ROLE FOR JANE FOSTER. NOW SHE WIELDS NOT THUNDER, BUT DEATH. AND LIFE. AND EVERYTHING IN BETWEEN.

SHE IS THE LAST OF THE VALKYRIES. AND THE FIRST OF HER KIND.

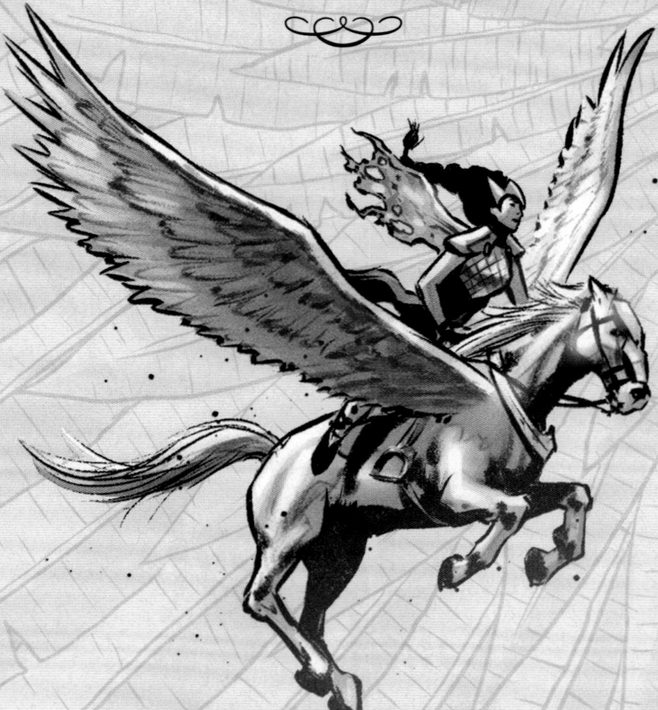

COLLECTION EDITOR **JENNIFER GRÜNWALD**
ASSOCIATE MANAGING EDITOR **KATERI WOODY**
VP PRODUCTION & SPECIAL PROJECTS **JEFF YOUNGQUIST**

CAITLIN O'CONNELL ASSISTANT EDITOR
MARK D. BEAZLEY EDITOR, SPECIAL PROJECTS
JAY BOWEN LOGO & BOOK DESIGNER

SVP PRINT, SALES & MARKETING **DAVID GABRIEL**
EDITOR IN CHIEF **C.B. CEBULSKI**
PRESIDENT **DAN BUCKLEY**

SVEN LARSEN DIRECTOR, LICENSED PUBLISHING
JOE QUESADA CHIEF CREATIVE OFFICER
ALAN FINE EXECUTIVE PRODUCER

VALKYRIE: JANE FOSTER: VOL. 1 — THE SACRED AND THE PROFANE. Contains material originally published in magazine form as VALKYRIE: JANE FOSTER (2019) #1-5 and WAR OF THE REALMS: OMEGA (2019) #1. First printing 2019. ISBN 978-1-302-92029-6. Published by MARVEL WORLDWIDE, INC., a subsidiary of MARVEL ENTERTAINMENT, LLC. OFFICE OF PUBLICATION: 135 West 50th Street, New York, NY 10020. **Printed in Canada.** DAN BUCKLEY, President, Marvel Entertainment; JOHN NEE, Publisher; JOE QUESADA, Chief Creative Officer; TOM BREVOORT, SVP of Publishing; DAVID BOGART, Associate Publisher & SVP of Talent Affairs; DAVID GABRIEL, VP of Print & Digital Publishing; JEFF YOUNGQUIST, VP of Production & Special Projects; DAN CARR, Executive Director of Publishing Technology; ALEX MORALES, Director of Publishing Operations; DAN EDINGTON, Managing Editor; SUSAN CRESP Production Manager; STAN LEE, Chairman Emeritus. For information regarding advertising in Marvel Comics or on Marvel.com, please contact Vit DeBellis, Custom Solutions & Integrated Advertising Manager, at vdebellis@marvel.com. For Marvel subscription inquiries, please call 888-511-5480. **Manufactured between 11/29/2019 and 12/31/2019 by SOLISCO PRINTERS, SCOTT, QC, CANADA.**

10 9 8 7 6 5 4 3 2 1

JANE FOSTER VALKYRIE

the Sacred and the Profane

AL EWING & JASON AARON
WRITERS

CAFU
WITH RAMÓN K. PÉREZ (#3),
CIAN TORMEY & ROBERTO POGGI (#3)
AND FRAZER IRVING (#3)
ARTISTS

JESUS ABURTOV
COLOR ARTIST

VC's JOE SABINO
LETTERER

MAHMUD ASRAR
WITH MATTHEW WILSON (#1-2, #4-5)
& DAVE McCAIG (#3)
COVER ART

WAR OF THE REALMS OMEGA
"GOD AND THE DEVIL WALK INTO A CHURCH"

WRITER **JASON AARON**
ARTIST **RON GARNEY**
COLOR ARTIST **MATT MILLA**
LETTERER **VC's JOE SABINO**
COVER ART **PHIL NOTO**

ASSOCIATE EDITOR **SARAH BRUNSTAD**
EDITOR **WIL MOSS**
SPECIAL THANKS TO **RUSSELL DAUTERMAN**

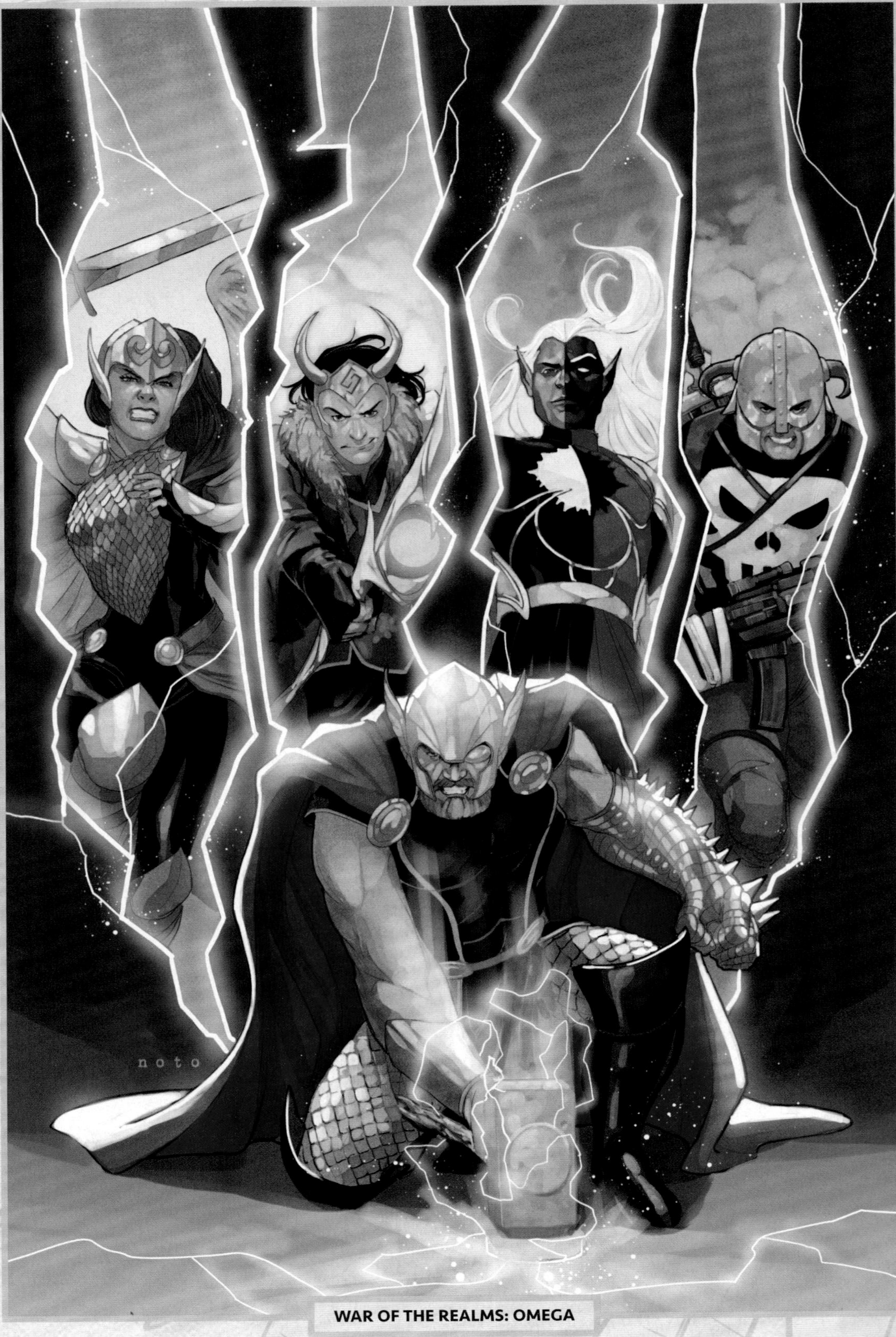
noto

WAR OF THE REALMS: OMEGA

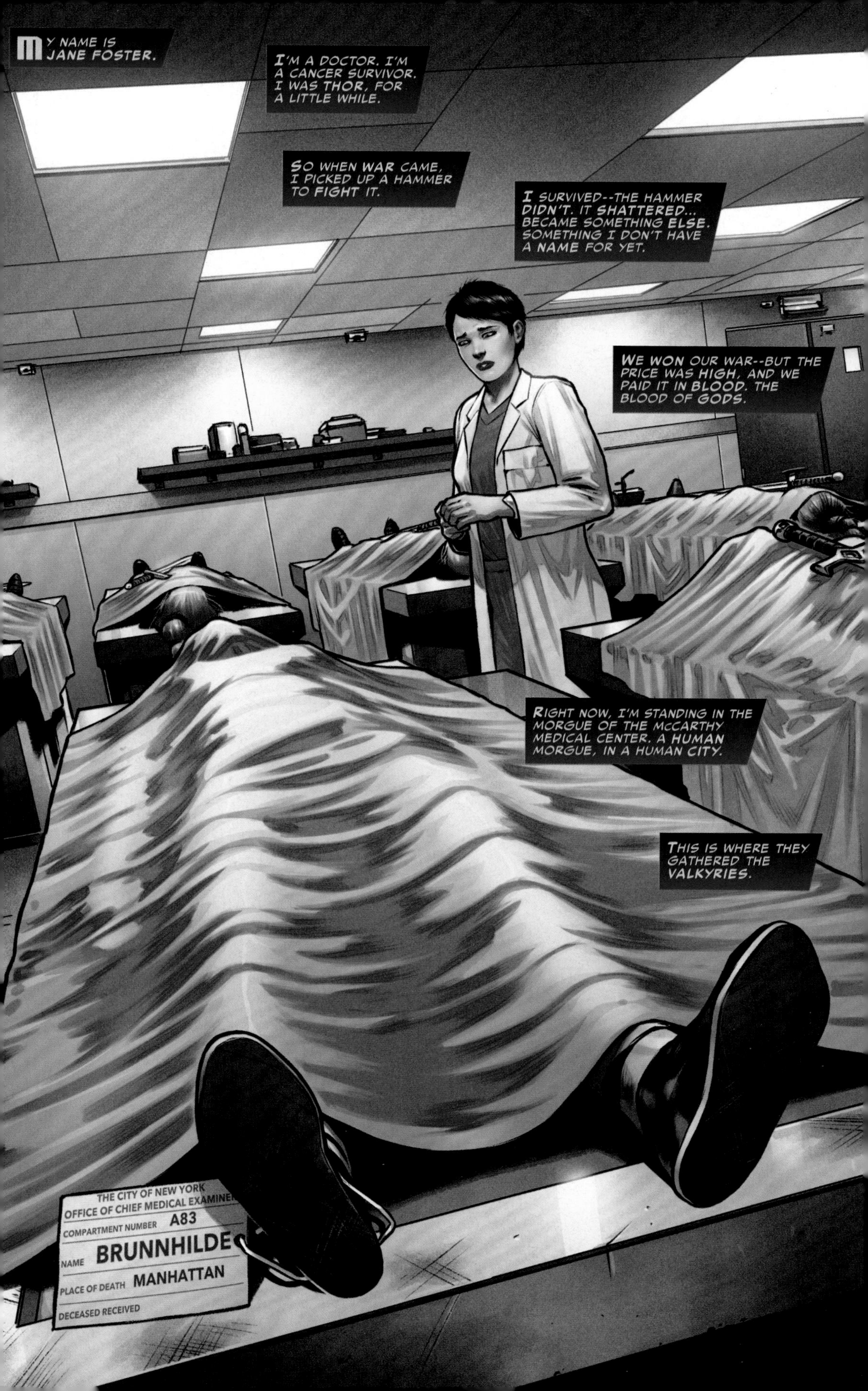
MY NAME IS JANE FOSTER.
I'M A DOCTOR. I'M A CANCER SURVIVOR. I WAS THOR, FOR A LITTLE WHILE.
SO WHEN WAR CAME, I PICKED UP A HAMMER TO FIGHT IT.
I SURVIVED--THE HAMMER DIDN'T. IT SHATTERED... BECAME SOMETHING ELSE. SOMETHING I DON'T HAVE A NAME FOR YET.
WE WON OUR WAR--BUT THE PRICE WAS HIGH, AND WE PAID IT IN BLOOD. THE BLOOD OF GODS.
RIGHT NOW, I'M STANDING IN THE MORGUE OF THE McCARTHY MEDICAL CENTER. A HUMAN MORGUE, IN A HUMAN CITY.
THIS IS WHERE THEY GATHERED THE VALKYRIES.
THE CITY OF NEW YORK
OFFICE OF CHIEF MEDICAL EXAMINER
COMPARTMENT NUMBER A83
NAME BRUNNHILDE
PLACE OF DEATH MANHATTAN
DECEASED RECEIVED

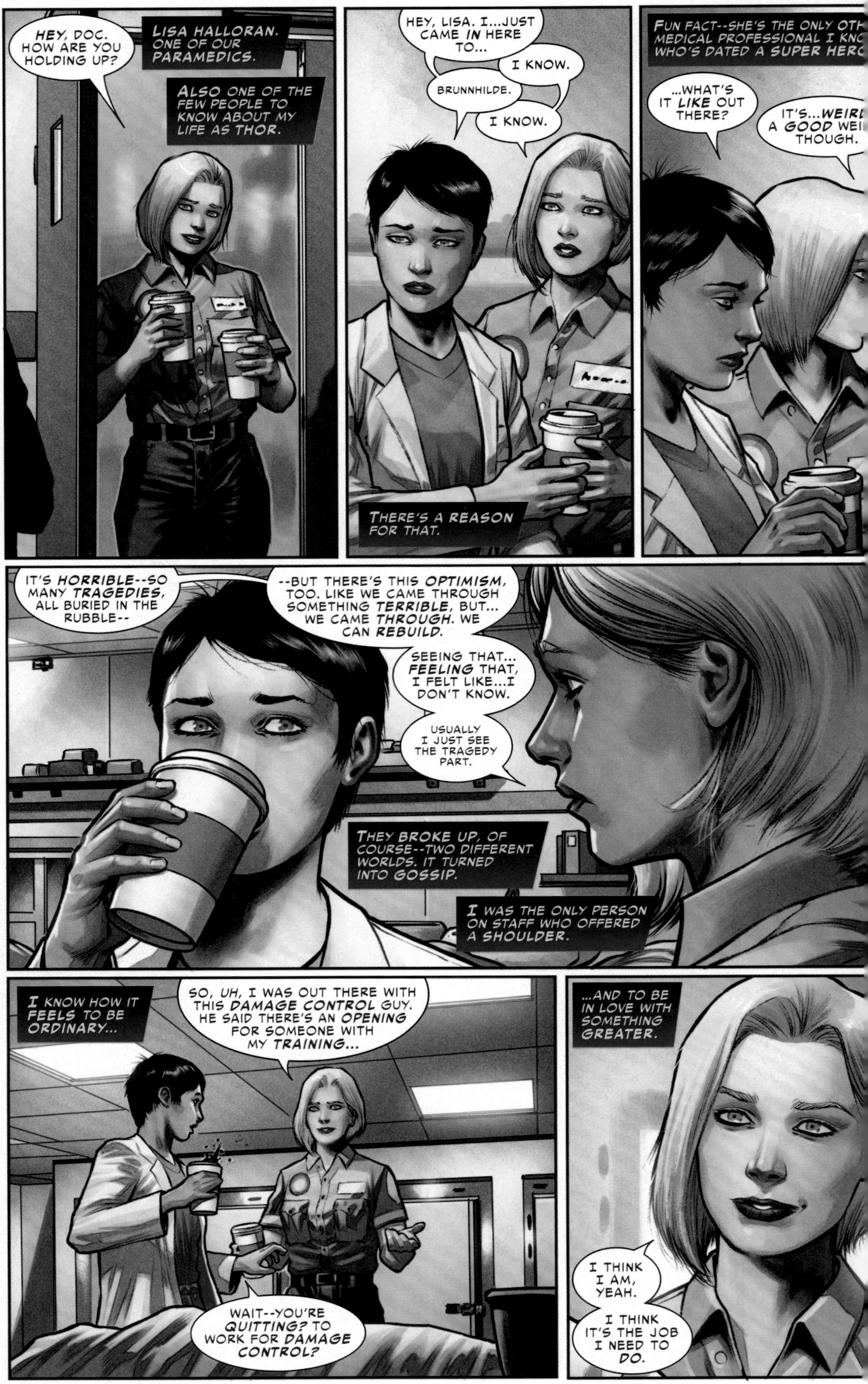
HEY, DOC. HOW ARE YOU HOLDING UP?
LISA HALLORAN. ONE OF OUR PARAMEDICS.
ALSO ONE OF THE FEW PEOPLE TO KNOW ABOUT MY LIFE AS THOR.
HEY, LISA. I...JUST CAME IN HERE TO...
I KNOW.
BRUNNHILDE.
I KNOW.
THERE'S A REASON FOR THAT.
FUN FACT--SHE'S THE ONLY OTH
MEDICAL PROFESSIONAL I KNO
WHO'S DATED A SUPER HERO
...WHAT'S IT LIKE OUT THERE?
IT'S...WEIRD
A GOOD WEI
THOUGH.
IT'S HORRIBLE--SO MANY TRAGEDIES, ALL BURIED IN THE RUBBLE--
--BUT THERE'S THIS OPTIMISM, TOO. LIKE WE CAME THROUGH SOMETHING TERRIBLE, BUT... WE CAME THROUGH. WE CAN REBUILD.
SEEING THAT... FEELING THAT, I FELT LIKE...I DON'T KNOW.
USUALLY I JUST SEE THE TRAGEDY PART.
THEY BROKE UP, OF COURSE--TWO DIFFERENT WORLDS. IT TURNED INTO GOSSIP.
I WAS THE ONLY PERSON ON STAFF WHO OFFERED A SHOULDER.
I KNOW HOW IT FEELS TO BE ORDINARY...
SO, UH, I WAS OUT THERE WITH THIS DAMAGE CONTROL GUY. HE SAID THERE'S AN OPENING FOR SOMEONE WITH MY TRAINING...
WAIT--YOU'RE QUITTING? TO WORK FOR DAMAGE CONTROL?
...AND TO BE IN LOVE WITH SOMETHING GREATER.
I THINK I AM, YEAH.
I THINK IT'S THE JOB I NEED TO DO.

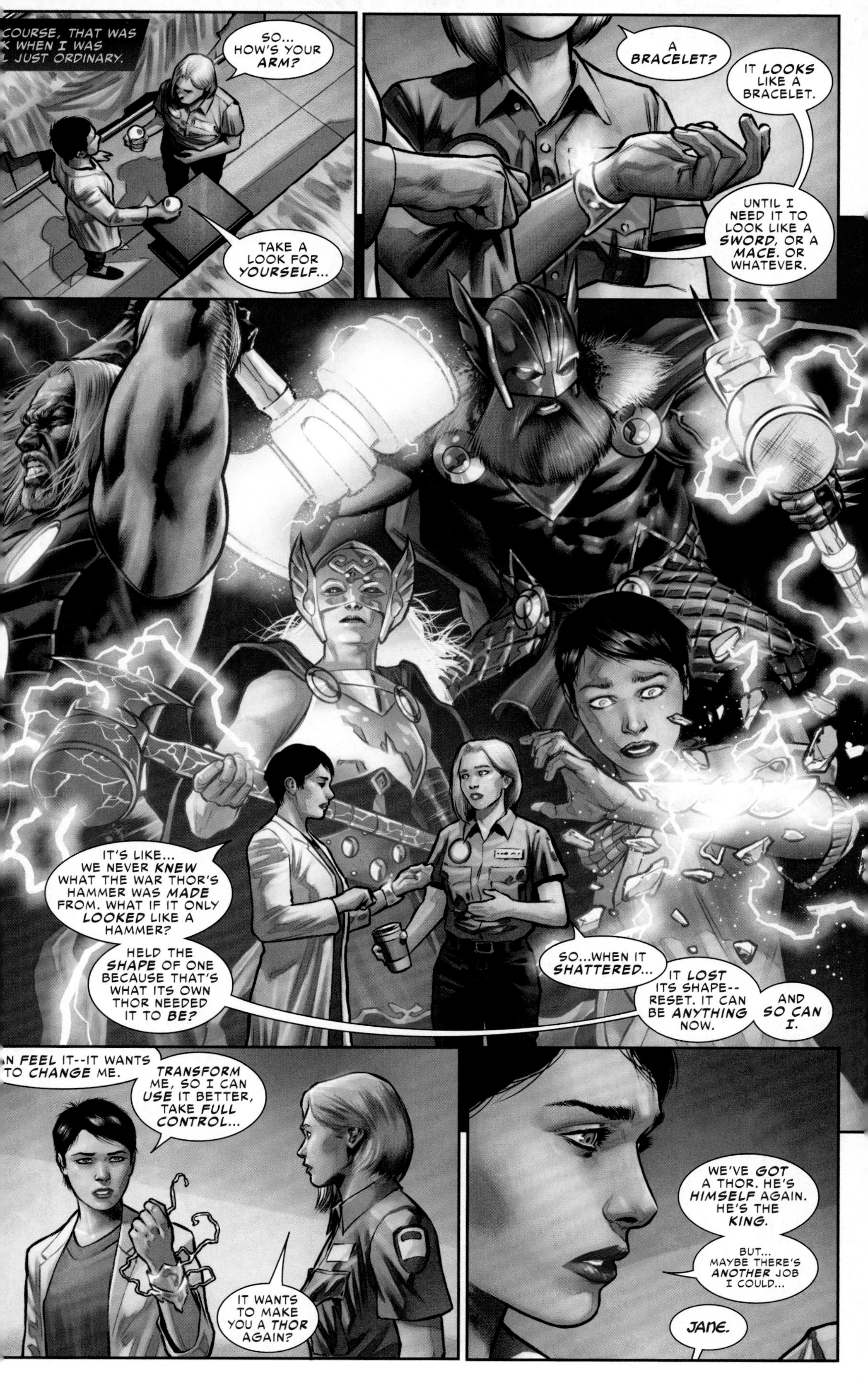
COURSE, THAT WAS
K WHEN I WAS
L JUST ORDINARY.
SO... HOW'S YOUR ARM?
TAKE A LOOK FOR YOURSELF...
A BRACELET?
IT LOOKS LIKE A BRACELET.
UNTIL I NEED IT TO LOOK LIKE A SWORD, OR A MACE. OR WHATEVER.
IT'S LIKE... WE NEVER KNEW WHAT THE WAR THOR'S HAMMER WAS MADE FROM. WHAT IF IT ONLY LOOKED LIKE A HAMMER?
HELD THE SHAPE OF ONE BECAUSE THAT'S WHAT ITS OWN THOR NEEDED IT TO BE?
SO...WHEN IT SHATTERED...
IT LOST ITS SHAPE-- RESET. IT CAN BE ANYTHING NOW.
AND SO CAN I.
N FEEL IT--IT WANTS TO CHANGE ME.
TRANSFORM ME, SO I CAN USE IT BETTER, TAKE FULL CONTROL...
IT WANTS TO MAKE YOU A THOR AGAIN?
WE'VE GOT A THOR. HE'S HIMSELF AGAIN. HE'S THE KING.
BUT... MAYBE THERE'S ANOTHER JOB I COULD...
JANE.

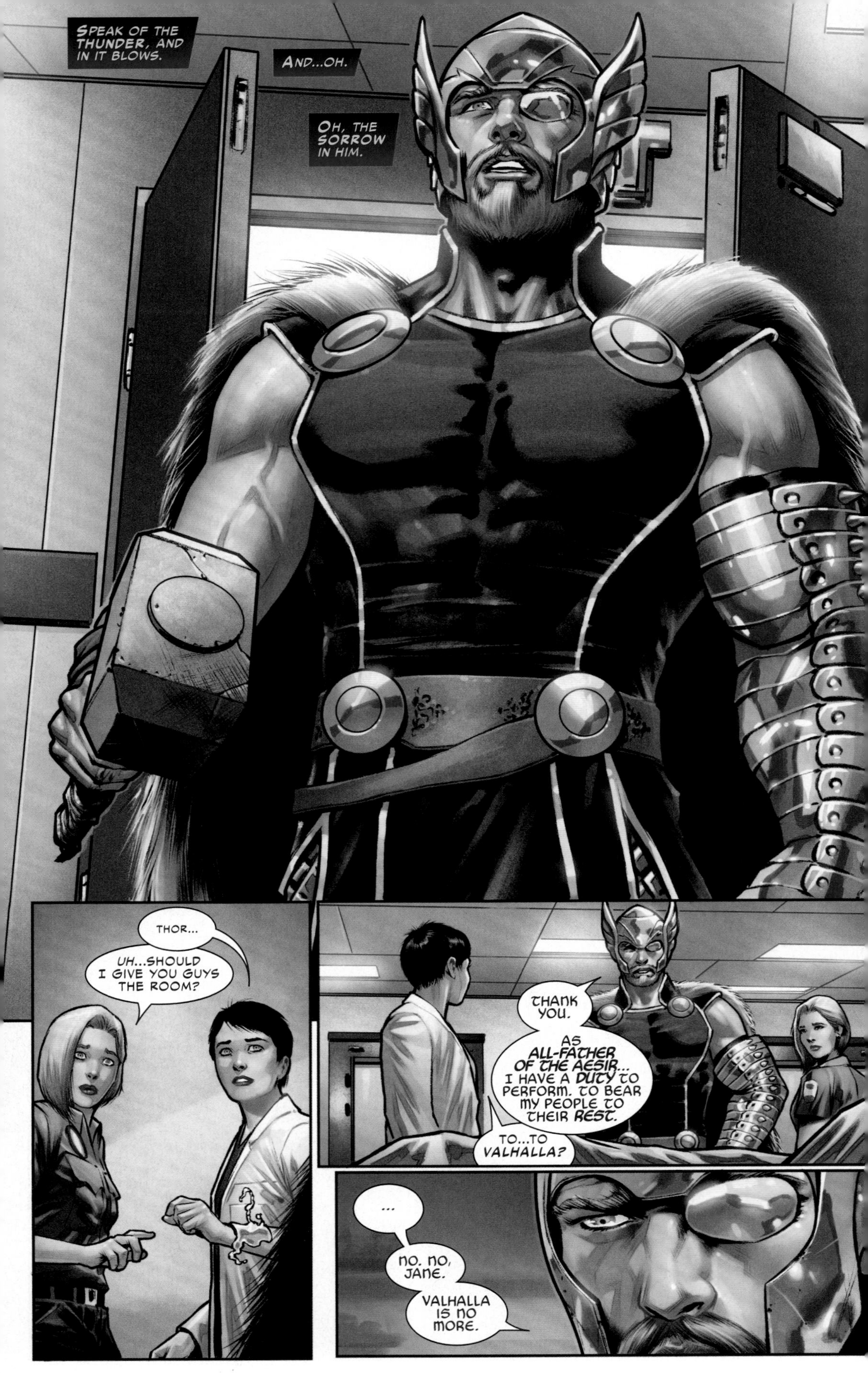
SPEAK OF THE THUNDER, AND IN IT BLOWS.
AND...OH.
OH, THE SORROW IN HIM.
THOR...
UH...SHOULD I GIVE YOU GUYS THE ROOM?
THANK YOU.
AS ALL-FATHER OF THE AESIR... I HAVE A DUTY TO PERFORM. TO BEAR MY PEOPLE TO THEIR REST.
TO...TO VALHALLA?
...
NO. NO, JANE.
VALHALLA IS NO MORE.

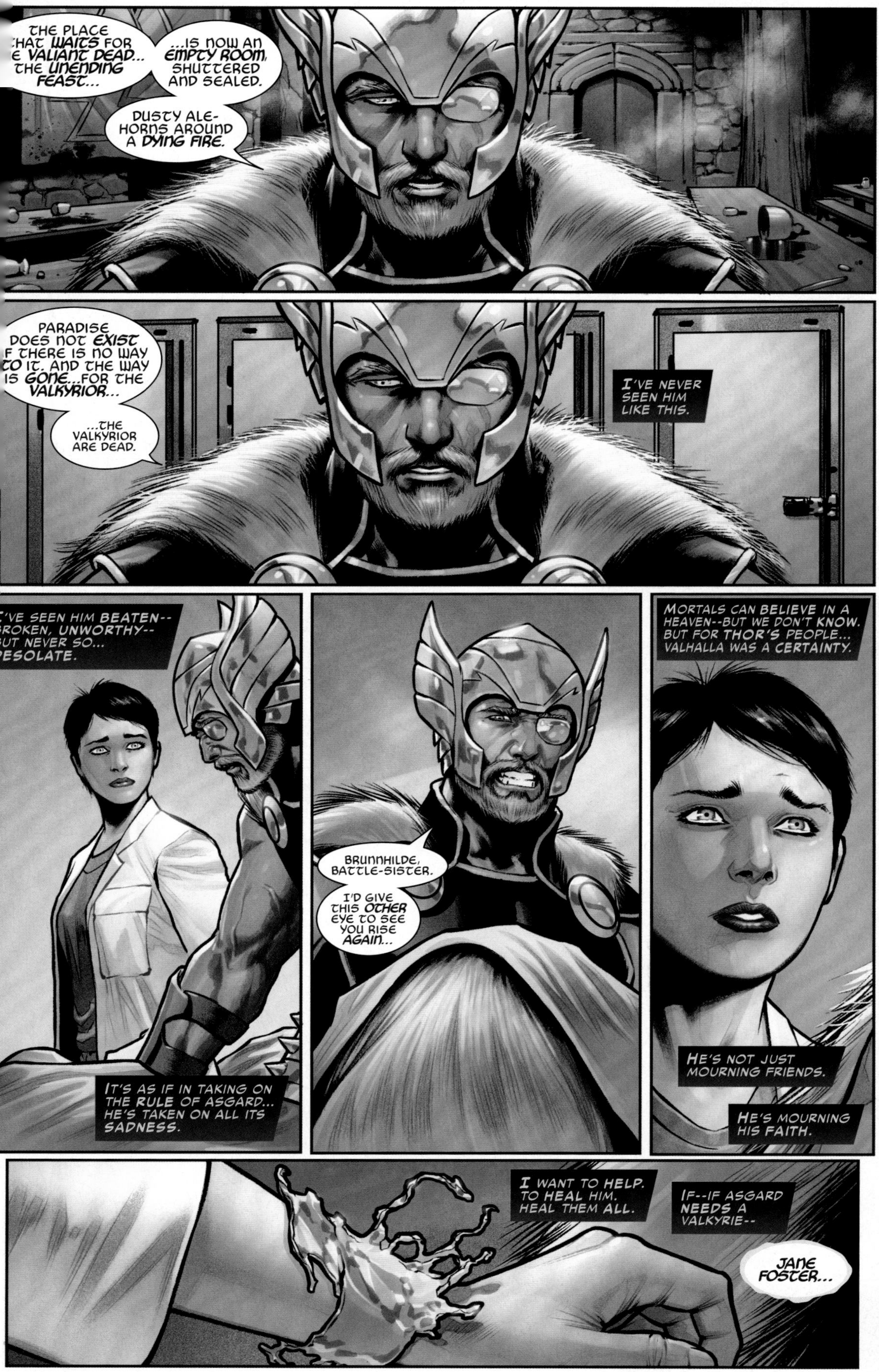
THE PLACE THAT WAITS FOR E VALIANT DEAD... THE UNENDING FEAST...
...IS NOW AN EMPTY ROOM, SHUTTERED AND SEALED.
DUSTY ALE-HORNS AROUND A DYING FIRE.
PARADISE DOES NOT EXIST F THERE IS NO WAY TO IT. AND THE WAY IS GONE...FOR THE VALKYRIOR...
...THE VALKYRIOR ARE DEAD.
I'VE NEVER SEEN HIM LIKE THIS.
I'VE SEEN HIM BEATEN-- BROKEN, UNWORTHY-- BUT NEVER SO... PESOLATE.
IT'S AS IF IN TAKING ON THE RULE OF ASGARD... HE'S TAKEN ON ALL ITS SADNESS.
BRUNNHILDE, BATTLE-SISTER.
I'D GIVE THIS OTHER EYE TO SEE YOU RISE AGAIN...
MORTALS CAN BELIEVE IN A HEAVEN--BUT WE DON'T KNOW. BUT FOR THOR'S PEOPLE... VALHALLA WAS A CERTAINTY.
HE'S NOT JUST MOURNING FRIENDS.
HE'S MOURNING HIS FAITH.
I WANT TO HELP. TO HEAL HIM. HEAL THEM ALL.
IF--IF ASGARD NEEDS A VALKYRIE--
JANE FOSTER...

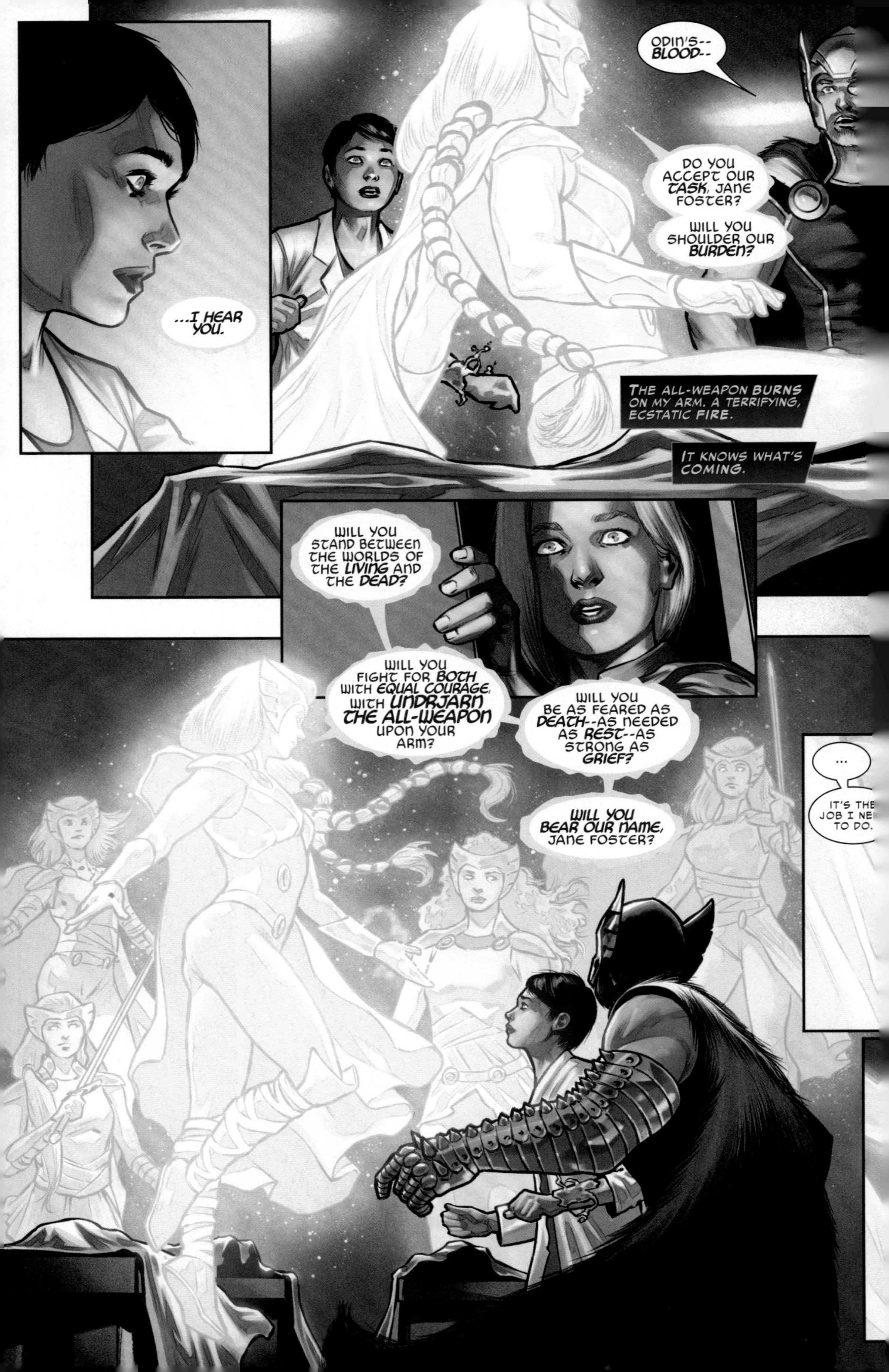
...I HEAR YOU.
ODIN'S-- BLOOD--
DO YOU ACCEPT OUR TASK, JANE FOSTER?
WILL YOU SHOULDER OUR BURDEN?
THE ALL-WEAPON BURNS ON MY ARM. A TERRIFYING, ECSTATIC FIRE.
IT KNOWS WHAT'S COMING.
WILL YOU STAND BETWEEN THE WORLDS OF THE LIVING AND THE DEAD?
WILL YOU FIGHT FOR BOTH WITH EQUAL COURAGE, WITH UNDRJARN THE ALL-WEAPON UPON YOUR ARM?
WILL YOU BE AS FEARED AS DEATH--AS NEEDED AS REST--AS STRONG AS GRIEF?
WILL YOU BEAR OUR NAME, JANE FOSTER?
...

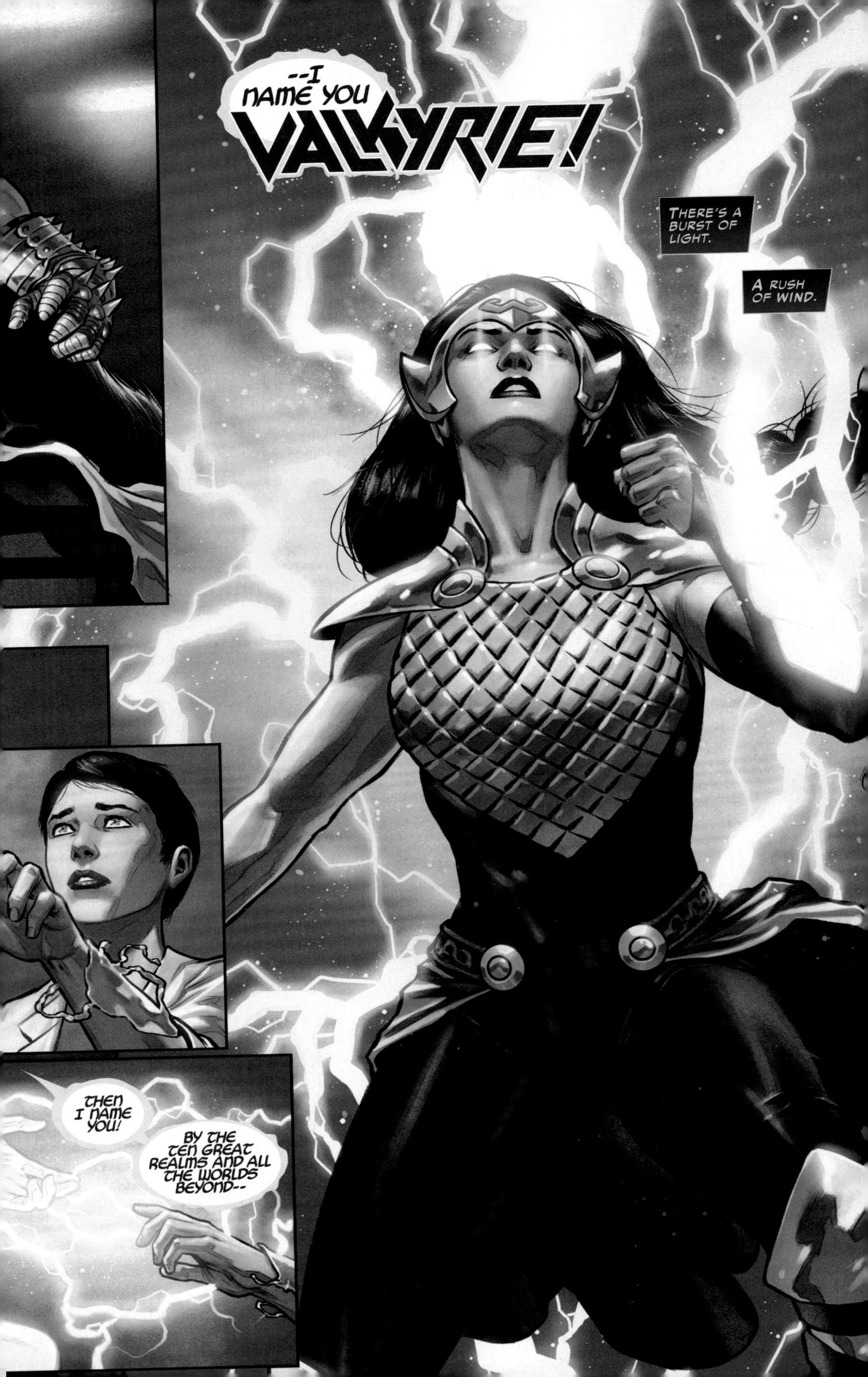
--I NAME YOU VALKYRIE!
THERE'S A BURST OF LIGHT.
A RUSH OF WIND.
THEN I NAME YOU!
BY THE TEN GREAT REALMS AND ALL THE WORLDS BEYOND--

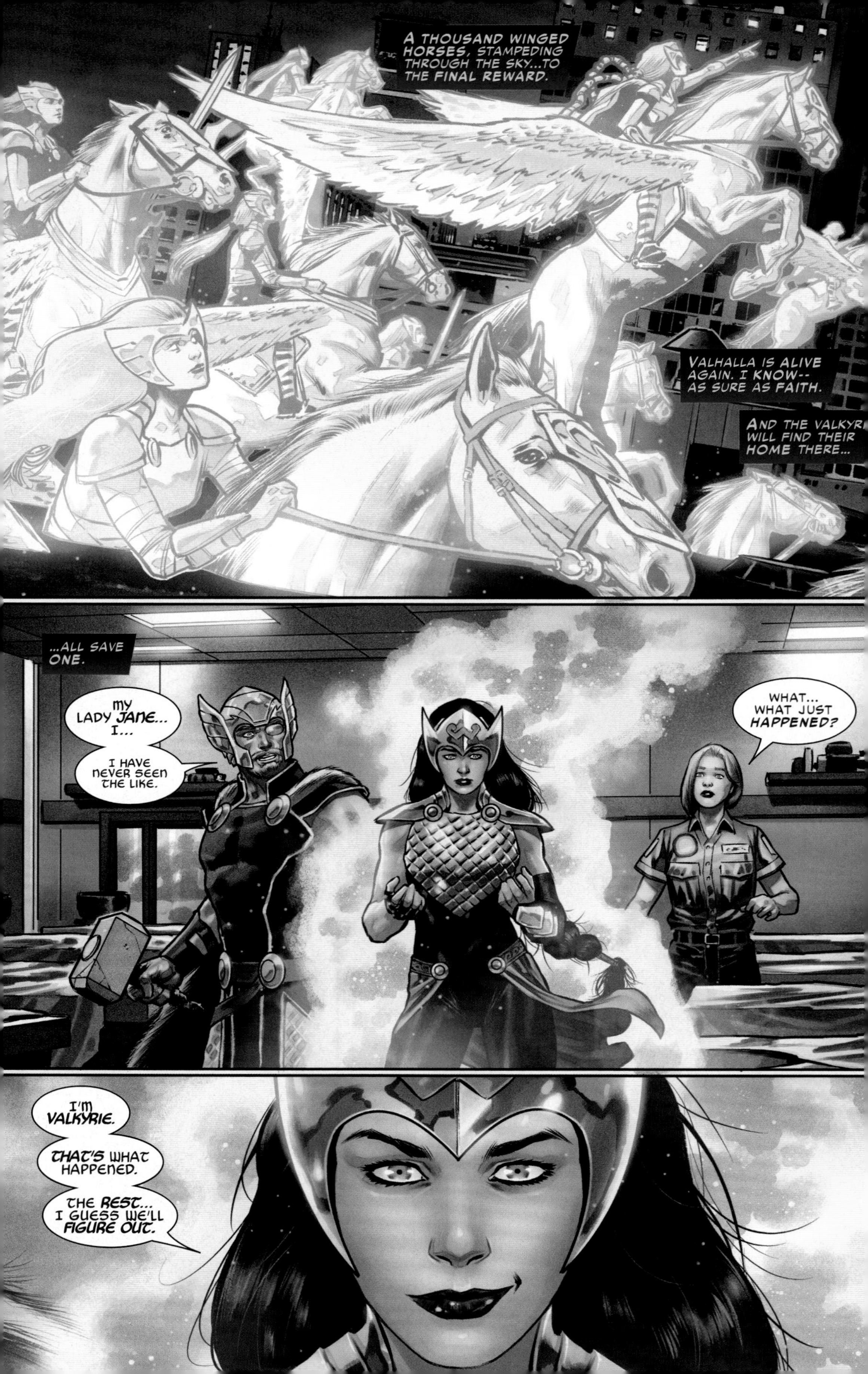
A THOUSAND WINGED HORSES, STAMPEDING THROUGH THE SKY...TO THE FINAL REWARD.
VALHALLA IS ALIVE AGAIN. I KNOW-- AS SURE AS FAITH.
AND THE VALKYR WILL FIND THEIR HOME THERE...
...ALL SAVE ONE.
MY LADY JANE... I...
I HAVE NEVER SEEN THE LIKE.
WHAT... WHAT JUST HAPPENED?
I'M VALKYRIE.
THAT'S WHAT HAPPENED.
THE REST... I GUESS WE'LL FIGURE OUT.

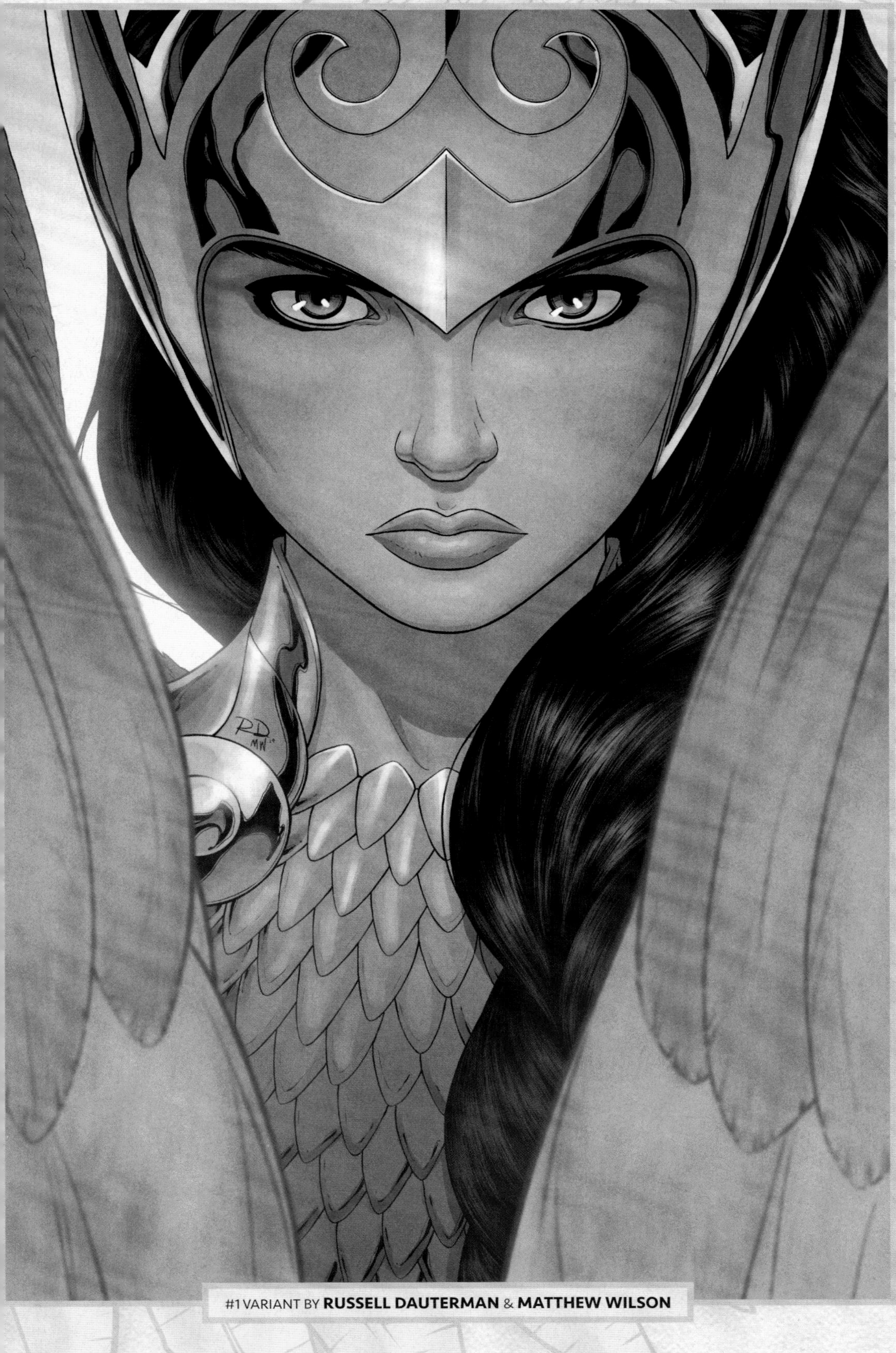

#1 VARIANT BY **RUSSELL DAUTERMAN** & **MATTHEW WILSON**

1.

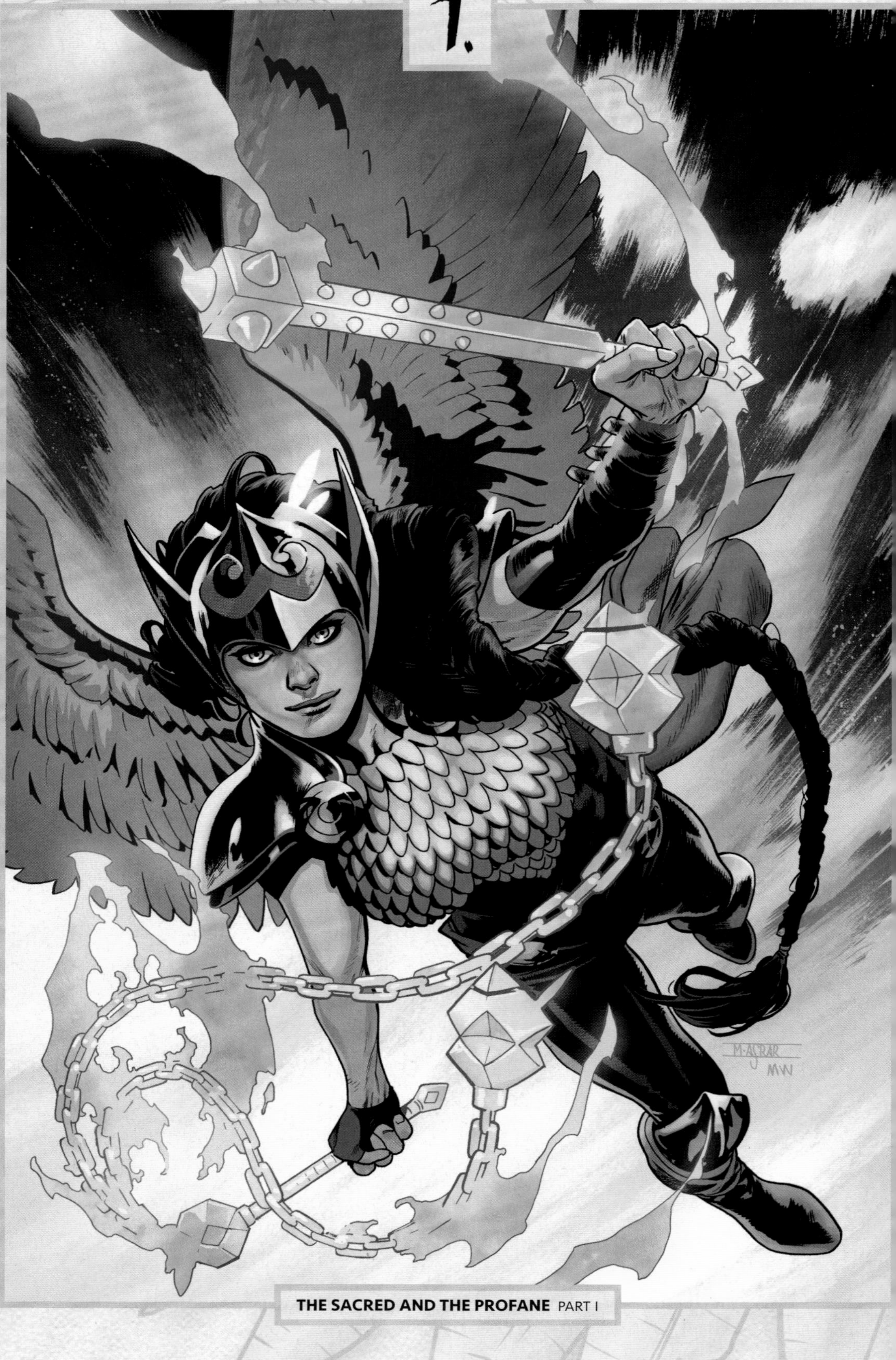

THE SACRED AND THE PROFANE PART I

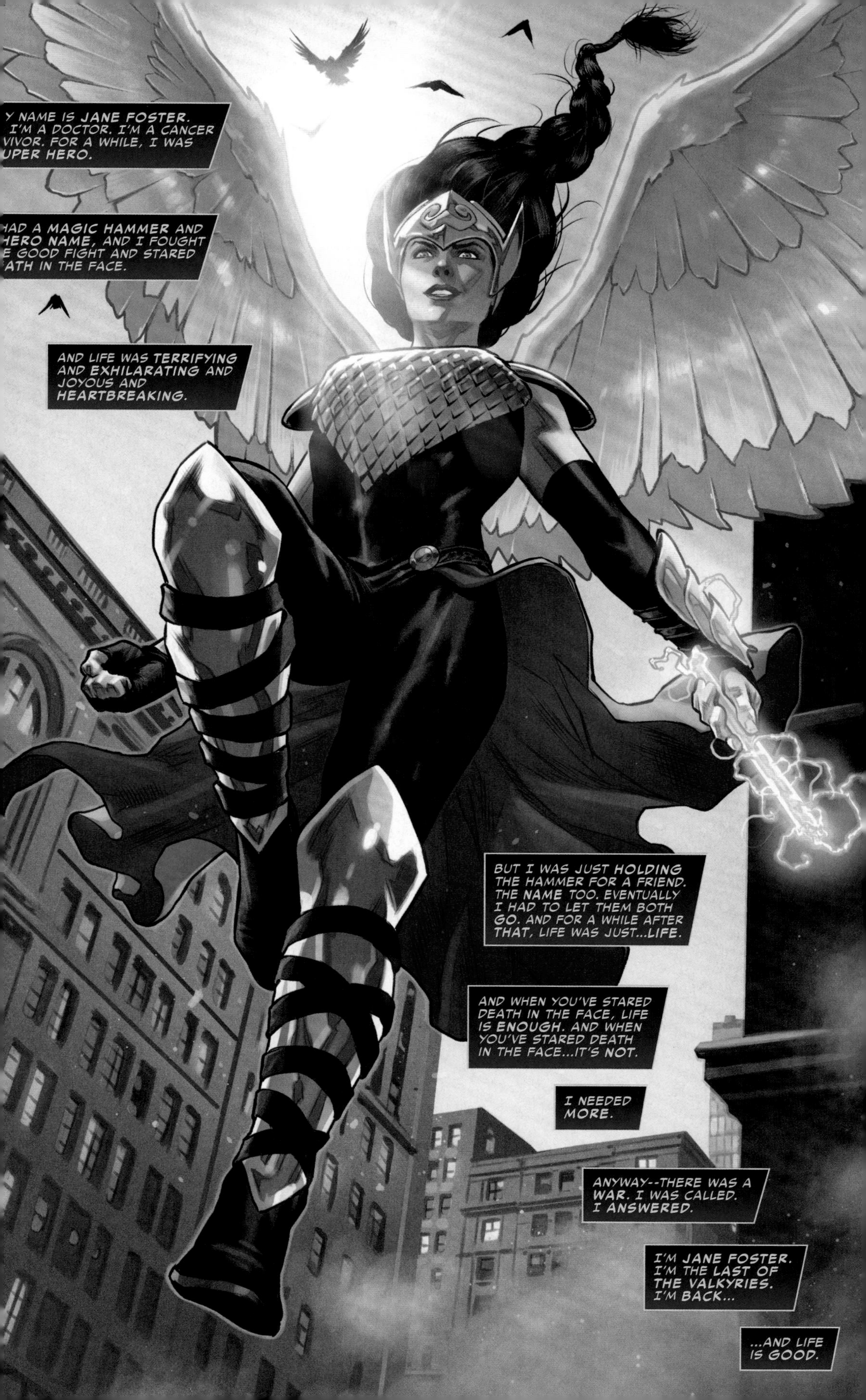

Y NAME IS JANE FOSTER. I'M A DOCTOR. I'M A CANCER VIVOR. FOR A WHILE, I WAS UPER HERO.
HAD A MAGIC HAMMER AND HERO NAME, AND I FOUGHT E GOOD FIGHT AND STARED ATH IN THE FACE.
AND LIFE WAS TERRIFYING AND EXHILARATING AND JOYOUS AND HEARTBREAKING.
BUT I WAS JUST HOLDING THE HAMMER FOR A FRIEND. THE NAME TOO. EVENTUALLY I HAD TO LET THEM BOTH GO. AND FOR A WHILE AFTER THAT, LIFE WAS JUST...LIFE.
AND WHEN YOU'VE STARED DEATH IN THE FACE, LIFE IS ENOUGH. AND WHEN YOU'VE STARED DEATH IN THE FACE...IT'S NOT.
I NEEDED MORE.
ANYWAY--THERE WAS A WAR. I WAS CALLED. I ANSWERED.
I'M JANE FOSTER. I'M THE LAST OF THE VALKYRIES. I'M BACK...
...AND LIFE IS GOOD.

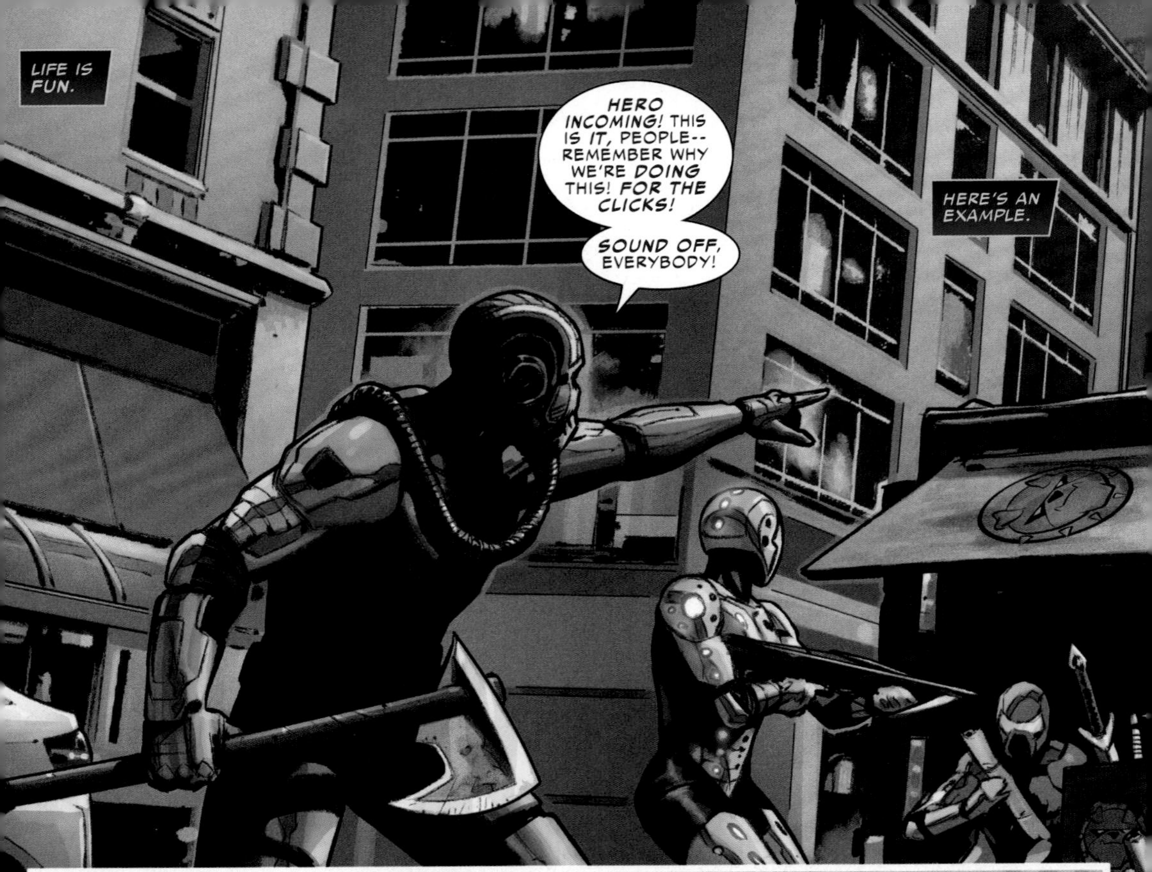
LIFE IS FUN.
HERO INCOMING! THIS IS IT, PEOPLE-- REMEMBER WHY WE'RE DOING THIS! FOR THE CLICKS!
SOUND OFF, EVERYBODY!
HERE'S AN EXAMPLE.

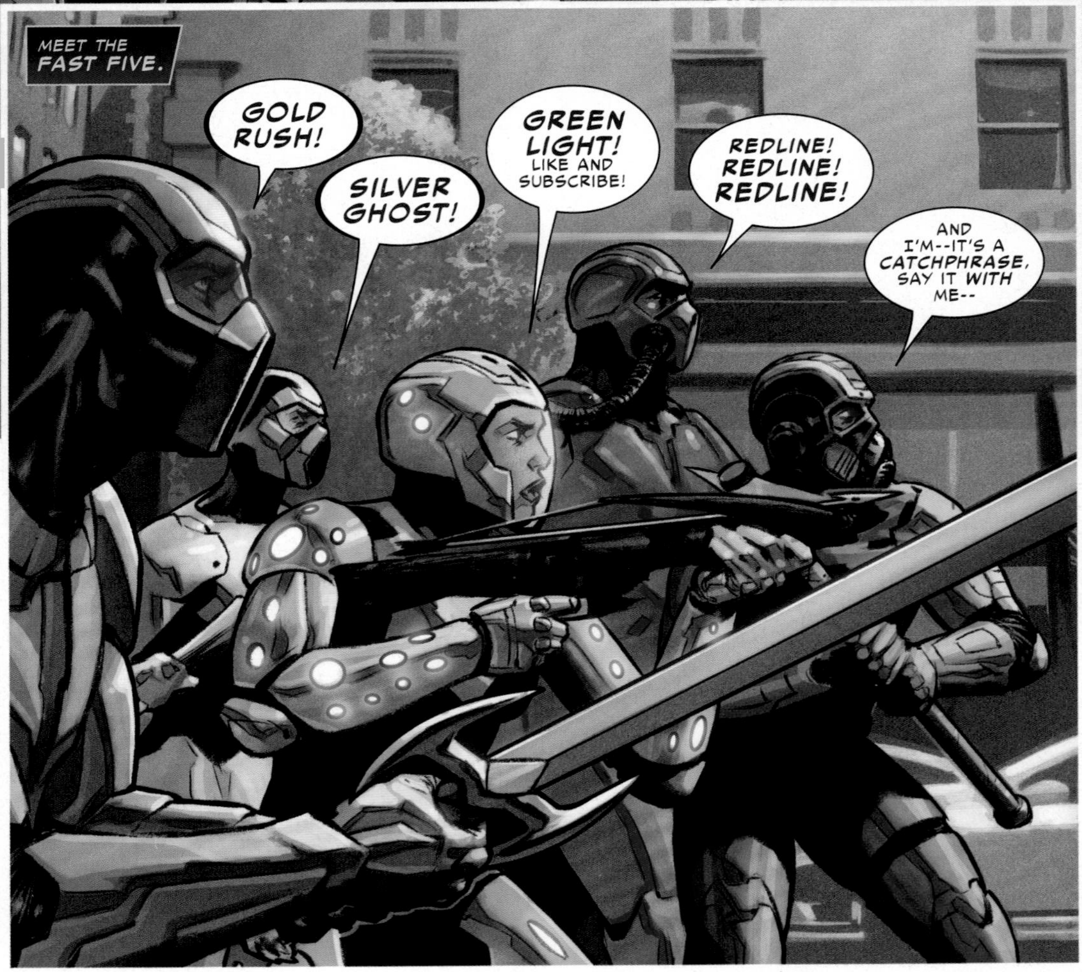
MEET THE FAST FIVE.
GOLD RUSH!
SILVER GHOST!
GREEN LIGHT! LIKE AND SUBSCRIBE!
REDLINE! REDLINE! REDLINE!
AND I'M--IT'S A CATCHPHRASE, SAY IT WITH ME--

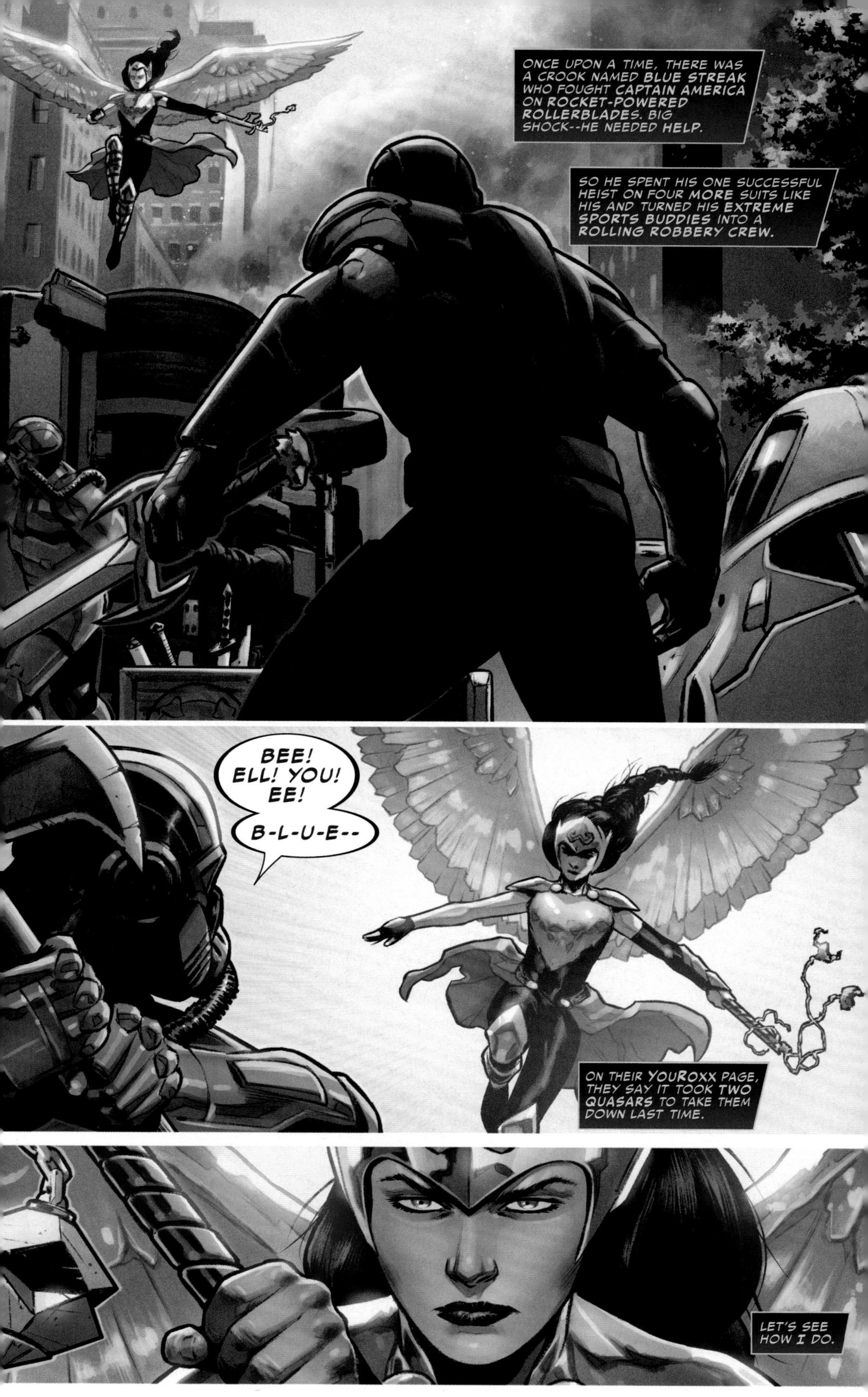

ONCE UPON A TIME, THERE WAS A CROOK NAMED BLUE STREAK WHO FOUGHT CAPTAIN AMERICA ON ROCKET-POWERED ROLLERBLADES. BIG SHOCK--HE NEEDED HELP.
SO HE SPENT HIS ONE SUCCESSFUL HEIST ON FOUR MORE SUITS LIKE HIS AND TURNED HIS EXTREME SPORTS BUDDIES INTO A ROLLING ROBBERY CREW.
BEE! ELL! YOU! EE!
B-L-U-E--
ON THEIR YOUROXX PAGE, THEY SAY IT TOOK TWO QUASARS TO TAKE THEM DOWN LAST TIME.
LET'S SEE HOW I DO.

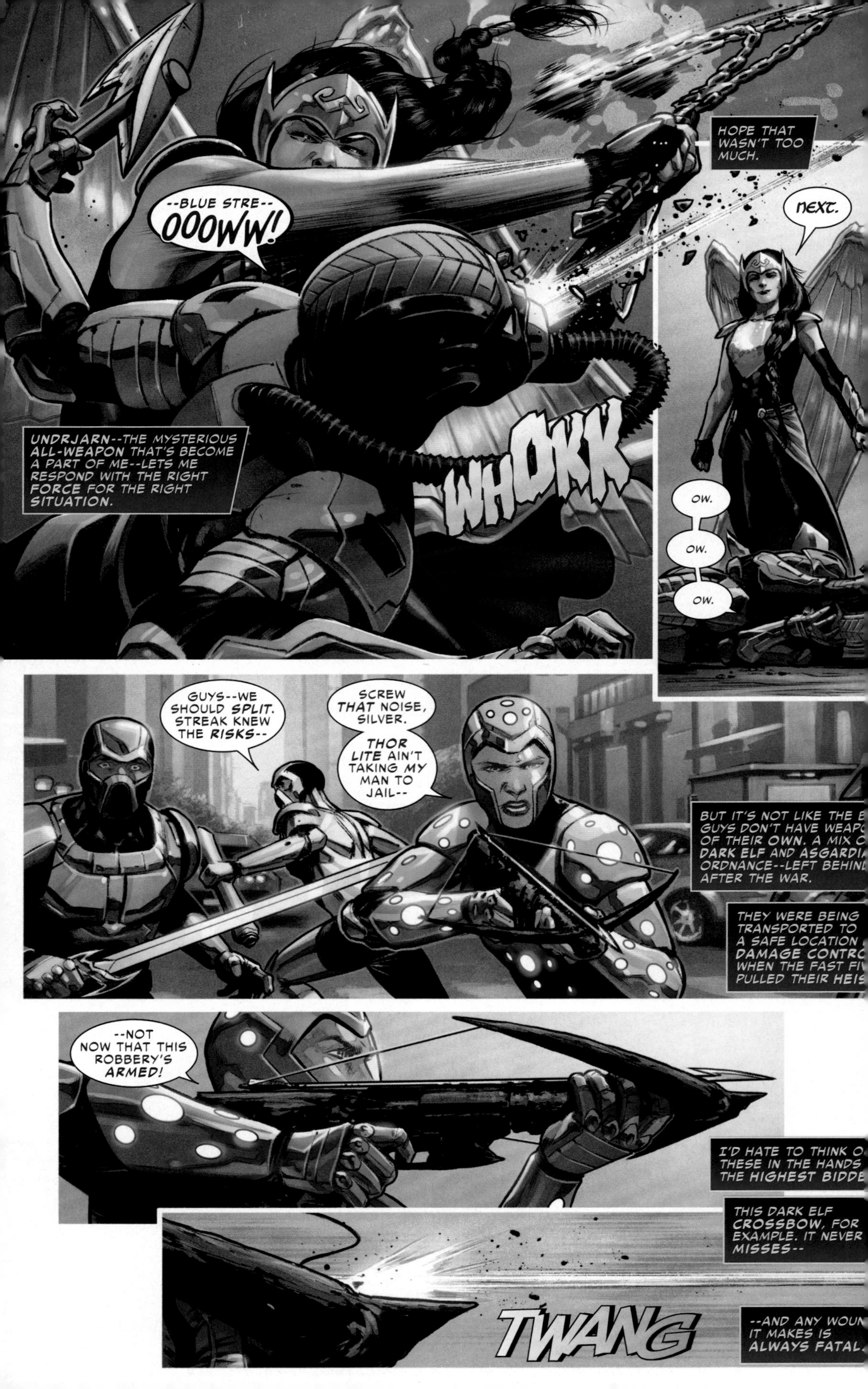
--BLUE STRE-- OOOWW!
UNDRJARN--THE MYSTERIOUS ALL-WEAPON THAT'S BECOME A PART OF ME--LETS ME RESPOND WITH THE RIGHT FORCE FOR THE RIGHT SITUATION.
WHOKK
HOPE THAT WASN'T TOO MUCH.
NEXT.
OW.
OW.
OW.
GUYS--WE SHOULD SPLIT. STREAK KNEW THE RISKS--
SCREW THAT NOISE, SILVER.
THOR LITE AIN'T TAKING MY MAN TO JAIL--
BUT IT'S NOT LIKE THE B GUYS DON'T HAVE WEAP OF THEIR OWN. A MIX O DARK ELF AND ASGARDI ORDNANCE--LEFT BEHIN AFTER THE WAR.
THEY WERE BEING TRANSPORTED TO A SAFE LOCATION DAMAGE CONTRO WHEN THE FAST FI PULLED THEIR HEIS
--NOT NOW THAT THIS ROBBERY'S ARMED!
I'D HATE TO THINK O THESE IN THE HANDS THE HIGHEST BIDDE
THIS DARK ELF CROSSBOW, FOR EXAMPLE. IT NEVER MISSES--
TWANG
--AND ANY WOUN IT MAKES IS ALWAYS FATAL

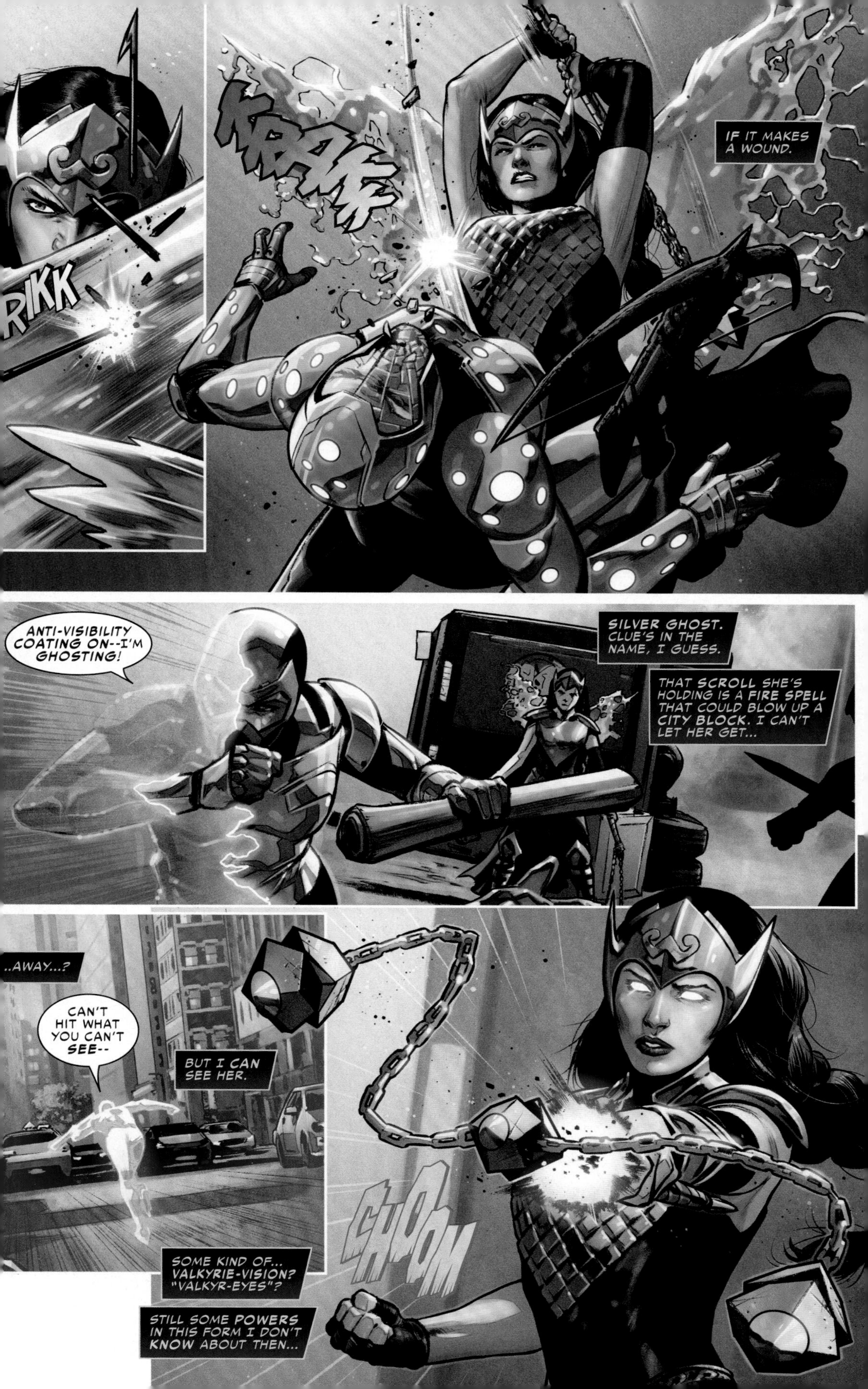
RIKK
KRAK
IF IT MAKES A WOUND.
ANTI-VISIBILITY COATING ON--I'M GHOSTING!
SILVER GHOST. CLUE'S IN THE NAME, I GUESS.
THAT SCROLL SHE'S HOLDING IS A FIRE SPELL THAT COULD BLOW UP A CITY BLOCK. I CAN'T LET HER GET...
..AWAY...?
CAN'T HIT WHAT YOU CAN'T SEE--
BUT I CAN SEE HER.
SOME KIND OF... VALKYRIE-VISION? "VALKYR-EYES"?
STILL SOME POWERS IN THIS FORM I DON'T KNOW ABOUT THEN...
CHOOM

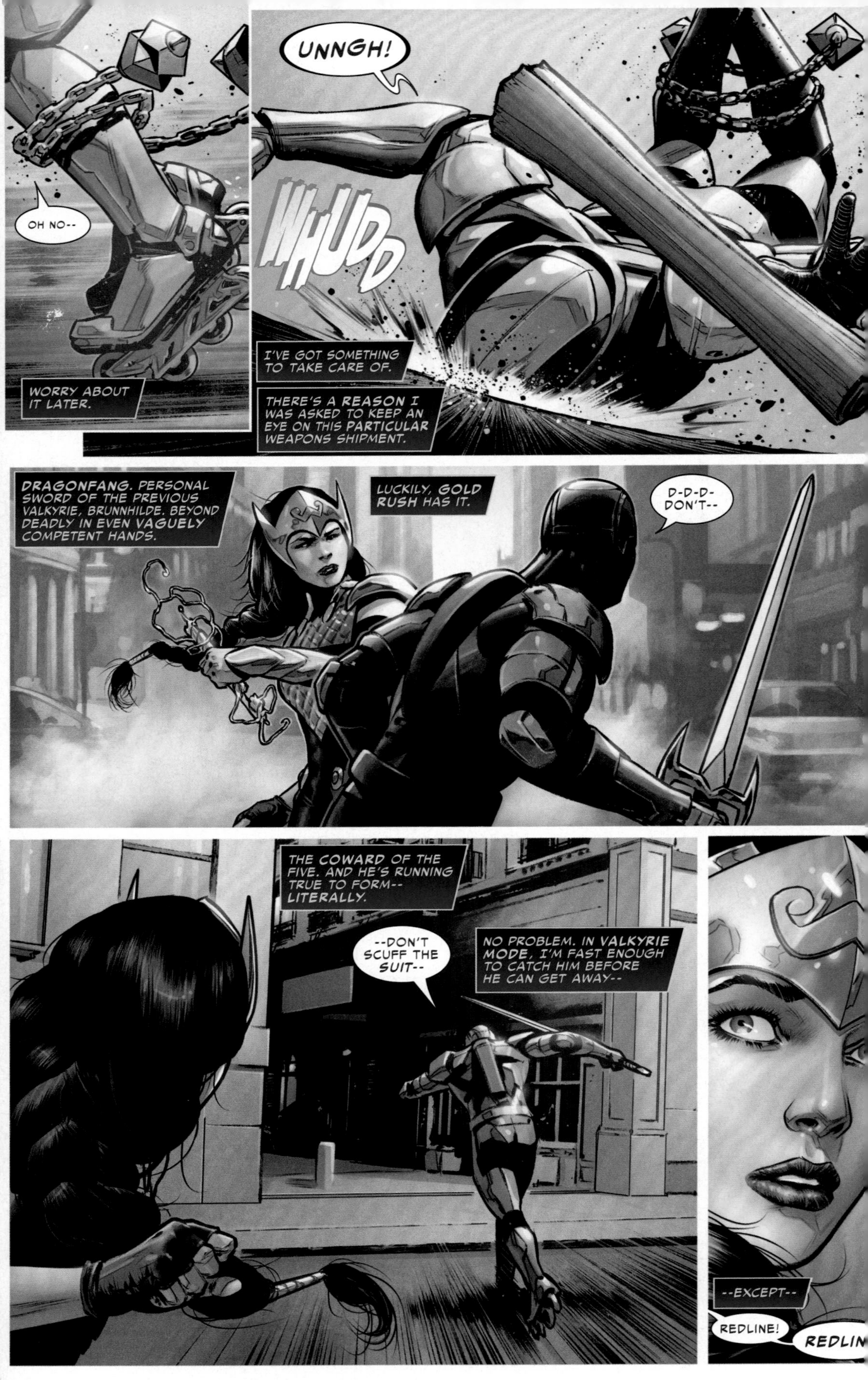
OH NO--
WORRY ABOUT IT LATER.
UNNGH!
WHUDD
I'VE GOT SOMETHING TO TAKE CARE OF.
THERE'S A REASON I WAS ASKED TO KEEP AN EYE ON THIS PARTICULAR WEAPONS SHIPMENT.
DRAGONFANG. PERSONAL SWORD OF THE PREVIOUS VALKYRIE, BRUNNHILDE. BEYOND DEADLY IN EVEN VAGUELY COMPETENT HANDS.
LUCKILY, GOLD RUSH HAS IT.
D-D-D-DON'T--
THE COWARD OF THE FIVE. AND HE'S RUNNING TRUE TO FORM--LITERALLY.
--DON'T SCUFF THE SUIT--
NO PROBLEM. IN VALKYRIE MODE, I'M FAST ENOUGH TO CATCH HIM BEFORE HE CAN GET AWAY--
--EXCEPT--
REDLINE!
REDLIN

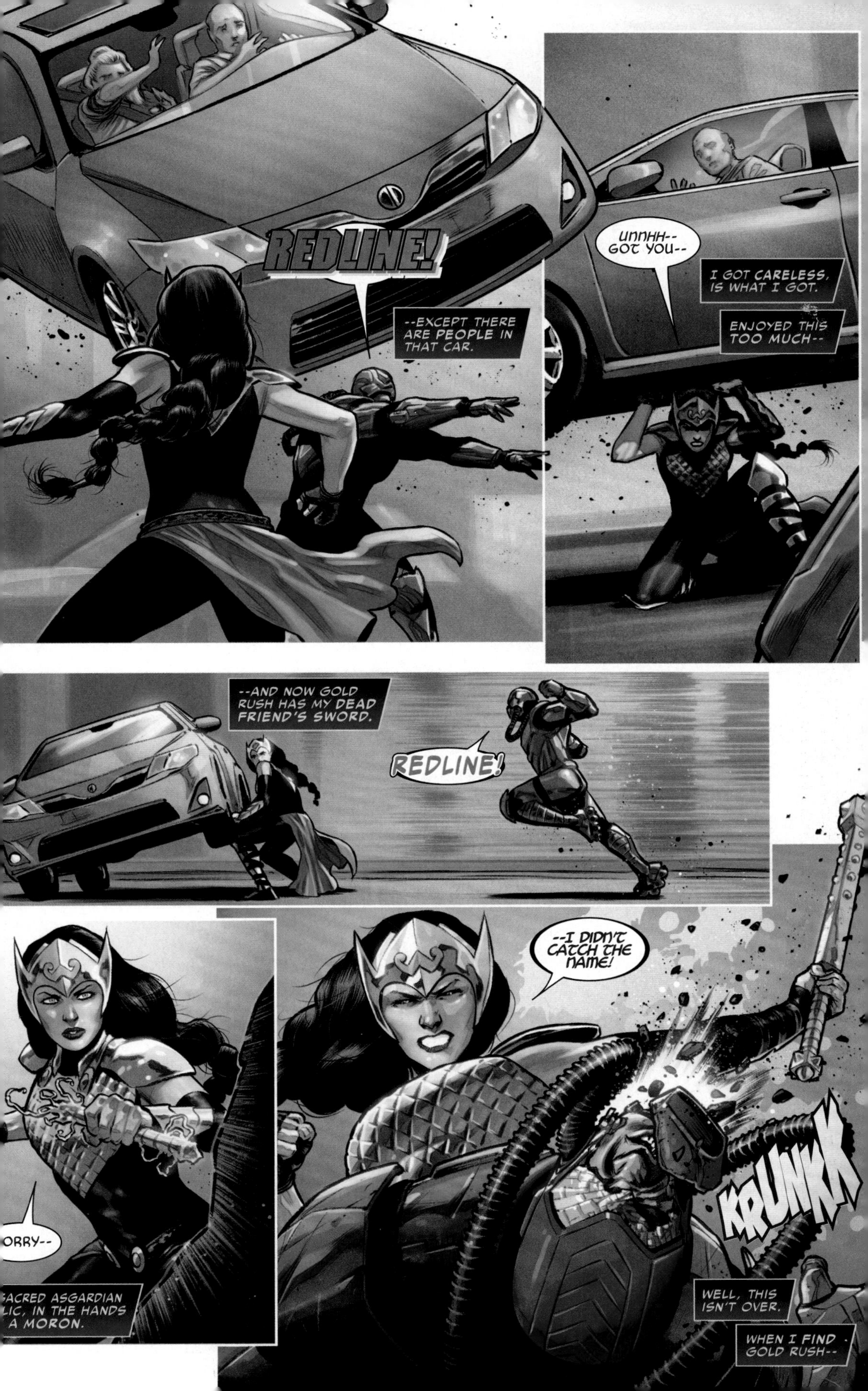

REDLINE!
--EXCEPT THERE ARE PEOPLE IN THAT CAR.
UNNHH-- GOT YOU--
I GOT CARELESS, IS WHAT I GOT.
ENJOYED THIS TOO MUCH--
--AND NOW GOLD RUSH HAS MY DEAD FRIEND'S SWORD.
REDLINE!
ORRY--
ACRED ASGARDIAN LIC, IN THE HANDS A MORON.
--I DIDN'T CATCH THE NAME!
KRUNKK
WELL, THIS ISN'T OVER.
WHEN I FIND GOLD RUSH--

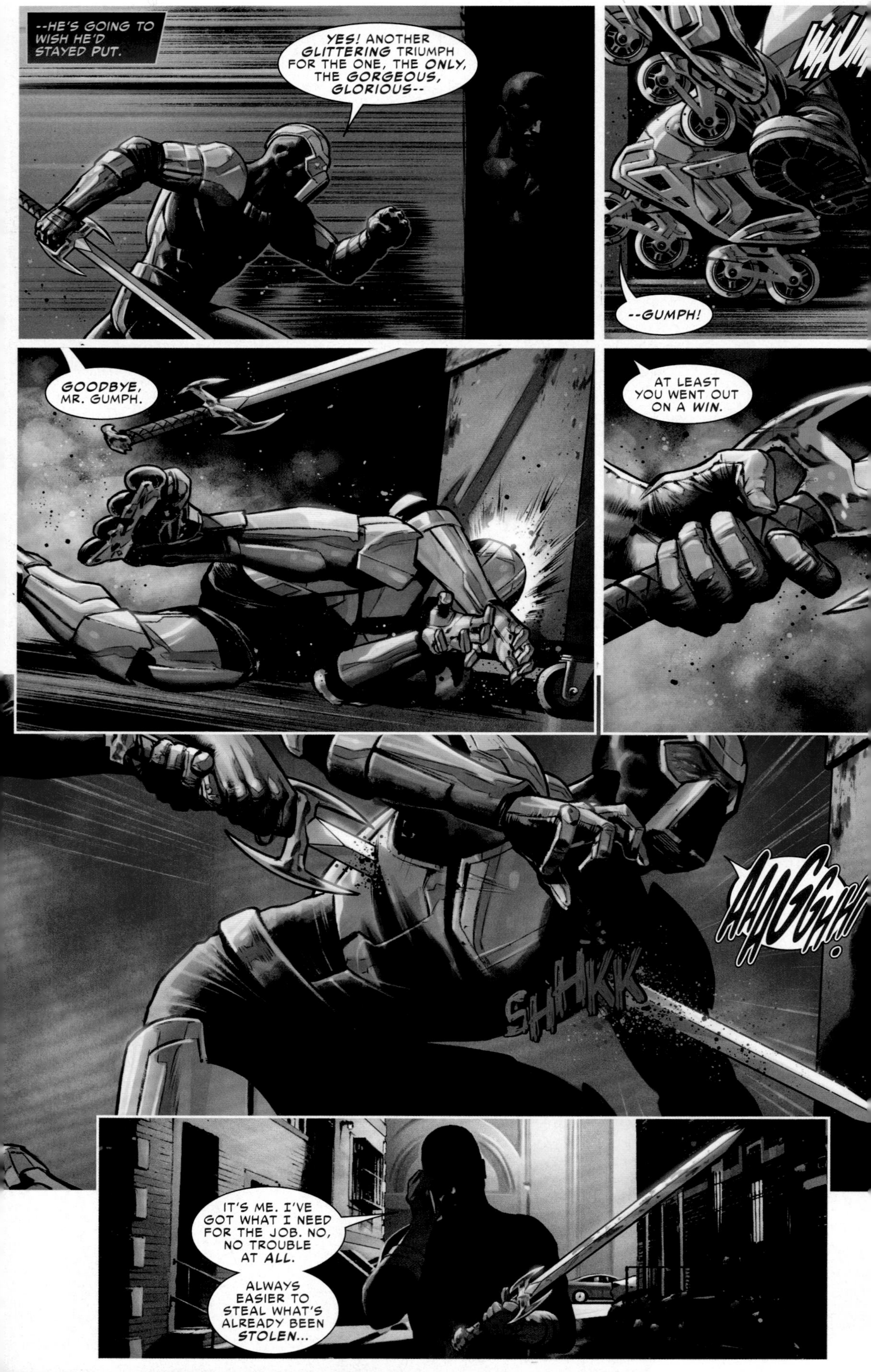
--HE'S GOING TO WISH HE'D STAYED PUT.
YES! ANOTHER GLITTERING TRIUMPH FOR THE ONE, THE ONLY, THE GORGEOUS, GLORIOUS--
WHUMP
--GUMPH!
GOODBYE, MR. GUMPH.
AT LEAST YOU WENT OUT ON A WIN.
AAAGGHH!
SHHKK
IT'S ME. I'VE GOT WHAT I NEED FOR THE JOB. NO, NO TROUBLE AT ALL.
ALWAYS EASIER TO STEAL WHAT'S ALREADY BEEN STOLEN...

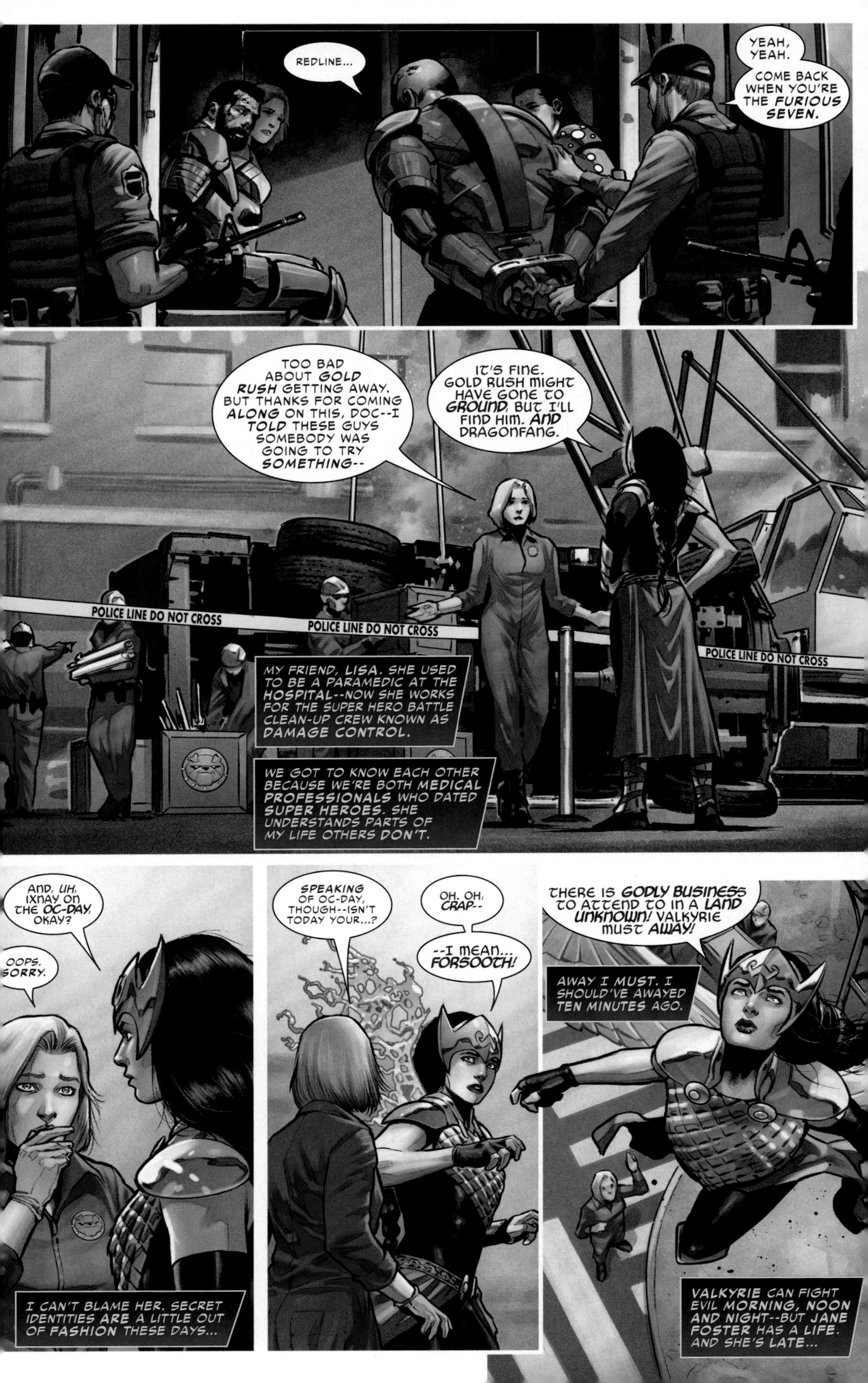

REDLINE...
YEAH, YEAH.
COME BACK WHEN YOU'RE THE FURIOUS SEVEN.
TOO BAD ABOUT GOLD RUSH GETTING AWAY. BUT THANKS FOR COMING ALONG ON THIS, DOC--I TOLD THESE GUYS SOMEBODY WAS GOING TO TRY SOMETHING--
IT'S FINE. GOLD RUSH MIGHT HAVE GONE TO GROUND, BUT I'LL FIND HIM. AND DRAGONFANG.
POLICE LINE DO NOT CROSS
POLICE LINE DO NOT CROSS
POLICE LINE DO NOT CROSS
MY FRIEND, LISA. SHE USED TO BE A PARAMEDIC AT THE HOSPITAL--NOW SHE WORKS FOR THE SUPER HERO BATTLE CLEAN-UP CREW KNOWN AS DAMAGE CONTROL.
WE GOT TO KNOW EACH OTHER BECAUSE WE'RE BOTH MEDICAL PROFESSIONALS WHO DATED SUPER HEROES. SHE UNDERSTANDS PARTS OF MY LIFE OTHERS DON'T.
AND, UH, IXNAY ON THE OC-DAY, OKAY?
OOPS. SORRY.
I CAN'T BLAME HER. SECRET IDENTITIES ARE A LITTLE OUT OF FASHION THESE DAYS...
SPEAKING OF OC-DAY, THOUGH--ISN'T TODAY YOUR...?
OH. OH, CRAP--
--I MEAN... FORSOOTH!
THERE IS GODLY BUSINESS TO ATTEND TO IN A LAND UNKNOWN! VALKYRIE MUST AWAY!
AWAY I MUST. I SHOULD'VE AWAYED TEN MINUTES AGO.
VALKYRIE CAN FIGHT EVIL MORNING, NOON AND NIGHT--BUT JANE FOSTER HAS A LIFE. AND SHE'S LATE...

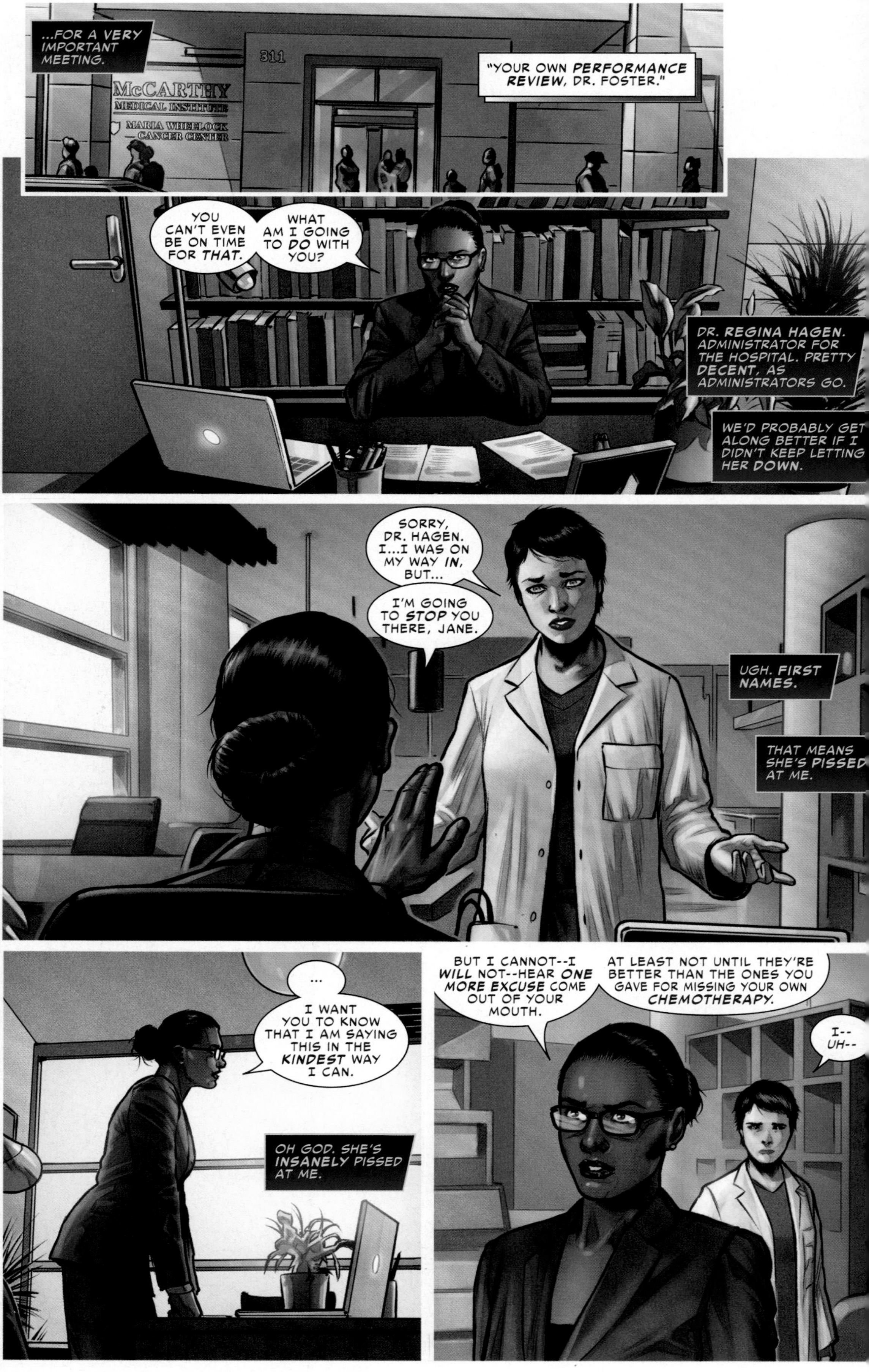
...FOR A VERY IMPORTANT MEETING.
311
McCARTHY MEDICAL INSTITUTE
MARIA WHEELOCK CANCER CENTER
"YOUR OWN PERFORMANCE REVIEW, DR. FOSTER."
YOU CAN'T EVEN BE ON TIME FOR THAT.
WHAT AM I GOING TO DO WITH YOU?
DR. REGINA HAGEN. ADMINISTRATOR FOR THE HOSPITAL. PRETTY DECENT, AS ADMINISTRATORS GO.
WE'D PROBABLY GET ALONG BETTER IF I DIDN'T KEEP LETTING HER DOWN.
SORRY, DR. HAGEN. I...I WAS ON MY WAY IN, BUT...
I'M GOING TO STOP YOU THERE, JANE.
UGH. FIRST NAMES.
THAT MEANS SHE'S PISSED AT ME.
...
I WANT YOU TO KNOW THAT I AM SAYING THIS IN THE KINDEST WAY I CAN.
OH GOD. SHE'S INSANELY PISSED AT ME.
BUT I CANNOT--I WILL NOT--HEAR ONE MORE EXCUSE COME OUT OF YOUR MOUTH.
AT LEAST NOT UNTIL THEY'RE BETTER THAN THE ONES YOU GAVE FOR MISSING YOUR OWN CHEMOTHERAPY.
I-- UH--

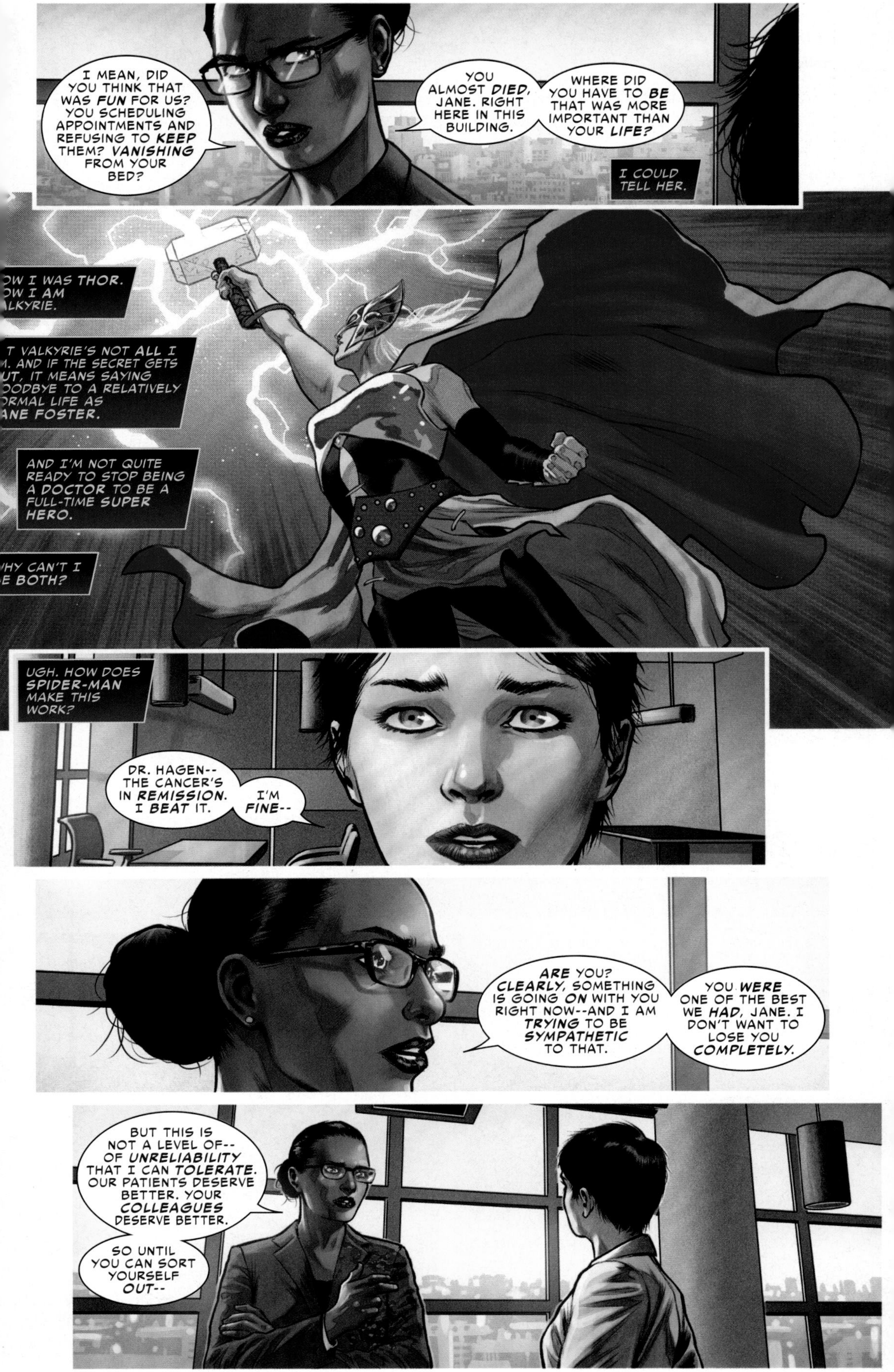
I MEAN, DID YOU THINK THAT WAS FUN FOR US? YOU SCHEDULING APPOINTMENTS AND REFUSING TO KEEP THEM? VANISHING FROM YOUR BED?
YOU ALMOST DIED, JANE. RIGHT HERE IN THIS BUILDING.
WHERE DID YOU HAVE TO BE THAT WAS MORE IMPORTANT THAN YOUR LIFE?
I COULD TELL HER.
OW I WAS THOR. OW I AM ALKYRIE.
T VALKYRIE'S NOT ALL I M. AND IF THE SECRET GETS UT, IT MEANS SAYING OODBYE TO A RELATIVELY ORMAL LIFE AS ANE FOSTER.
AND I'M NOT QUITE READY TO STOP BEING A DOCTOR TO BE A FULL-TIME SUPER HERO.
HY CAN'T I E BOTH?
UGH. HOW DOES SPIDER-MAN MAKE THIS WORK?
DR. HAGEN-- THE CANCER'S IN REMISSION. I BEAT IT.
I'M FINE--
ARE YOU? CLEARLY, SOMETHING IS GOING ON WITH YOU RIGHT NOW--AND I AM TRYING TO BE SYMPATHETIC TO THAT.
YOU WERE ONE OF THE BEST WE HAD, JANE. I DON'T WANT TO LOSE YOU COMPLETELY.
BUT THIS IS NOT A LEVEL OF-- OF UNRELIABILITY THAT I CAN TOLERATE. OUR PATIENTS DESERVE BETTER. YOUR COLLEAGUES DESERVE BETTER.
SO UNTIL YOU CAN SORT YOURSELF OUT--

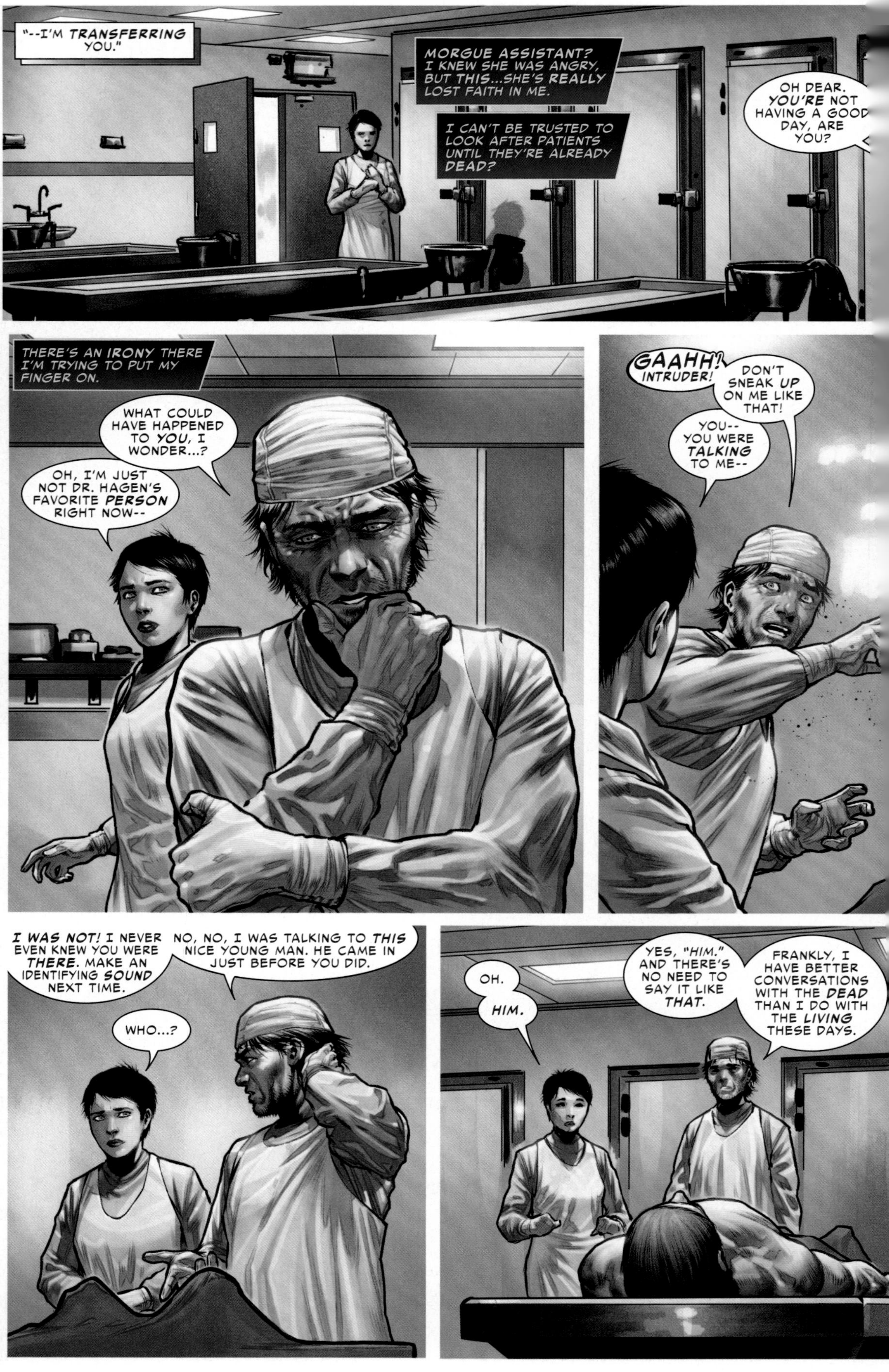
"--I'M TRANSFERRING YOU."
MORGUE ASSISTANT? I KNEW SHE WAS ANGRY, BUT THIS...SHE'S REALLY LOST FAITH IN ME.
I CAN'T BE TRUSTED TO LOOK AFTER PATIENTS UNTIL THEY'RE ALREADY DEAD?
OH DEAR. YOU'RE NOT HAVING A GOOD DAY, ARE YOU?
THERE'S AN IRONY THERE I'M TRYING TO PUT MY FINGER ON.
WHAT COULD HAVE HAPPENED TO YOU, I WONDER...?
OH, I'M JUST NOT DR. HAGEN'S FAVORITE PERSON RIGHT NOW--
GAAHH! INTRUDER!
DON'T SNEAK UP ON ME LIKE THAT!
YOU-- YOU WERE TALKING TO ME--
I WAS NOT! I NEVER EVEN KNEW YOU WERE THERE. MAKE AN IDENTIFYING SOUND NEXT TIME.
NO, NO, I WAS TALKING TO THIS NICE YOUNG MAN. HE CAME IN JUST BEFORE YOU DID.
WHO...?
OH.
HIM.
YES, "HIM." AND THERE'S NO NEED TO SAY IT LIKE THAT.
FRANKLY, I HAVE BETTER CONVERSATIONS WITH THE DEAD THAN I DO WITH THE LIVING THESE DAYS.

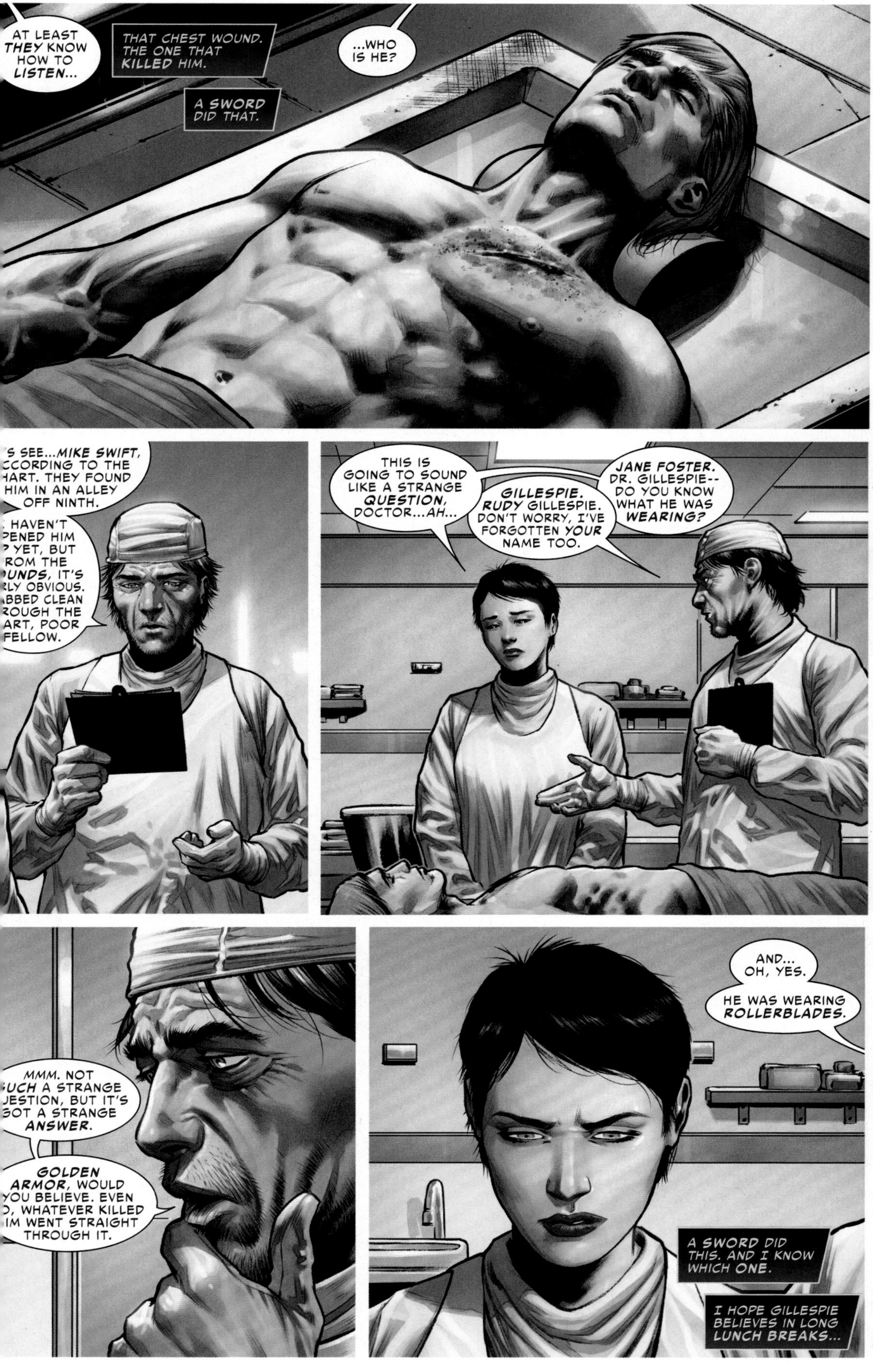

AT LEAST THEY KNOW HOW TO LISTEN...
THAT CHEST WOUND. THE ONE THAT KILLED HIM.
A SWORD DID THAT.
...WHO IS HE?
'S SEE...MIKE SWIFT, CCORDING TO THE HART. THEY FOUND HIM IN AN ALLEY OFF NINTH.
HAVEN'T PENED HIM P YET, BUT ROM THE OUNDS, IT'S RLY OBVIOUS. BBED CLEAN ROUGH THE ART, POOR FELLOW.
THIS IS GOING TO SOUND LIKE A STRANGE QUESTION, DOCTOR...AH...
GILLESPIE. RUDY GILLESPIE. DON'T WORRY, I'VE FORGOTTEN YOUR NAME TOO.
JANE FOSTER. DR. GILLESPIE-- DO YOU KNOW WHAT HE WAS WEARING?
MMM. NOT UCH A STRANGE UESTION, BUT IT'S GOT A STRANGE ANSWER.
GOLDEN ARMOR, WOULD YOU BELIEVE. EVEN O, WHATEVER KILLED IM WENT STRAIGHT THROUGH IT.
AND... OH, YES.
HE WAS WEARING ROLLERBLADES.
A SWORD DID THIS. AND I KNOW WHICH ONE.
I HOPE GILLESPIE BELIEVES IN LONG LUNCH BREAKS...

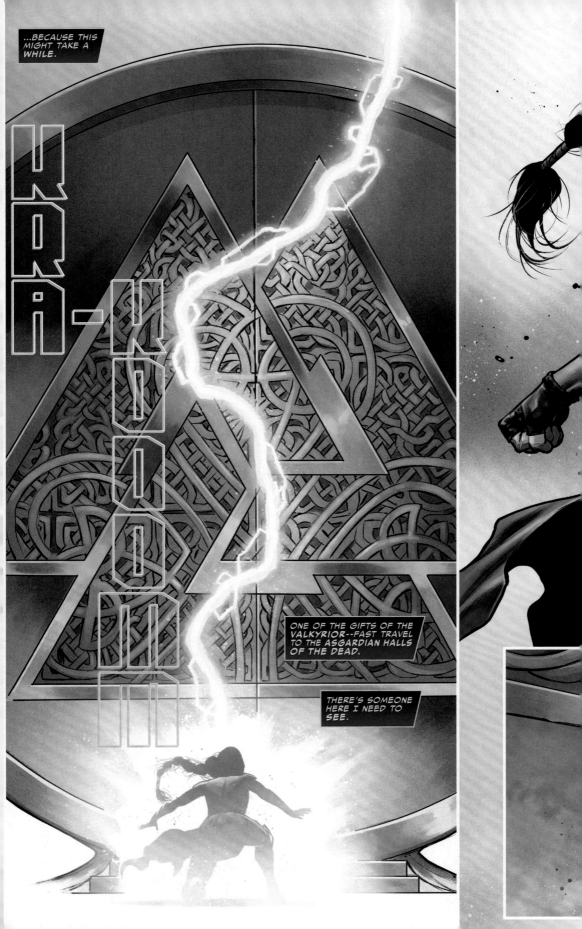

...BECAUSE THIS MIGHT TAKE A WHILE.

KRA-KOOOM!

ONE OF THE GIFTS OF THE VALKYRIOR--FAST TRAVEL TO THE ASGARDIAN HALLS OF THE DEAD.

THERE'S SOMEONE HERE I NEED TO SEE.

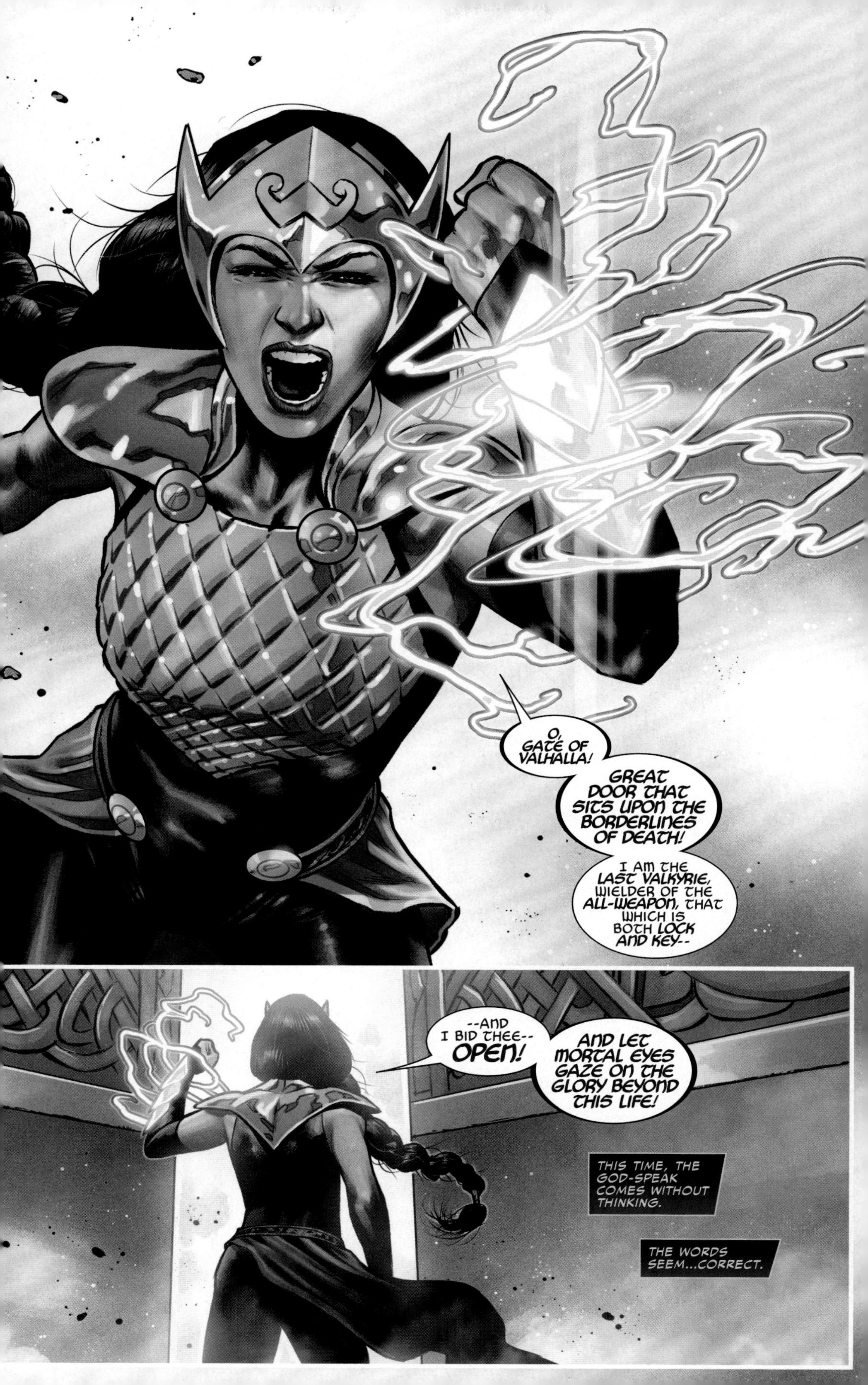
O, GATE OF VALHALLA!
GREAT DOOR THAT SITS UPON THE BORDERLINES OF DEATH!
I AM THE LAST VALKYRIE, WIELDER OF THE ALL-WEAPON, THAT WHICH IS BOTH LOCK AND KEY--
--AND I BID THEE-- OPEN!
AND LET MORTAL EYES GAZE ON THE GLORY BEYOND THIS LIFE!
THIS TIME, THE GOD-SPEAK COMES WITHOUT THINKING.
THE WORDS SEEM...CORRECT.

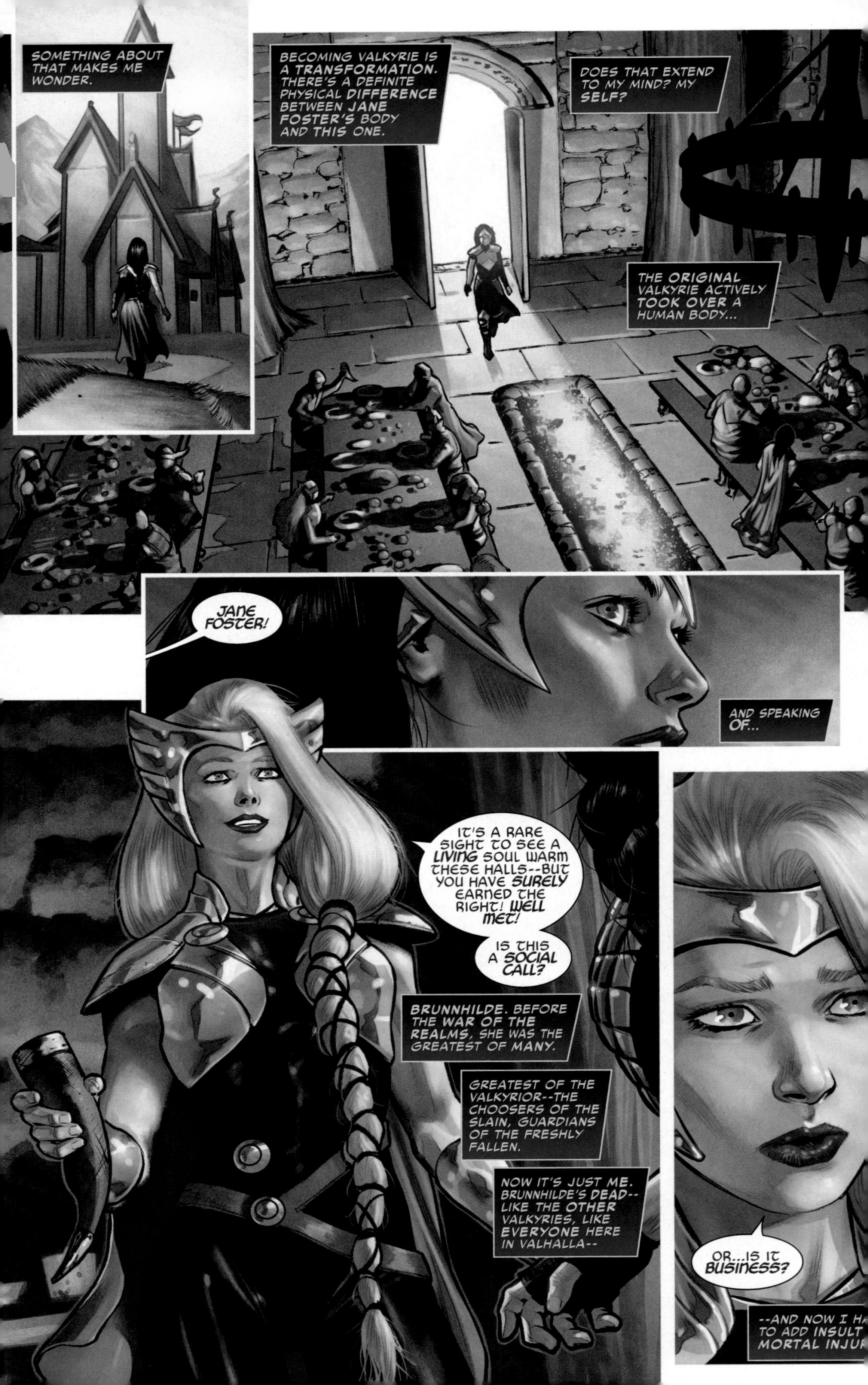
SOMETHING ABOUT THAT MAKES ME WONDER.
BECOMING VALKYRIE IS A TRANSFORMATION. THERE'S A DEFINITE PHYSICAL DIFFERENCE BETWEEN JANE FOSTER'S BODY AND THIS ONE.
DOES THAT EXTEND TO MY MIND? MY SELF?
THE ORIGINAL VALKYRIE ACTIVELY TOOK OVER A HUMAN BODY...
JANE FOSTER!
AND SPEAKING OF...
IT'S A RARE SIGHT TO SEE A LIVING SOUL WARM THESE HALLS--BUT YOU HAVE SURELY EARNED THE RIGHT! WELL MET!
IS THIS A SOCIAL CALL?
BRUNNHILDE. BEFORE THE WAR OF THE REALMS, SHE WAS THE GREATEST OF MANY.
GREATEST OF THE VALKYRIOR--THE CHOOSERS OF THE SLAIN, GUARDIANS OF THE FRESHLY FALLEN.
NOW IT'S JUST ME. BRUNNHILDE'S DEAD--LIKE THE OTHER VALKYRIES, LIKE EVERYONE HERE IN VALHALLA--
OR...IS IT BUSINESS?
--AND NOW I HA TO ADD INSULT MORTAL INJUR

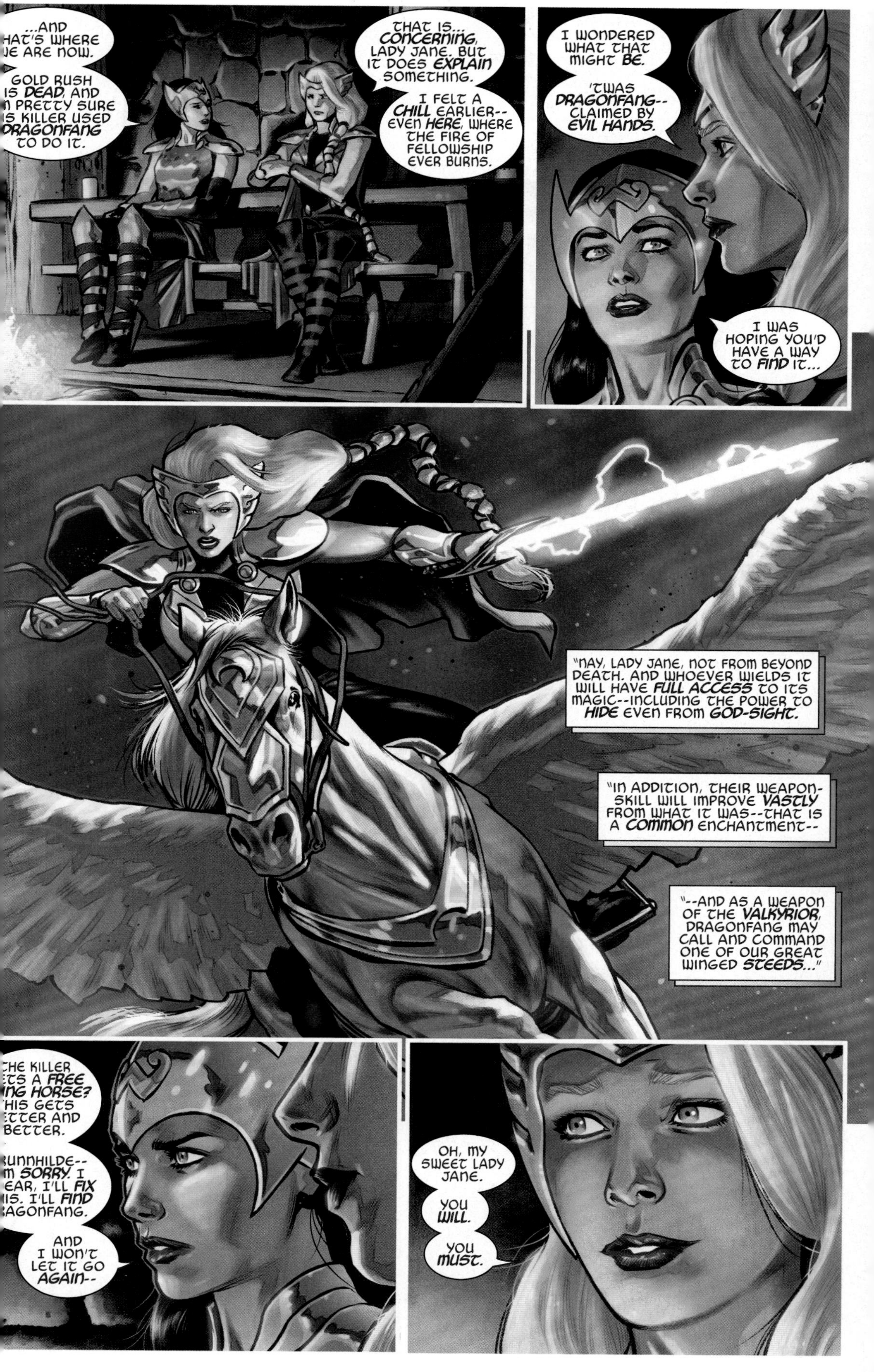

...AND HAT'S WHERE E ARE NOW.
GOLD RUSH IS DEAD, AND N PRETTY SURE S KILLER USED DRAGONFANG TO DO IT.
THAT IS... CONCERNING, LADY JANE. BUT IT DOES EXPLAIN SOMETHING.
I FELT A CHILL EARLIER-- EVEN HERE, WHERE THE FIRE OF FELLOWSHIP EVER BURNS.
I WONDERED WHAT THAT MIGHT BE.
'TWAS DRAGONFANG-- CLAIMED BY EVIL HANDS.
I WAS HOPING YOU'D HAVE A WAY TO FIND IT...
"NAY, LADY JANE, NOT FROM BEYOND DEATH. AND WHOEVER WIELDS IT WILL HAVE FULL ACCESS TO ITS MAGIC--INCLUDING THE POWER TO HIDE EVEN FROM GOD-SIGHT.
"IN ADDITION, THEIR WEAPON-SKILL WILL IMPROVE VASTLY FROM WHAT IT WAS--THAT IS A COMMON ENCHANTMENT--
"--AND AS A WEAPON OF THE VALKYRIOR, DRAGONFANG MAY CALL AND COMMAND ONE OF OUR GREAT WINGED STEEDS..."
THE KILLER ETS A FREE ING HORSE? THIS GETS ETTER AND BETTER.
RUNNHILDE-- M SORRY. I EAR, I'LL FIX IS. I'LL FIND AGONFANG.
AND I WON'T LET IT GO AGAIN--
OH, MY SWEET LADY JANE.
YOU WILL.
YOU MUST.

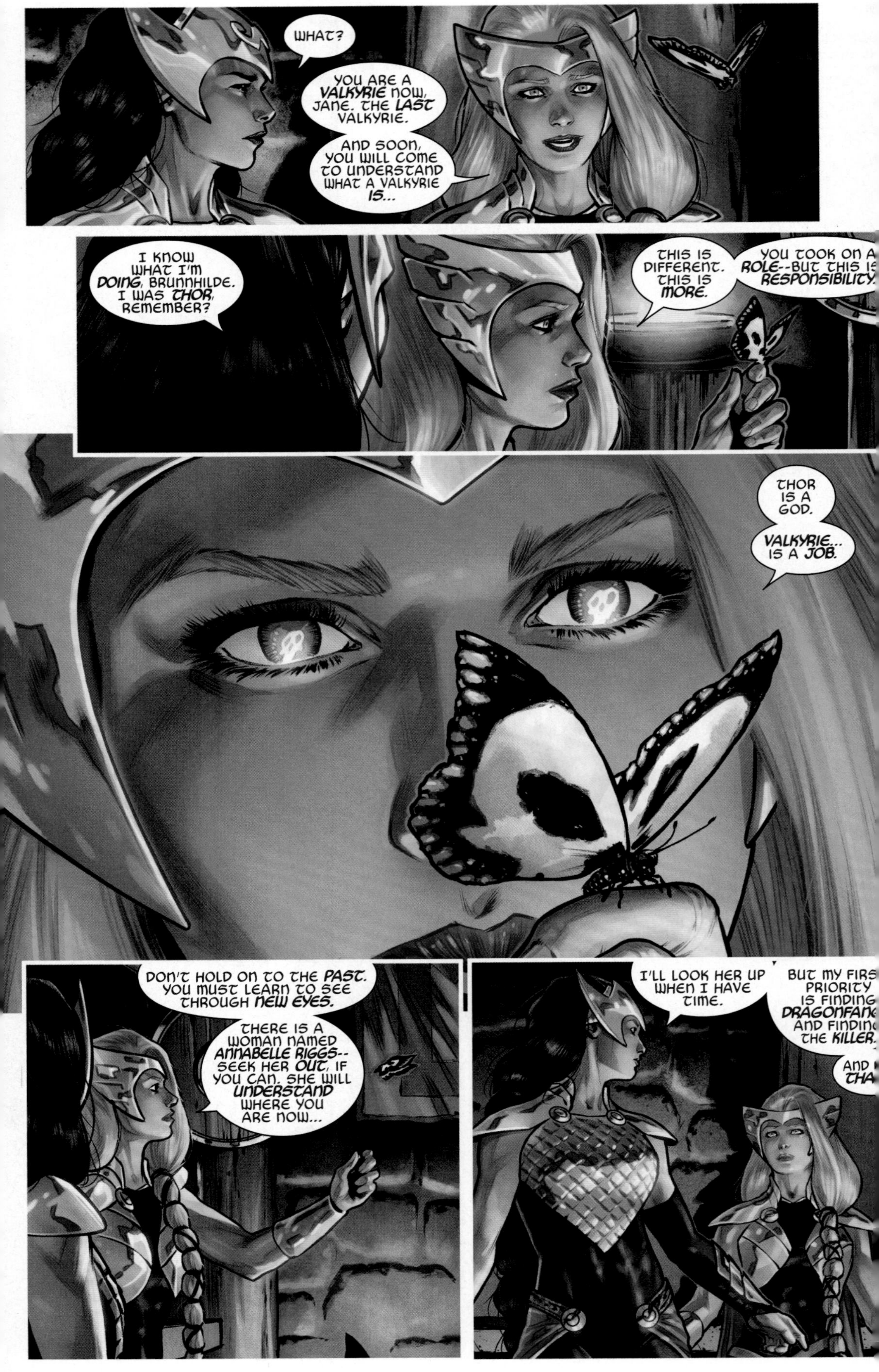
WHAT?
YOU ARE A VALKYRIE NOW, JANE. THE LAST VALKYRIE.
AND SOON, YOU WILL COME TO UNDERSTAND WHAT A VALKYRIE IS...
I KNOW WHAT I'M DOING, BRUNNHILDE. I WAS THOR, REMEMBER?
THIS IS DIFFERENT. THIS IS MORE.
YOU TOOK ON A ROLE--BUT THIS IS RESPONSIBILITY.
THOR IS A GOD.
VALKYRIE... IS A JOB.
DON'T HOLD ON TO THE PAST. YOU MUST LEARN TO SEE THROUGH NEW EYES.
THERE IS A WOMAN NAMED ANNABELLE RIGGS--SEEK HER OUT, IF YOU CAN. SHE WILL UNDERSTAND WHERE YOU ARE NOW...
I'LL LOOK HER UP WHEN I HAVE TIME.
BUT MY FIRS PRIORITY IS FINDING DRAGONFAN AND FINDING THE KILLER.
AND THA

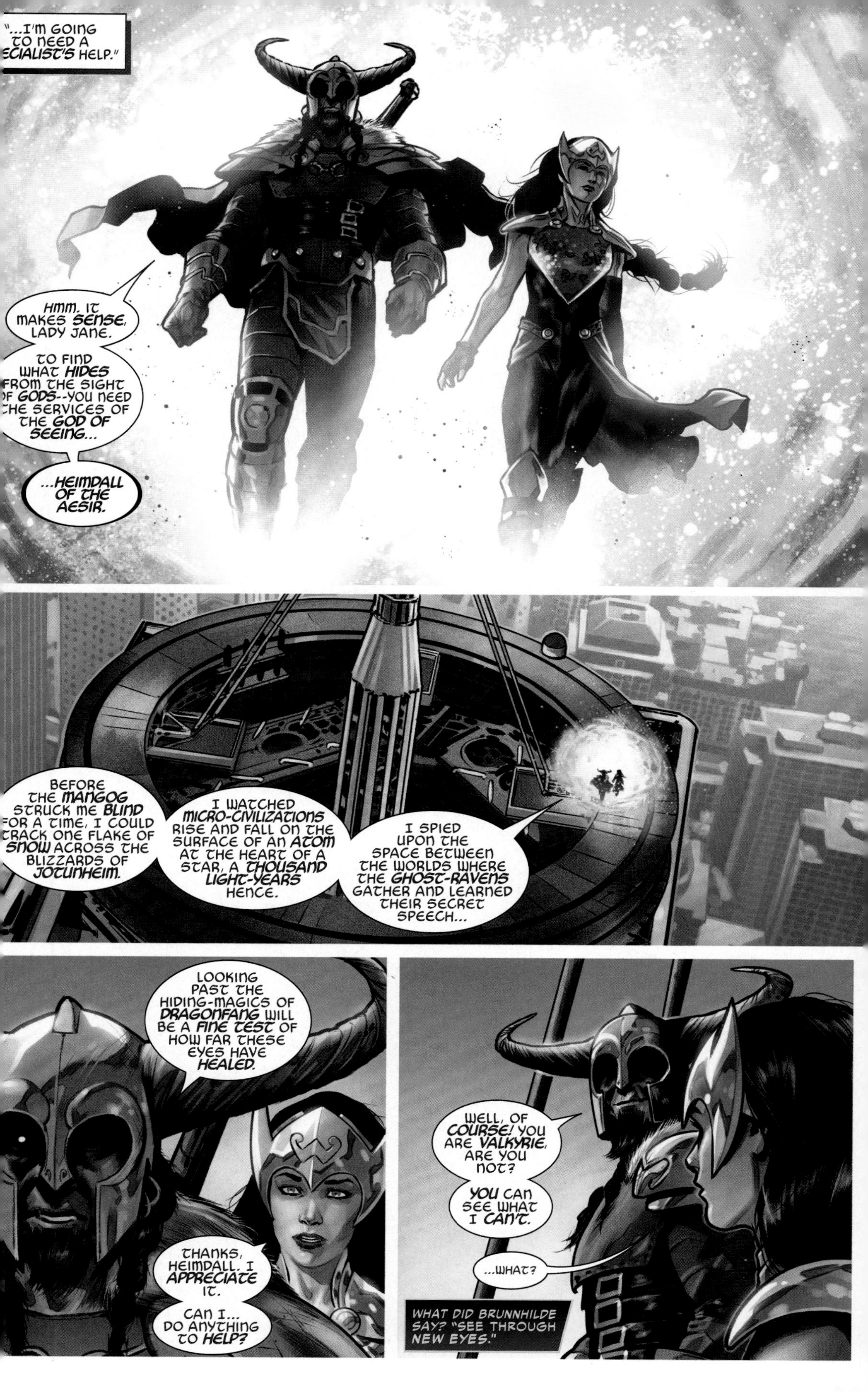
"...I'M GOING TO NEED A ECIALIST'S HELP."
HMM. IT MAKES SENSE, LADY JANE.
TO FIND WHAT HIDES FROM THE SIGHT F GODS--YOU NEED THE SERVICES OF THE GOD OF SEEING...
...HEIMDALL OF THE AESIR.
BEFORE THE MANGOG STRUCK ME BLIND FOR A TIME, I COULD TRACK ONE FLAKE OF SNOW ACROSS THE BLIZZARDS OF JOTUNHEIM.
I WATCHED MICRO-CIVILIZATIONS RISE AND FALL ON THE SURFACE OF AN ATOM AT THE HEART OF A STAR, A THOUSAND LIGHT-YEARS HENCE.
I SPIED UPON THE SPACE BETWEEN THE WORLDS WHERE THE GHOST-RAVENS GATHER AND LEARNED THEIR SECRET SPEECH...
LOOKING PAST THE HIDING-MAGICS OF DRAGONFANG WILL BE A FINE TEST OF HOW FAR THESE EYES HAVE HEALED.
THANKS, HEIMDALL. I APPRECIATE IT.
CAN I... DO ANYTHING TO HELP?
WELL, OF COURSE! YOU ARE VALKYRIE, ARE YOU NOT?
YOU CAN SEE WHAT I CAN'T.
...WHAT?
WHAT DID BRUNNHILDE SAY? "SEE THROUGH NEW EYES."

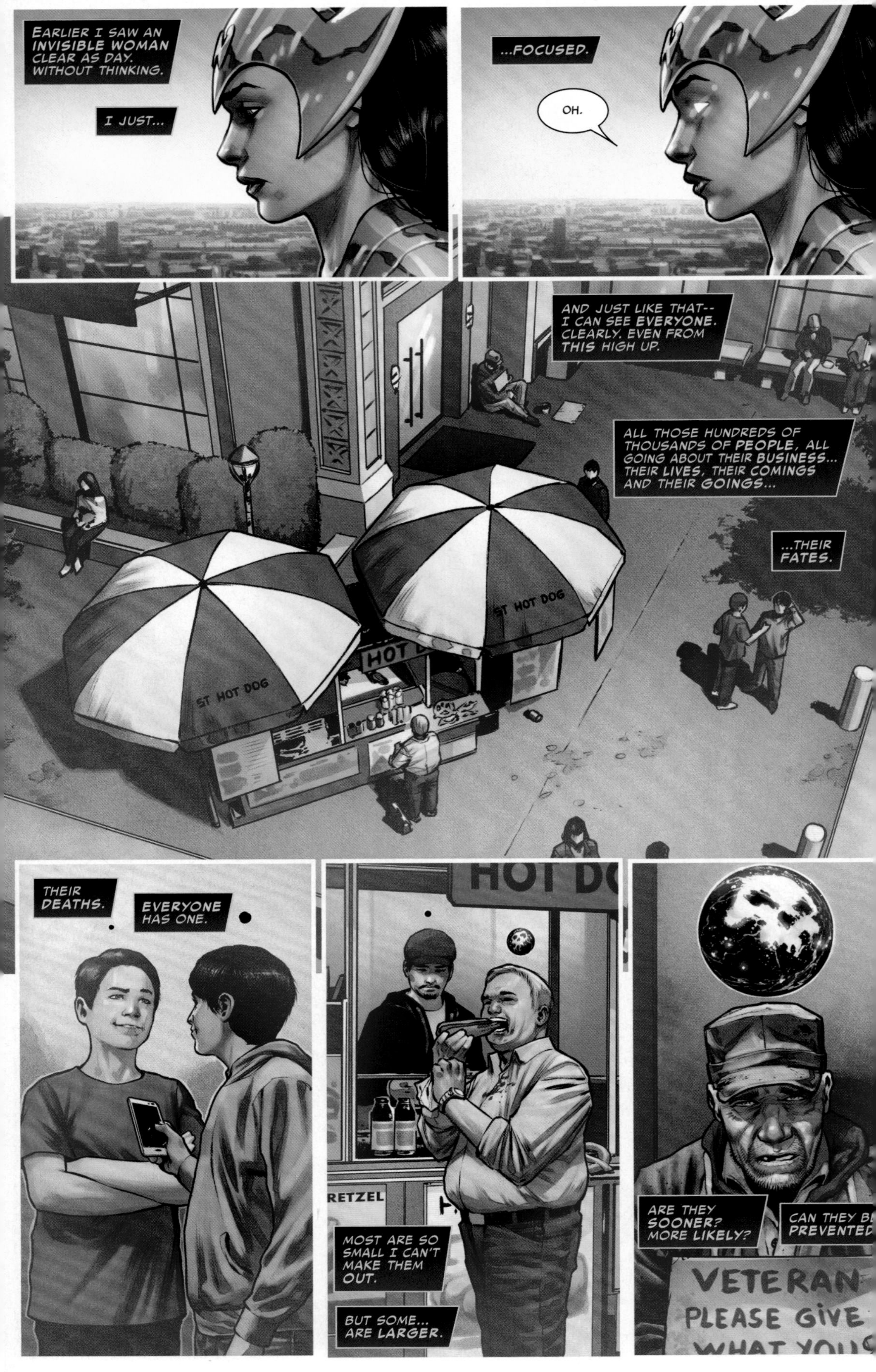
EARLIER I SAW AN INVISIBLE WOMAN CLEAR AS DAY. WITHOUT THINKING.
I JUST...
...FOCUSED.
OH.
AND JUST LIKE THAT-- I CAN SEE EVERYONE. CLEARLY. EVEN FROM THIS HIGH UP.
ALL THOSE HUNDREDS OF THOUSANDS OF PEOPLE, ALL GOING ABOUT THEIR BUSINESS... THEIR LIVES, THEIR COMINGS AND THEIR GOINGS...
...THEIR FATES.
ST HOT DOG
ST HOT DOG
THEIR DEATHS.
EVERYONE HAS ONE.
MOST ARE SO SMALL I CAN'T MAKE THEM OUT.
BUT SOME... ARE LARGER.
ARE THEY SOONER? MORE LIKELY?
CAN THEY B PREVENTED
VETERAN
PLEASE GIVE

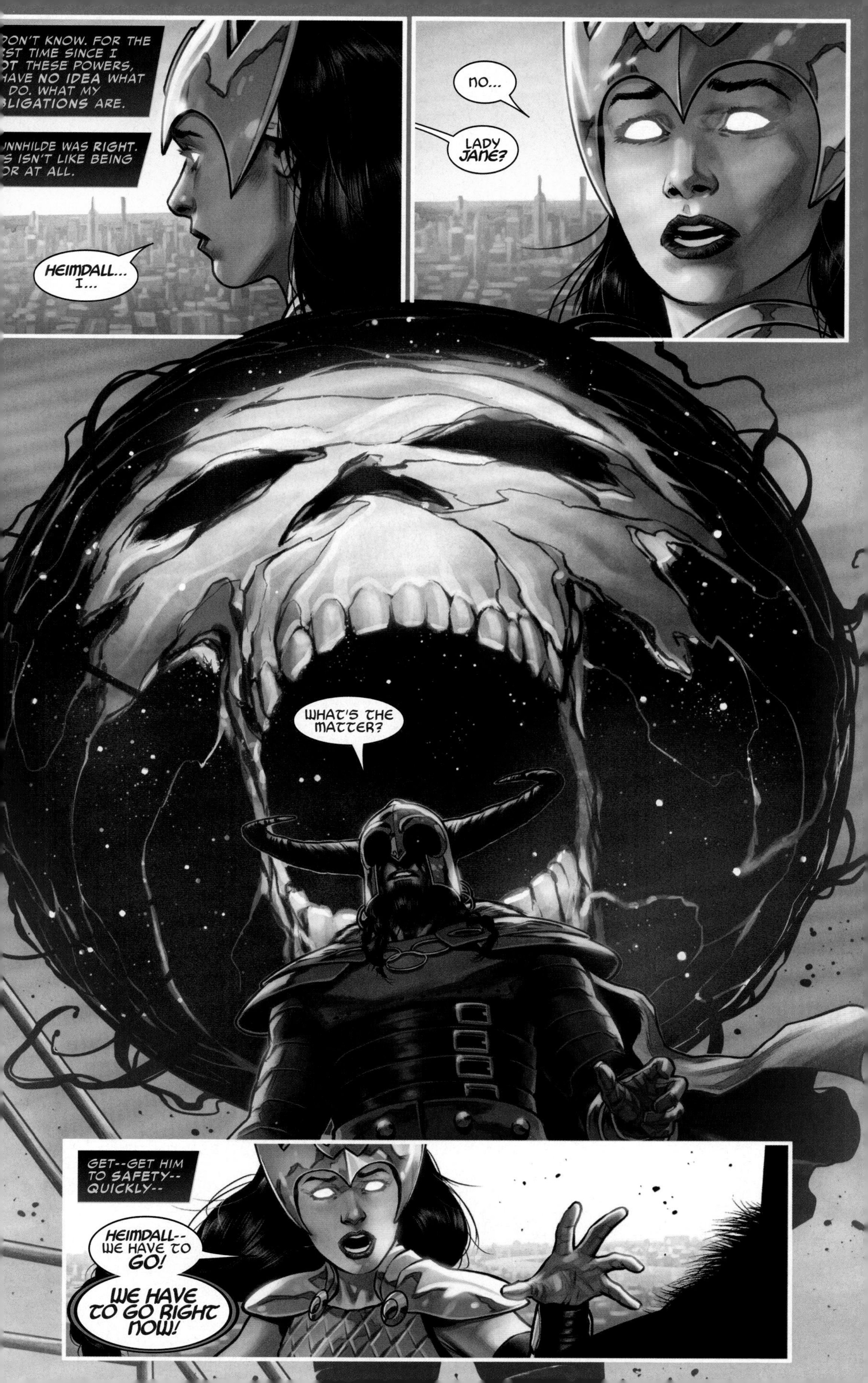

DON'T KNOW. FOR THE
ST TIME SINCE I
OT THESE POWERS,
HAVE NO IDEA WHAT
DO. WHAT MY
BLIGATIONS ARE.
UNNHILDE WAS RIGHT.
S ISN'T LIKE BEING
OR AT ALL.
HEIMDALL... I...
no...
LADY JANE?
WHAT'S THE MATTER?
GET--GET HIM TO SAFETY-- QUICKLY--
HEIMDALL-- WE HAVE TO GO!
WE HAVE TO GO RIGHT NOW!

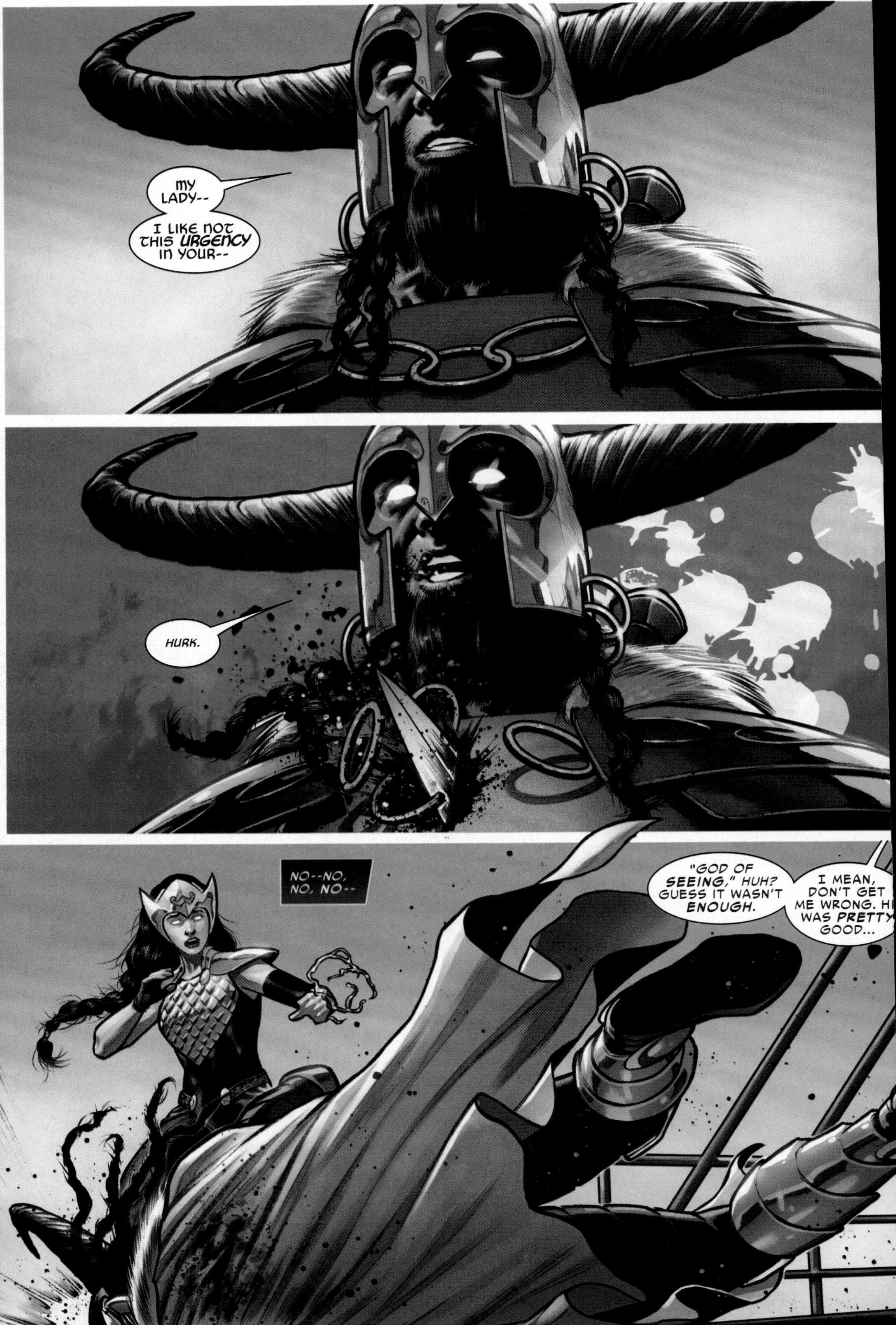
MY LADY--
I LIKE NOT THIS URGENCY IN YOUR--
HURK.
NO--NO, NO, NO--
"GOD OF SEEING," HUH? GUESS IT WASN'T ENOUGH.
I MEAN, DON'T GET ME WRONG. HE WAS PRETTY GOOD...

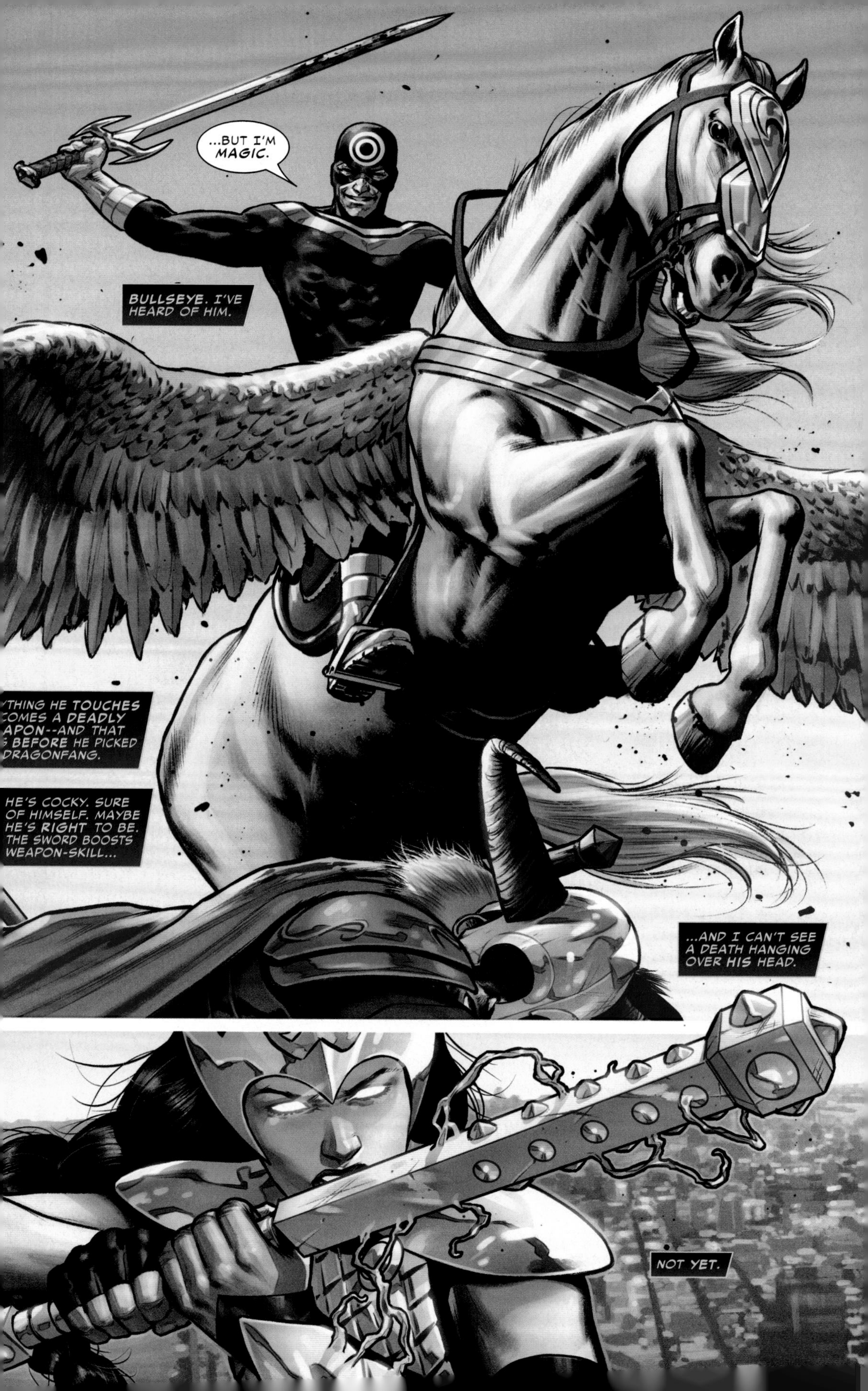

...BUT I'M MAGIC.
BULLSEYE. I'VE HEARD OF HIM.
YTHING HE TOUCHES COMES A DEADLY APON--AND THAT S BEFORE HE PICKED DRAGONFANG.
HE'S COCKY. SURE OF HIMSELF. MAYBE HE'S RIGHT TO BE. THE SWORD BOOSTS WEAPON-SKILL...
...AND I CAN'T SEE A DEATH HANGING OVER HIS HEAD.
NOT YET.

2.

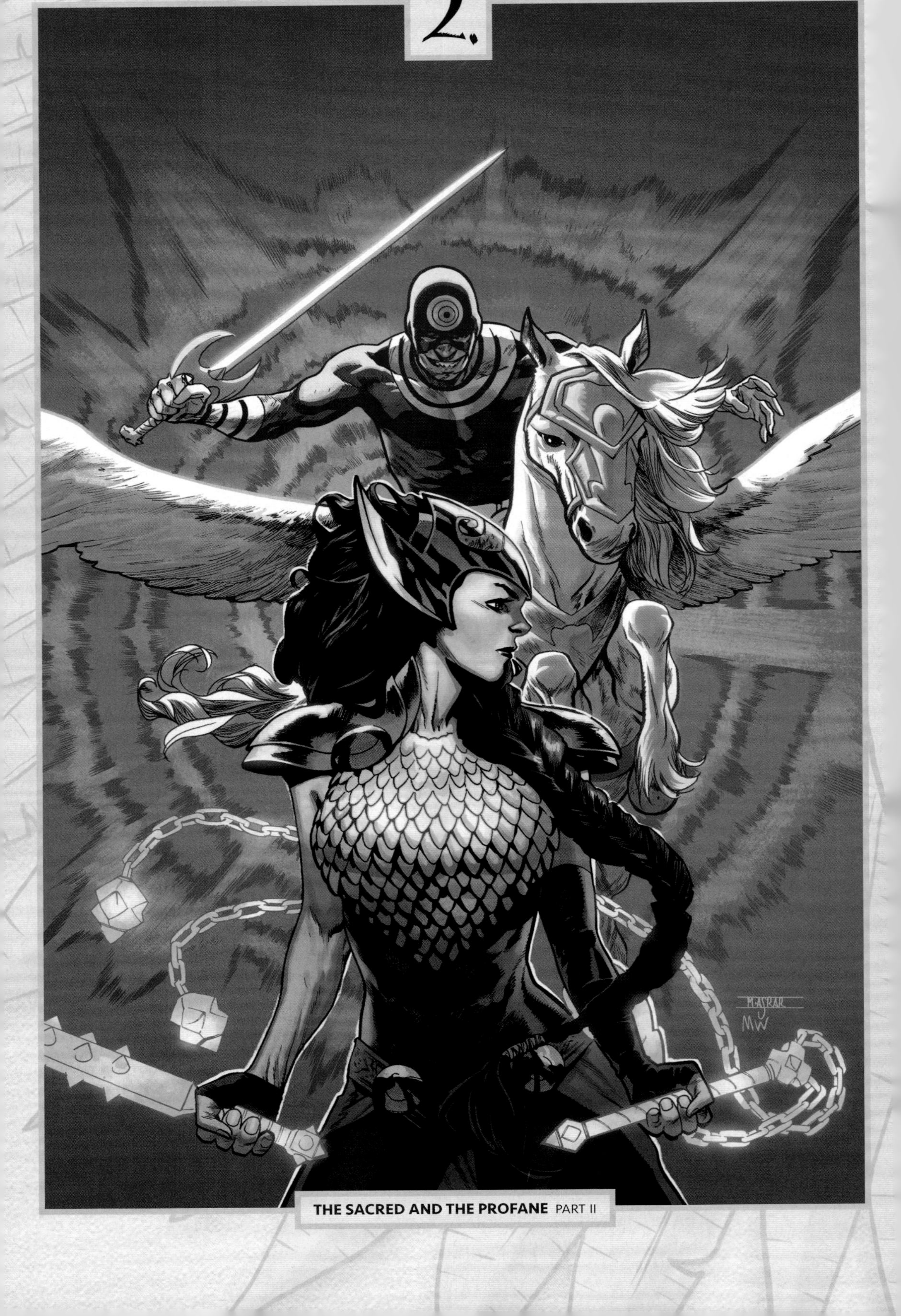

THE SACRED AND THE PROFANE PART II

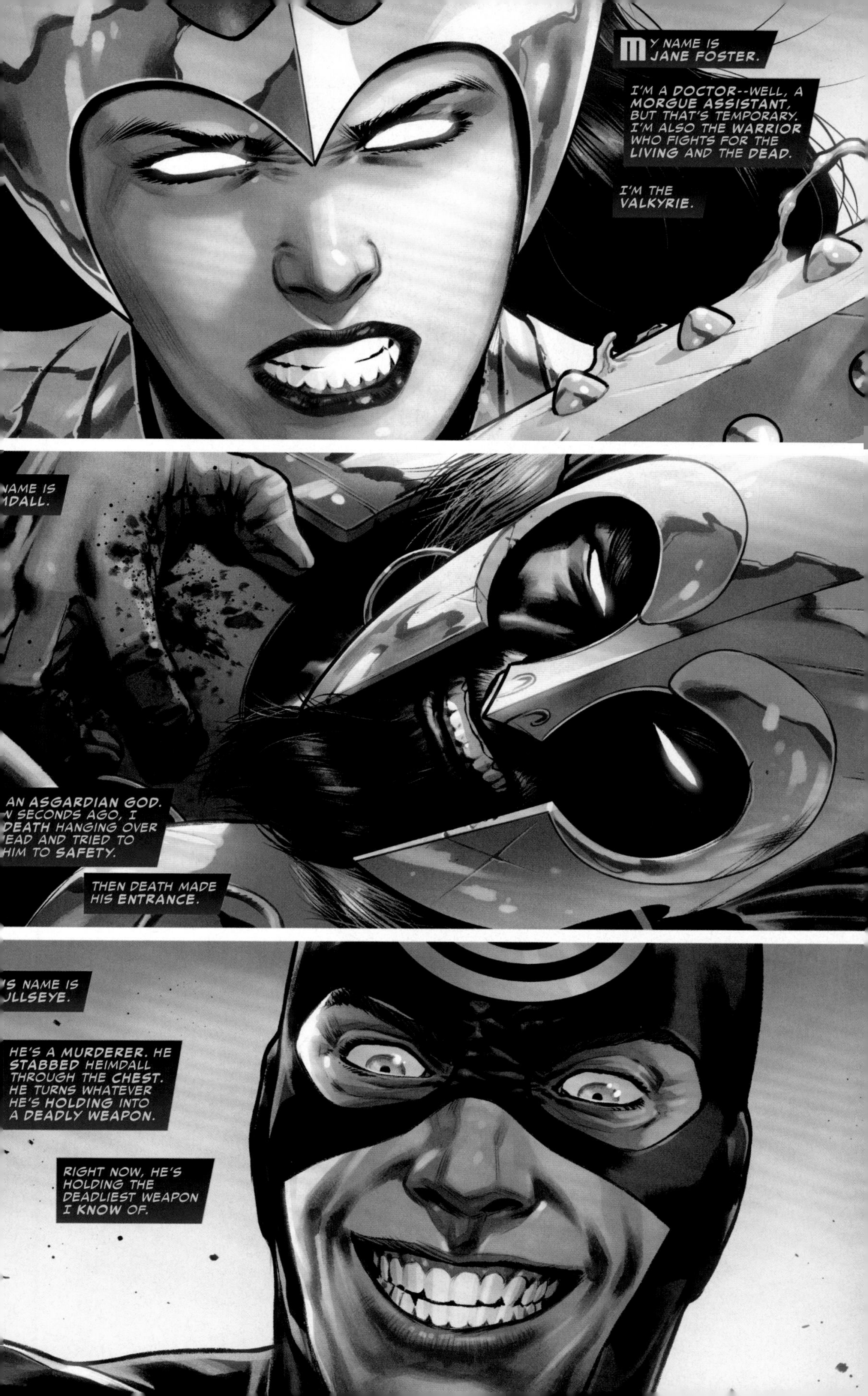
MY NAME IS JANE FOSTER.
I'M A DOCTOR--WELL, A MORGUE ASSISTANT, BUT THAT'S TEMPORARY. I'M ALSO THE WARRIOR WHO FIGHTS FOR THE LIVING AND THE DEAD.
I'M THE VALKYRIE.
NAME IS DALL.
AN ASGARDIAN GOD. N SECONDS AGO, I DEATH HANGING OVER EAD AND TRIED TO HIM TO SAFETY.
THEN DEATH MADE HIS ENTRANCE.
S NAME IS JLLSEYE.
HE'S A MURDERER. HE STABBED HEIMDALL THROUGH THE CHEST. HE TURNS WHATEVER HE'S HOLDING INTO A DEADLY WEAPON.
RIGHT NOW, HE'S HOLDING THE DEADLIEST WEAPON I KNOW OF.

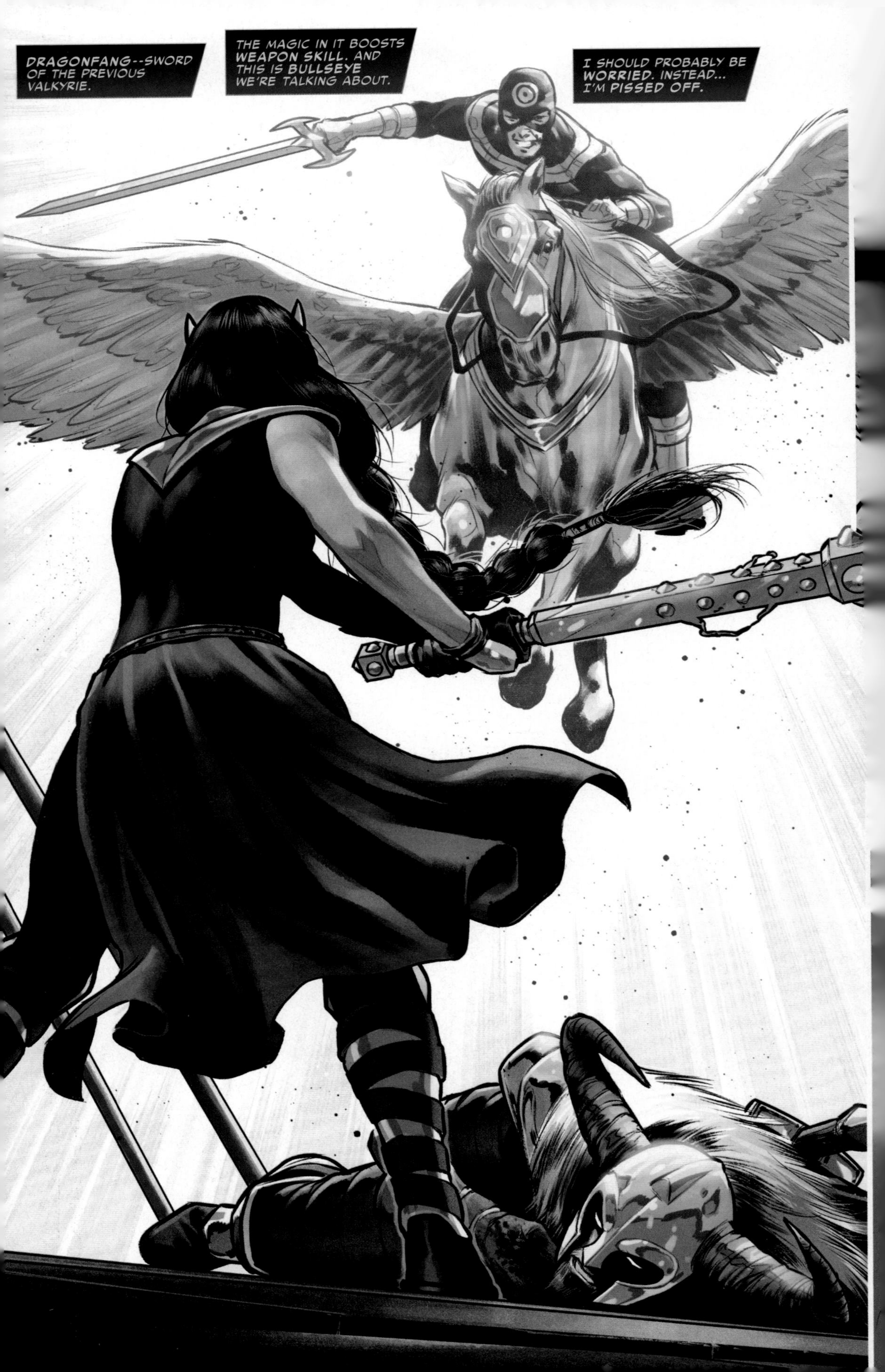
DRAGONFANG--SWORD OF THE PREVIOUS VALKYRIE.
THE MAGIC IN IT BOOSTS WEAPON SKILL. AND THIS IS BULLSEYE WE'RE TALKING ABOUT.
I SHOULD PROBABLY BE WORRIED. INSTEAD... I'M PISSED OFF.

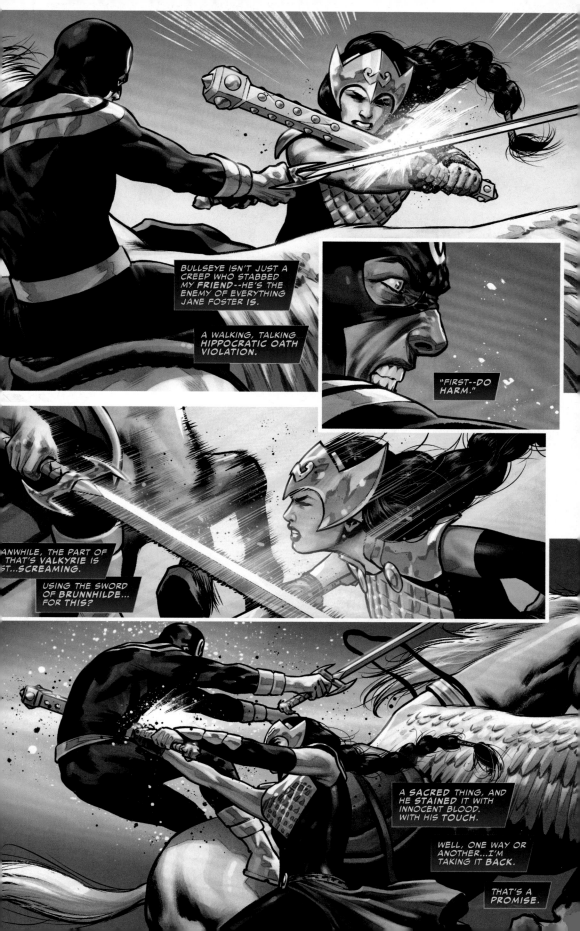

BULLSEYE ISN'T JUST A CREEP WHO STABBED MY FRIEND--HE'S THE ENEMY OF EVERYTHING JANE FOSTER IS.

A WALKING, TALKING HIPPOCRATIC OATH VIOLATION.

"FIRST--DO HARM."

ANWHILE, THE PART OF T THAT'S VALKYRIE IS ST...SCREAMING.

USING THE SWORD OF BRUNNHILDE... FOR THIS?

A SACRED THING, AND HE STAINED IT WITH INNOCENT BLOOD. WITH HIS TOUCH.

WELL, ONE WAY OR ANOTHER...I'M TAKING IT BACK.

THAT'S A PROMISE.

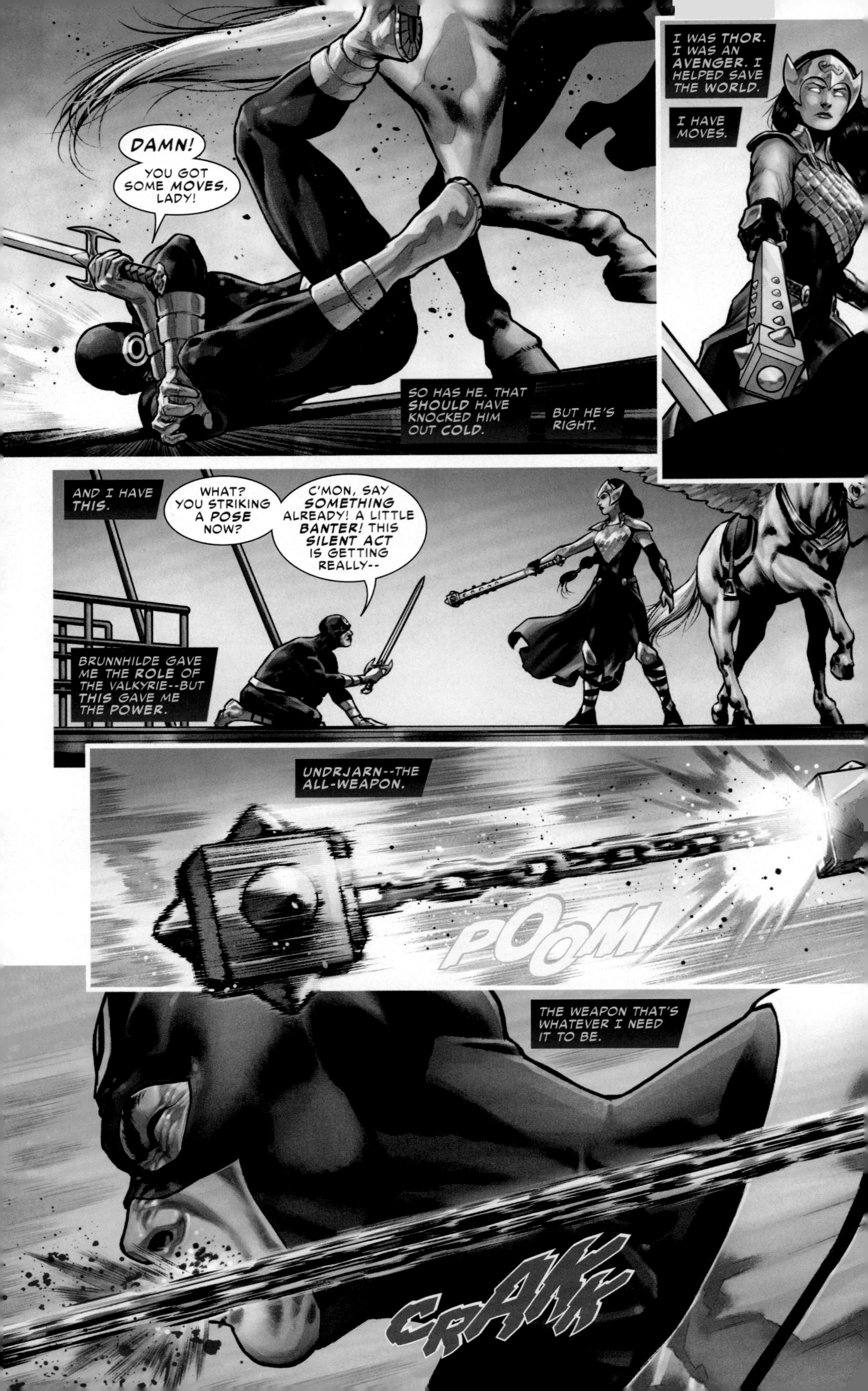
DAMN! YOU GOT SOME MOVES, LADY!
SO HAS HE. THAT SHOULD HAVE KNOCKED HIM OUT COLD.
BUT HE'S RIGHT.
I WAS THOR. I WAS AN AVENGER. I HELPED SAVE THE WORLD.
I HAVE MOVES.
AND I HAVE THIS.
WHAT? YOU STRIKING A POSE NOW?
C'MON, SAY SOMETHING ALREADY! A LITTLE BANTER! THIS SILENT ACT IS GETTING REALLY--
BRUNNHILDE GAVE ME THE ROLE OF THE VALKYRIE--BUT THIS GAVE ME THE POWER.
UNDRJARN--THE ALL-WEAPON.
POOOM
THE WEAPON THAT'S WHATEVER I NEED IT TO BE.
CRAAK

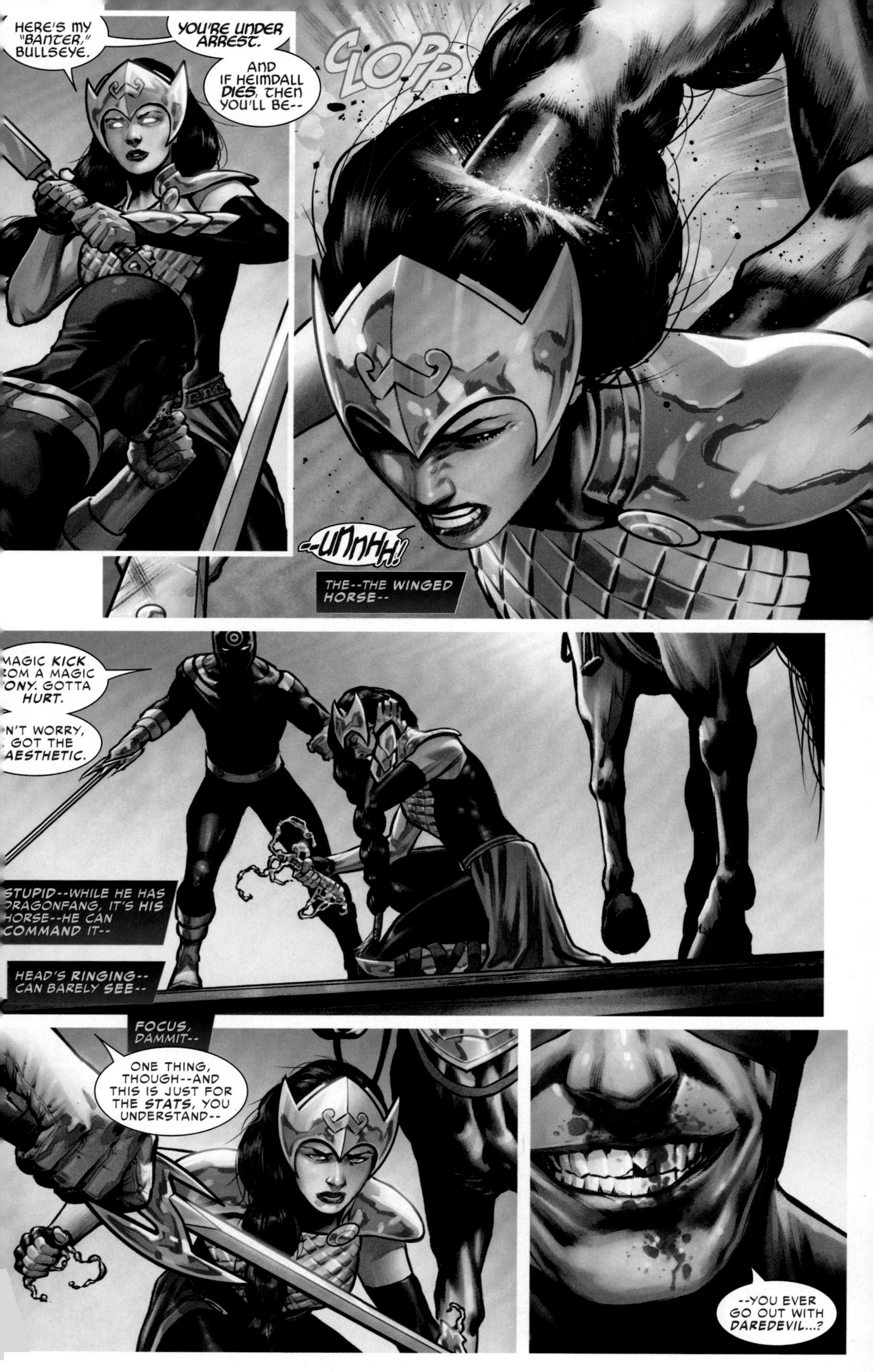
HERE'S MY "BANTER," BULLSEYE.
YOU'RE UNDER ARREST.
AND IF HEIMDALL DIES, THEN YOU'LL BE--
CLOPP
--UNNHH!
THE--THE WINGED HORSE--
MAGIC KICK ROM A MAGIC ONY. GOTTA HURT.
N'T WORRY, GOT THE AESTHETIC.
STUPID--WHILE HE HAS RAGONFANG, IT'S HIS HORSE--HE CAN COMMAND IT--
HEAD'S RINGING--CAN BARELY SEE--
FOCUS, DAMMIT--
ONE THING, THOUGH--AND THIS IS JUST FOR THE STATS, YOU UNDERSTAND--
--YOU EVER GO OUT WITH DAREDEVIL...?

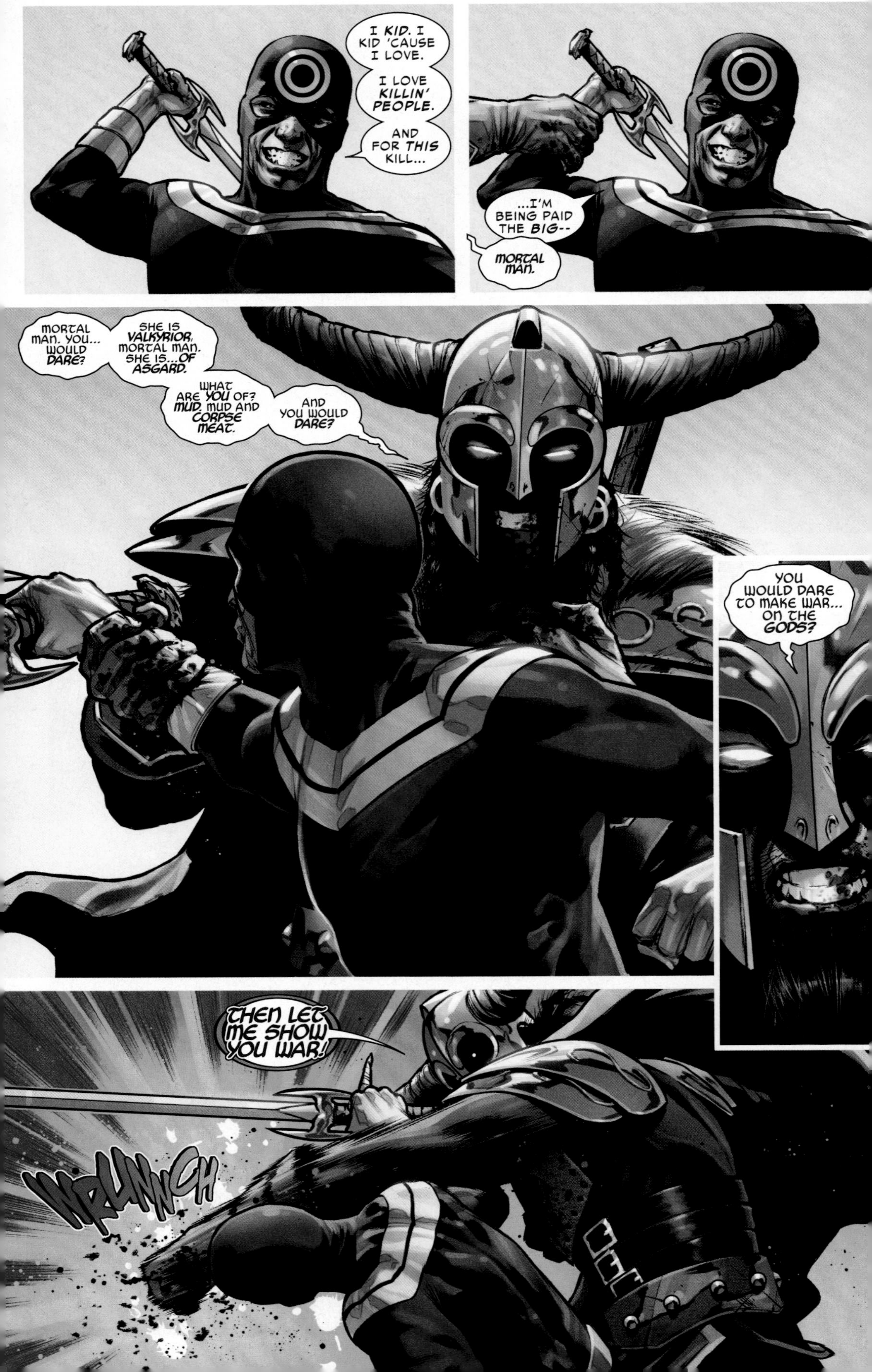

I KID. I KID 'CAUSE I LOVE.
I LOVE KILLIN' PEOPLE.
AND FOR THIS KILL...
...I'M BEING PAID THE BIG--
MORTAL MAN.
MORTAL MAN. YOU... WOULD DARE?
SHE IS VALKYRIOR, MORTAL MAN. SHE IS...OF ASGARD.
WHAT ARE YOU OF? MUD. MUD AND CORPSE MEAT.
AND YOU WOULD DARE?
YOU WOULD DARE TO MAKE WAR... ON THE GODS?
THEN LET ME SHOW YOU WAR!
WRUNNCH

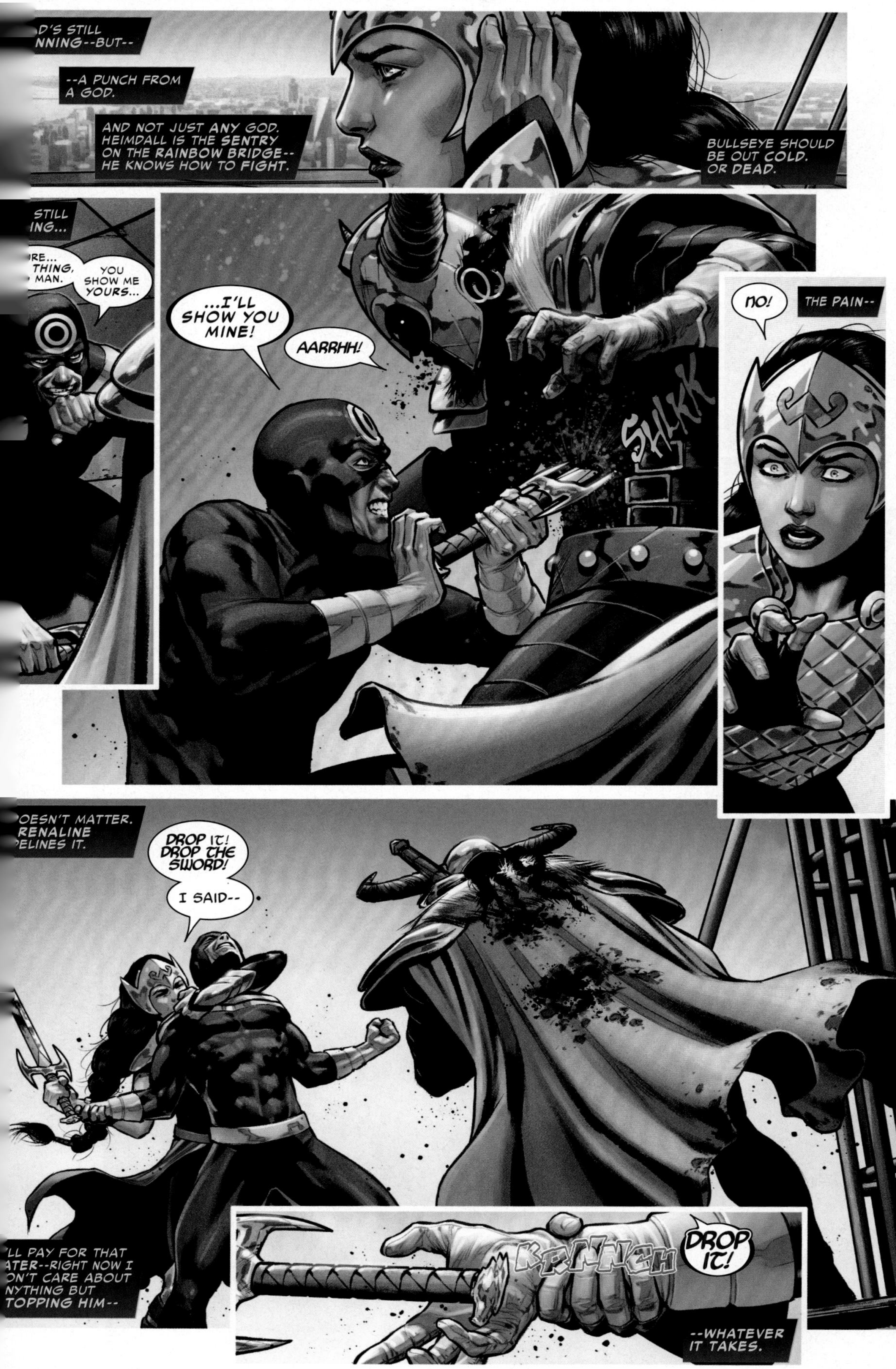

D'S STILL
NNING--BUT--
--A PUNCH FROM A GOD.
AND NOT JUST ANY GOD. HEIMDALL IS THE SENTRY ON THE RAINBOW BRIDGE--HE KNOWS HOW TO FIGHT.
BULLSEYE SHOULD BE OUT COLD. OR DEAD.
STILL
ING...
RE...
THING,
MAN.
YOU SHOW ME YOURS...
...I'LL SHOW YOU MINE!
AARRHH!
SHLKK
NO!
THE PAIN--
OESN'T MATTER.
RENALINE
PELINES IT.
DROP IT! DROP THE SWORD!
I SAID--
LL PAY FOR THAT
ATER--RIGHT NOW I
ON'T CARE ABOUT
NYTHING BUT
TOPPING HIM--
KRNNCH
DROP IT!
--WHATEVER IT TAKES.

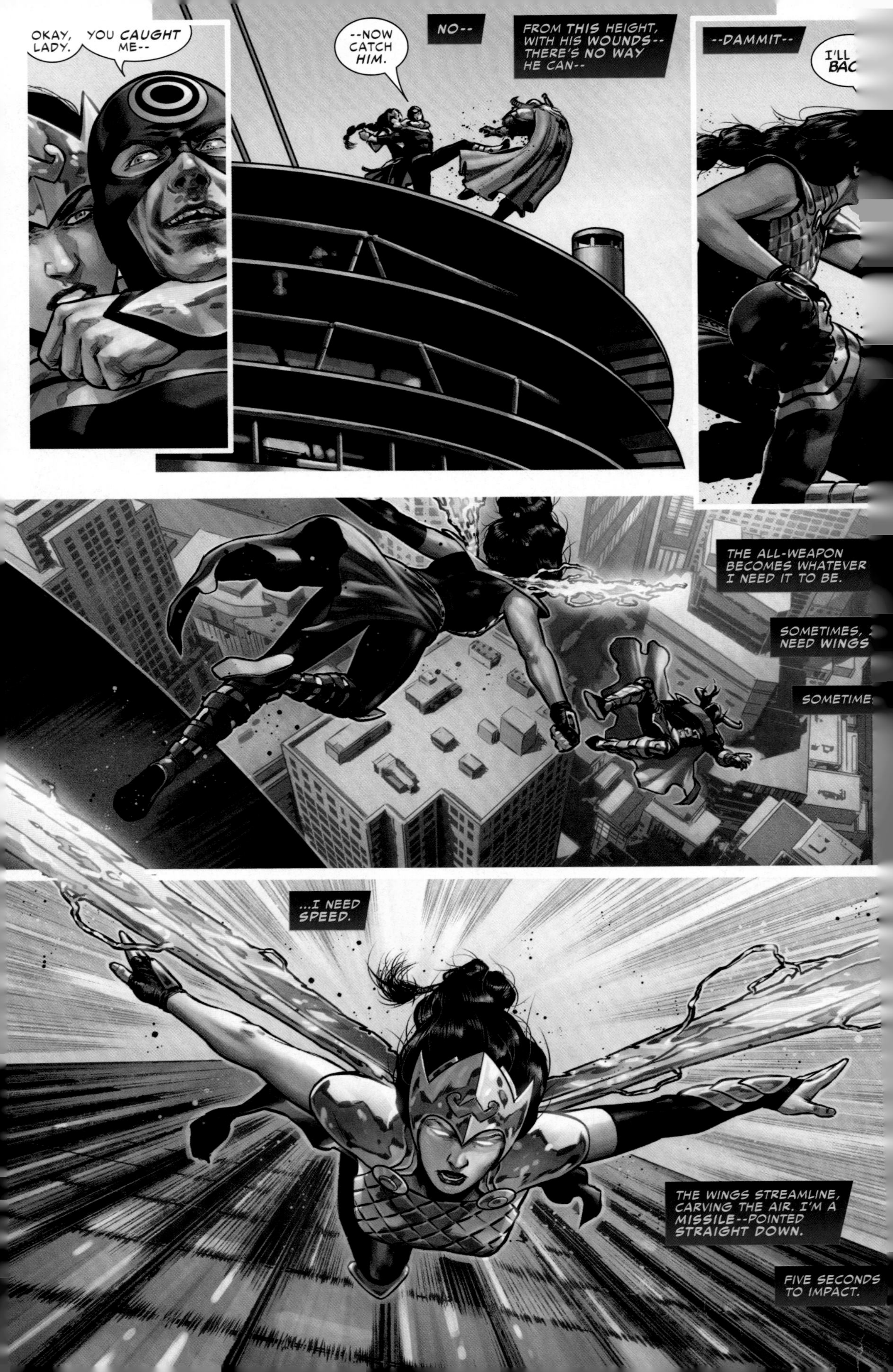
OKAY, LADY.
YOU CAUGHT ME--
--NOW CATCH HIM.
NO--
FROM THIS HEIGHT, WITH HIS WOUNDS-- THERE'S NO WAY HE CAN--
--DAMMIT--
I'LL BAC
THE ALL-WEAPON BECOMES WHATEVER I NEED IT TO BE.
SOMETIMES, NEED WINGS
SOMETIME
...I NEED SPEED.
THE WINGS STREAMLINE, CARVING THE AIR. I'M A MISSILE--POINTED STRAIGHT DOWN.
FIVE SECONDS TO IMPACT.

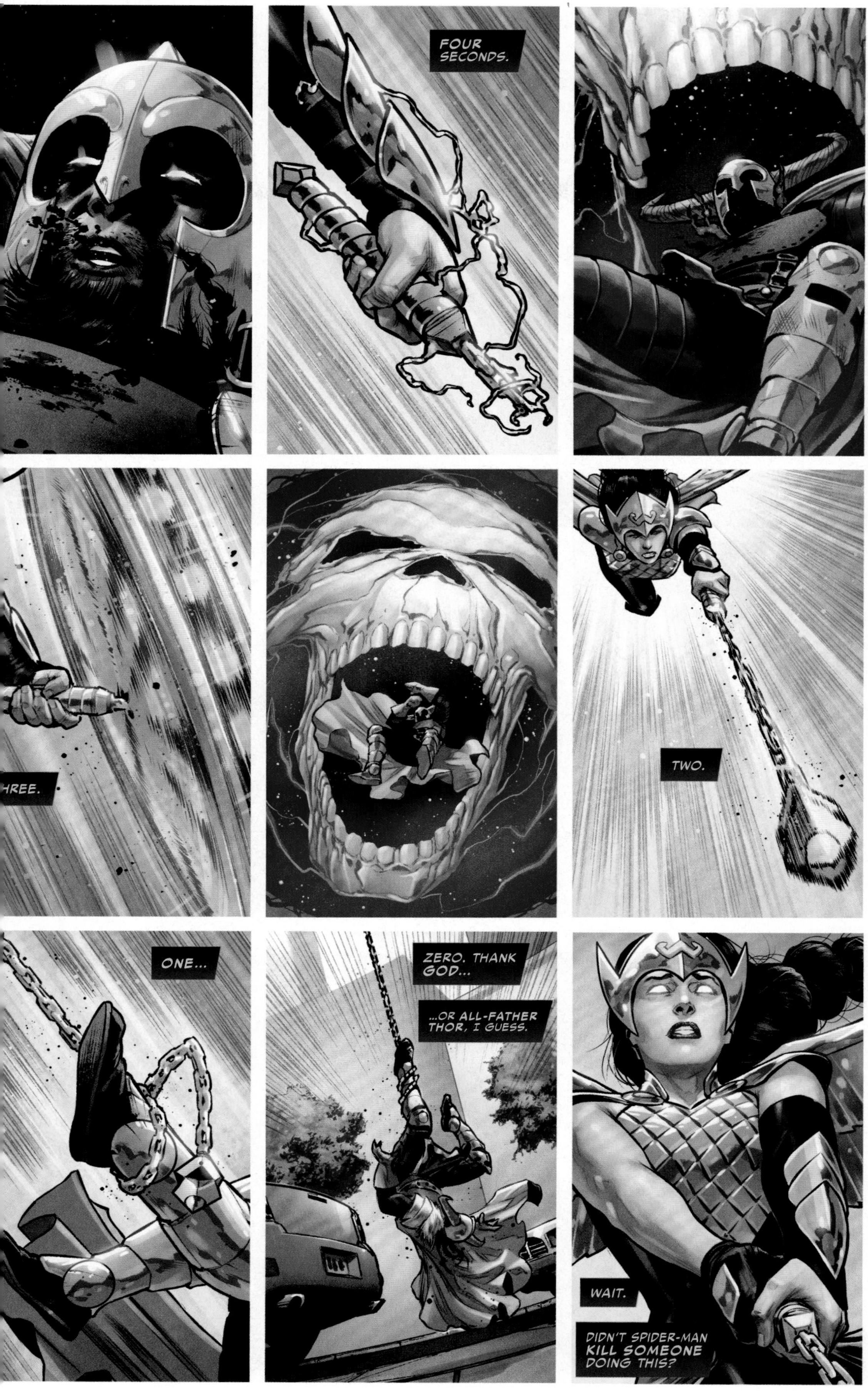
FOUR SECONDS.
HREE.
TWO.
ONE...
ZERO. THANK GOD...
...OR ALL-FATHER THOR, I GUESS.
WAIT.
DIDN'T SPIDER-MAN KILL SOMEONE DOING THIS?

HEIMDALL'S STILL WITH US. HE'S TOUGH--BUT EVEN A GOD IS ONLY *SO* TOUGH. THAT STUNT DIDN'T DO HIM ANY FAVORS.

AND HE'S BLEEDING OUT...

WE NEED TO GET YOU TO A *HOSPITAL,* HEIMDALL. RIGHT *NOW.*

NOT-- KAFF--NOT WHILE HE'S OUT THERE.

HE HOLDS DRAGONFANG, VALKYRIE.

HE...HOLDS DRAGONFANG.

I *KNOW.* I'LL...I'LL GET IT *BACK.* I *SWEAR.*

I--I KNOW IT'S *SACRED--*

IS IT? *METAL* AND *SPELLS*--IS *THAT* THE SACRED THING?

IF... IF *HE* HOLDS DRAGONFANG... A MAN LIKE *THAT...*

HE'S RAMBLIN[G] IS IT EVEN SA[FE] TO MOVE HIM[?]

IF I USE THE *DEATH SIGHT,* MAYBE I CAN...

SOMETIMES... YOU HAVE TO *LET GO.* LADY *JANE* KNOWS THAT LESSON.

VETERAN

...FIND OUT...

CAN THE *VALKYRIE* LEARN...?

VETERAN

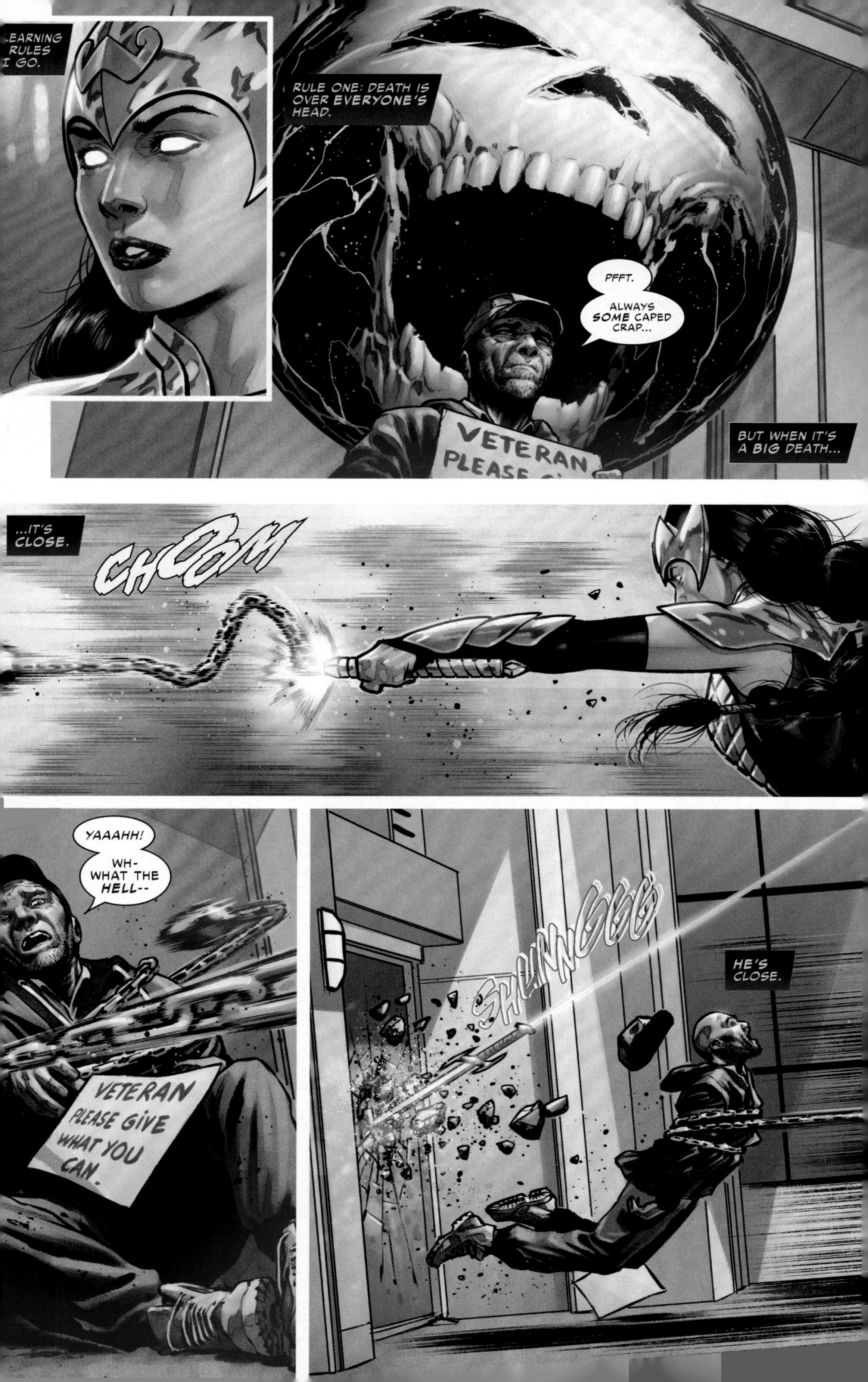
EARNING
RULES
I GO.
RULE ONE: DEATH IS OVER EVERYONE'S HEAD.
PFFT.
ALWAYS SOME CAPED CRAP...
VETERAN PLEASE
BUT WHEN IT'S A BIG DEATH...
...IT'S CLOSE.
CHOOM
YAAAHH!
WH- WHAT THE HELL--
VETERAN PLEASE GIVE WHAT YOU CAN.
SHUNNGGG
HE'S CLOSE.

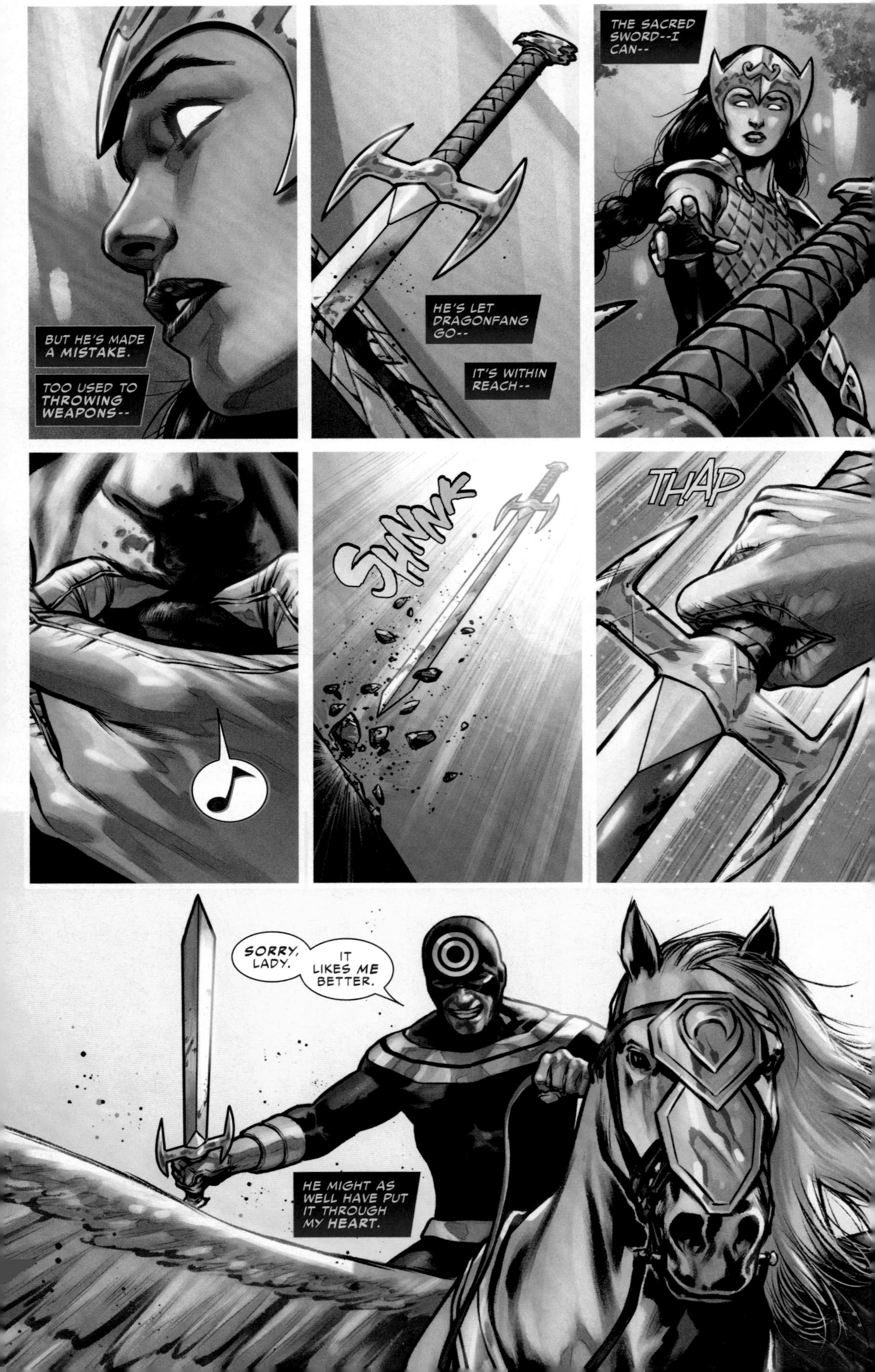

BUT HE'S MADE A MISTAKE.
TOO USED TO THROWING WEAPONS--
HE'S LET DRAGONFANG GO--
IT'S WITHIN REACH--
THE SACRED SWORD--I CAN--
SHNNK
THAP
SORRY, LADY.
IT LIKES ME BETTER.
HE MIGHT AS WELL HAVE PUT IT THROUGH MY HEART.

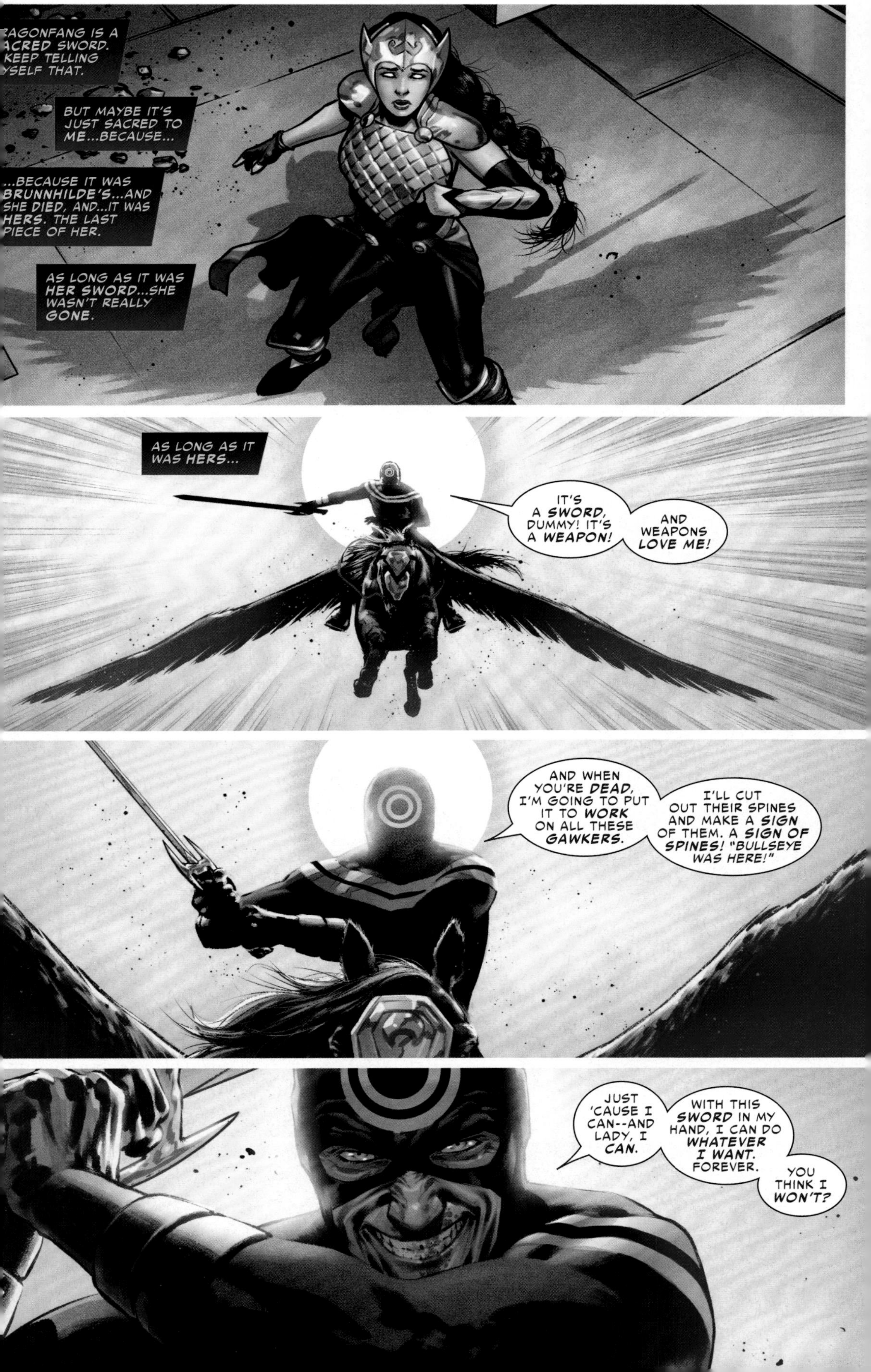
AGONFANG IS A ACRED SWORD. KEEP TELLING YSELF THAT.
BUT MAYBE IT'S JUST SACRED TO ME...BECAUSE...
...BECAUSE IT WAS BRUNNHILDE'S...AND SHE DIED, AND...IT WAS HERS. THE LAST PIECE OF HER.
AS LONG AS IT WAS HER SWORD...SHE WASN'T REALLY GONE.
AS LONG AS IT WAS HERS...
IT'S A SWORD, DUMMY! IT'S A WEAPON!
AND WEAPONS LOVE ME!
AND WHEN YOU'RE DEAD, I'M GOING TO PUT IT TO WORK ON ALL THESE GAWKERS.
I'LL CUT OUT THEIR SPINES AND MAKE A SIGN OF THEM. A SIGN OF SPINES! "BULLSEYE WAS HERE!"
JUST 'CAUSE I CAN--AND LADY, I CAN.
WITH THIS SWORD IN MY HAND, I CAN DO WHATEVER I WANT. FOREVER.
YOU THINK I WON'T?

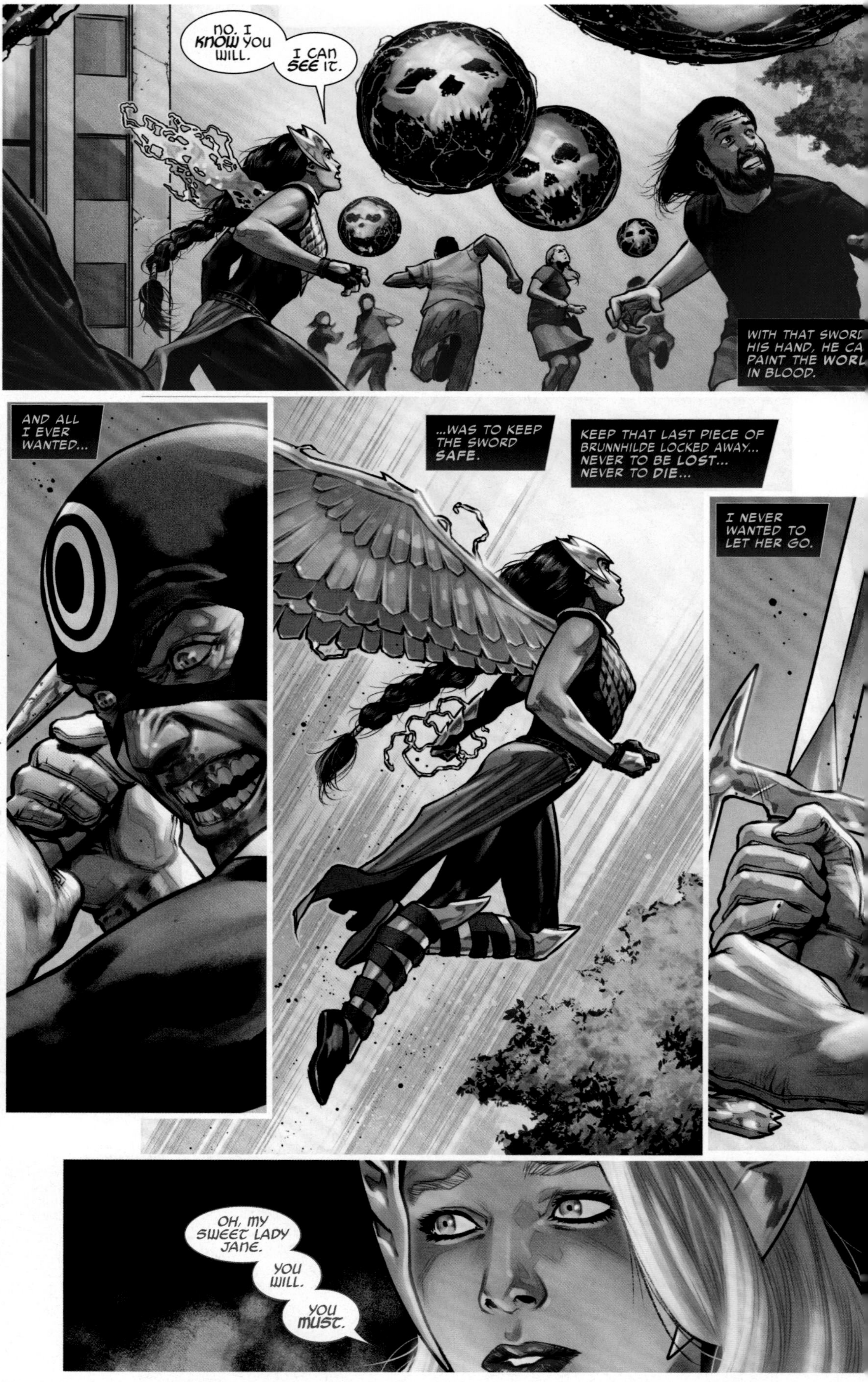
NO. I KNOW YOU WILL.
I CAN SEE IT.
WITH THAT SWORD HIS HAND, HE CA PAINT THE WORL IN BLOOD.
AND ALL I EVER WANTED...
...WAS TO KEEP THE SWORD SAFE.
KEEP THAT LAST PIECE OF BRUNNHILDE LOCKED AWAY... NEVER TO BE LOST... NEVER TO DIE...
I NEVER WANTED TO LET HER GO.
OH, MY SWEET LADY JANE.
YOU WILL.
YOU MUST.

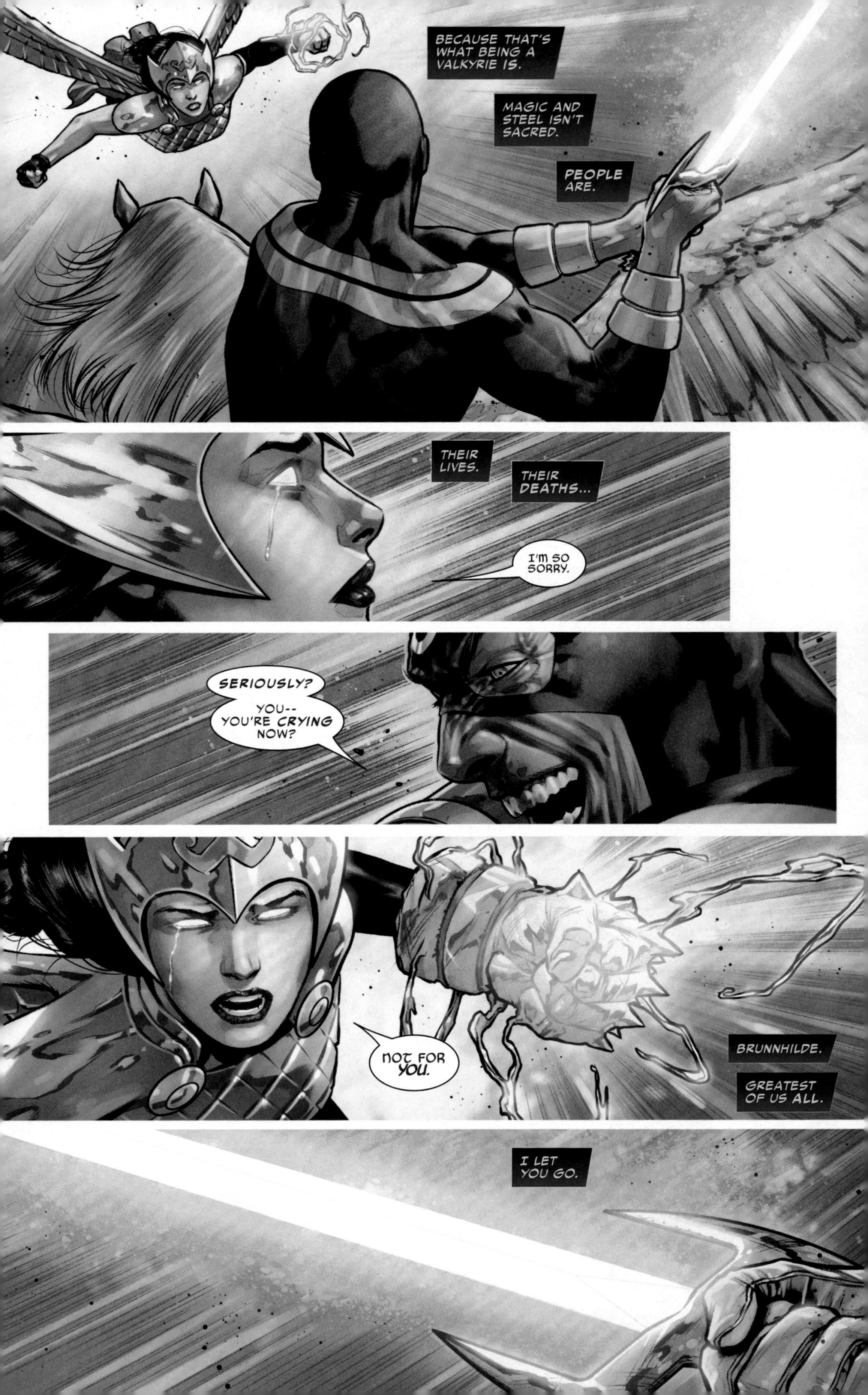

BECAUSE THAT'S WHAT BEING A VALKYRIE IS.
MAGIC AND STEEL ISN'T SACRED.
PEOPLE ARE.
THEIR LIVES.
THEIR DEATHS...
I'M SO SORRY.
SERIOUSLY?
YOU-- YOU'RE CRYING NOW?
NOT FOR YOU.
BRUNNHILDE.
GREATEST OF US ALL.
I LET YOU GO.

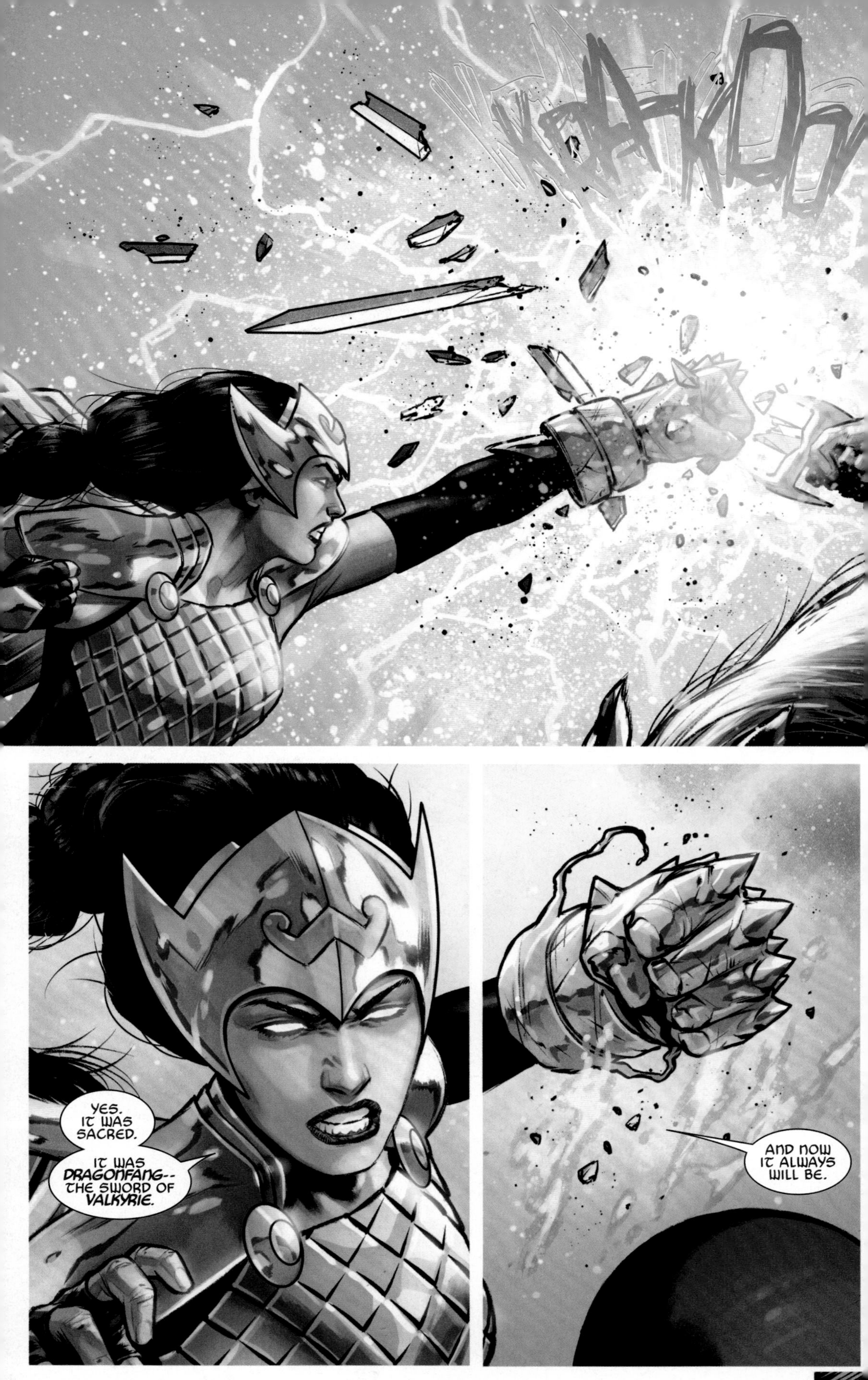
YES. IT WAS SACRED.
IT WAS DRAGONFANG-- THE SWORD OF VALKYRIE.
AND NOW IT ALWAYS WILL BE.

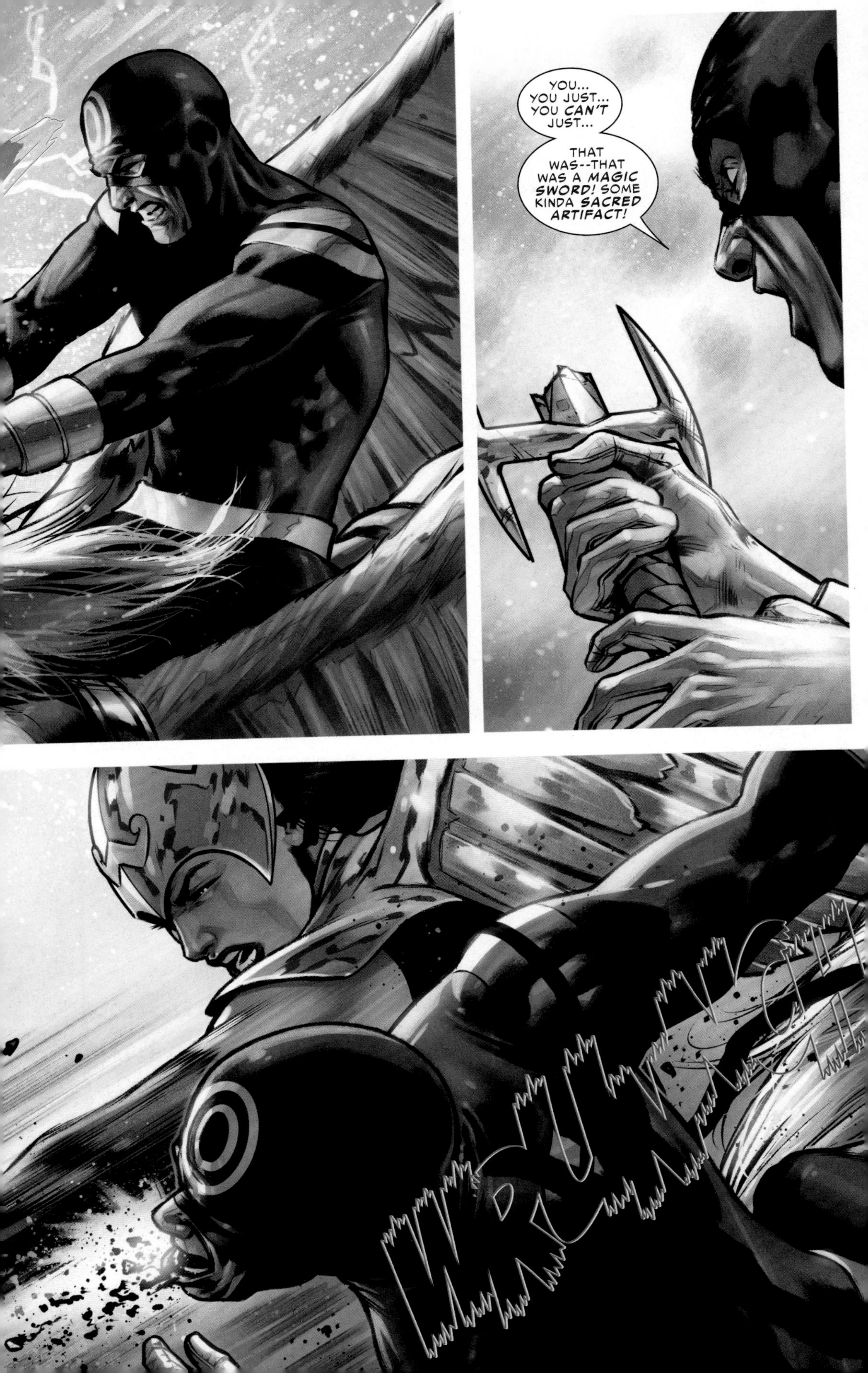
YOU... YOU JUST... YOU *CAN'T* JUST...
THAT WAS--THAT WAS A *MAGIC SWORD!* SOME KINDA *SACRED ARTIFACT!*
WRUNCH

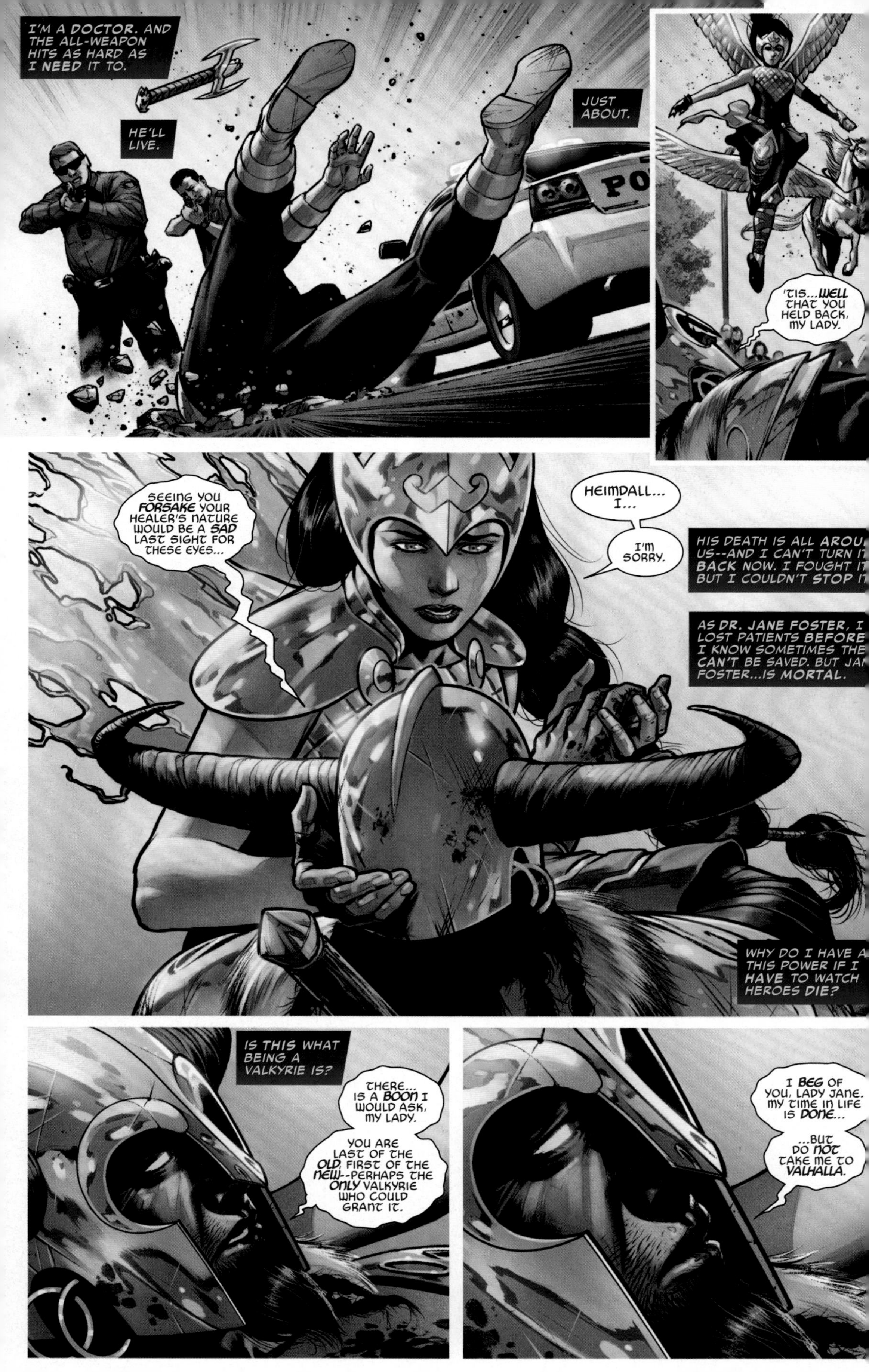

I'M A DOCTOR. AND THE ALL-WEAPON HITS AS HARD AS I NEED IT TO.
HE'LL LIVE.
JUST ABOUT.
PO
'TIS...WELL THAT YOU HELD BACK, MY LADY.
SEEING YOU FORSAKE YOUR HEALER'S NATURE WOULD BE A SAD LAST SIGHT FOR THESE EYES...
HEIMDALL... I...
I'M SORRY.
HIS DEATH IS ALL AROU US--AND I CAN'T TURN I BACK NOW. I FOUGHT I BUT I COULDN'T STOP I
AS DR. JANE FOSTER, I LOST PATIENTS BEFORE I KNOW SOMETIMES THE CAN'T BE SAVED. BUT JA FOSTER...IS MORTAL.
WHY DO I HAVE A THIS POWER IF I HAVE TO WATCH HEROES DIE?
IS THIS WHAT BEING A VALKYRIE IS?
THERE... IS A BOON I WOULD ASK, MY LADY.
YOU ARE LAST OF THE OLD, FIRST OF THE NEW--PERHAPS THE ONLY VALKYRIE WHO COULD GRANT IT.
I BEG OF YOU, LADY JANE. MY TIME IN LIFE IS DONE...
...BUT DO NOT TAKE ME TO VALHALLA.

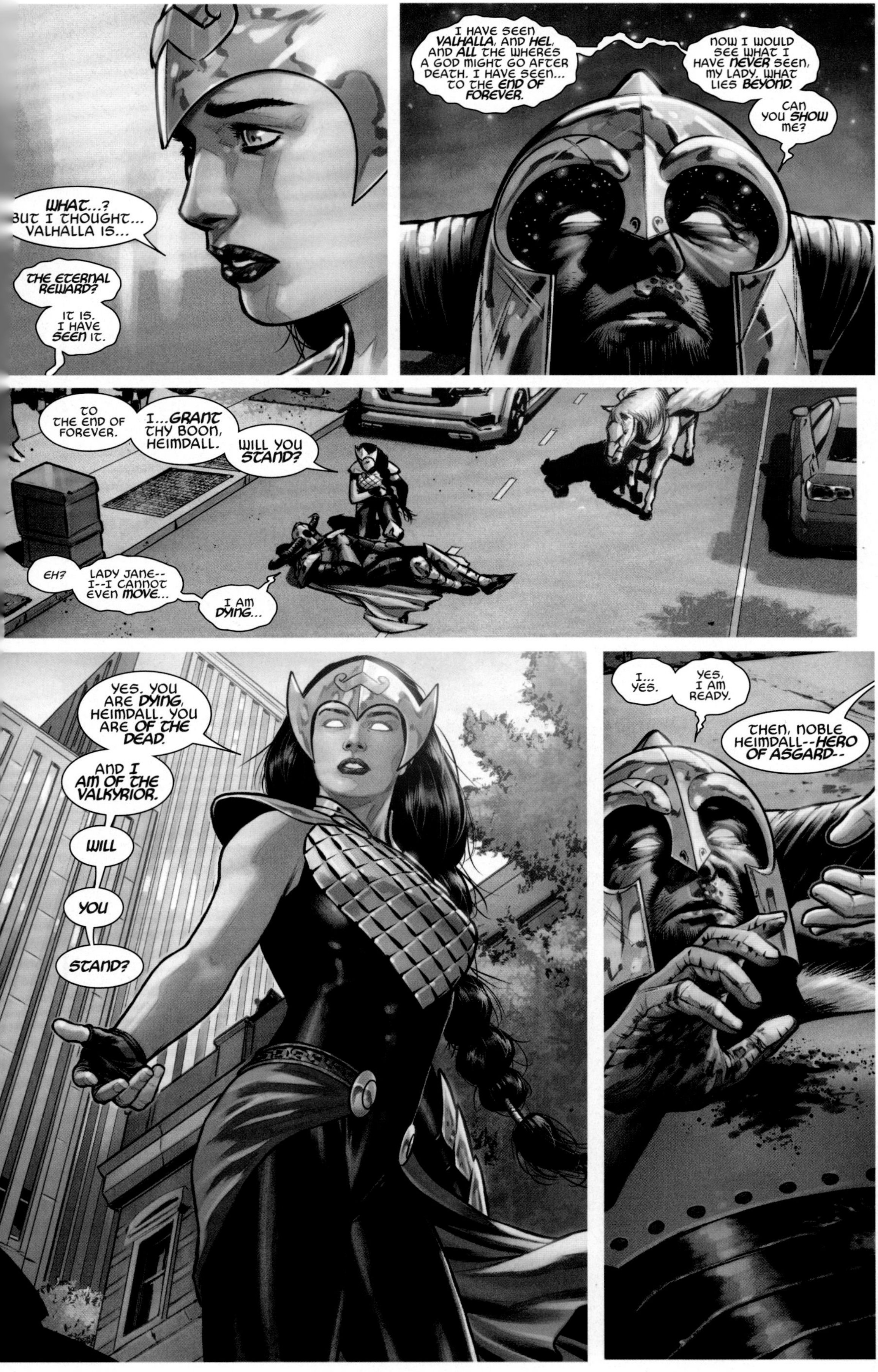
WHAT...? BUT I THOUGHT... VALHALLA IS...
THE ETERNAL REWARD?
IT IS. I HAVE SEEN IT.
I HAVE SEEN VALHALLA, AND HEL, AND ALL THE WHERES A GOD MIGHT GO AFTER DEATH. I HAVE SEEN... TO THE END OF FOREVER.
NOW I WOULD SEE WHAT I HAVE NEVER SEEN, MY LADY. WHAT LIES BEYOND.
CAN YOU SHOW ME?
TO THE END OF FOREVER.
I...GRANT THY BOON, HEIMDALL.
WILL YOU STAND?
EH?
LADY JANE-- I--I CANNOT EVEN MOVE...
I AM DYING...
YES. YOU ARE DYING, HEIMDALL. YOU ARE OF THE DEAD.
AND I AM OF THE VALKYRIOR.
WILL
YOU
STAND?
I... YES.
YES, I AM READY.
THEN, NOBLE HEIMDALL--HERO OF ASGARD--

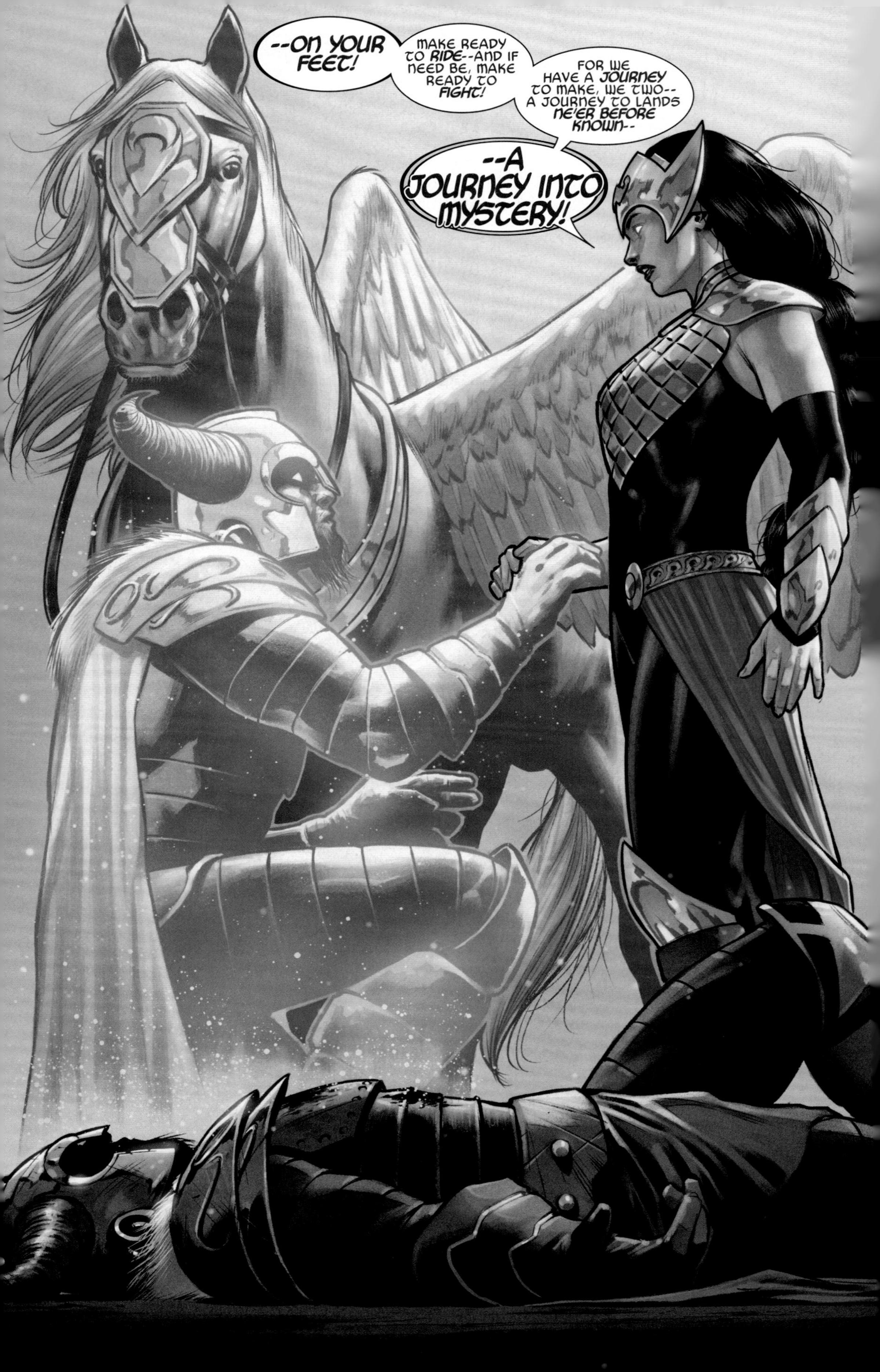
--ON YOUR FEET!
MAKE READY TO RIDE--AND IF NEED BE, MAKE READY TO FIGHT!
FOR WE HAVE A JOURNEY TO MAKE, WE TWO-- A JOURNEY TO LANDS NE'ER BEFORE KNOWN--
--A JOURNEY INTO MYSTERY!

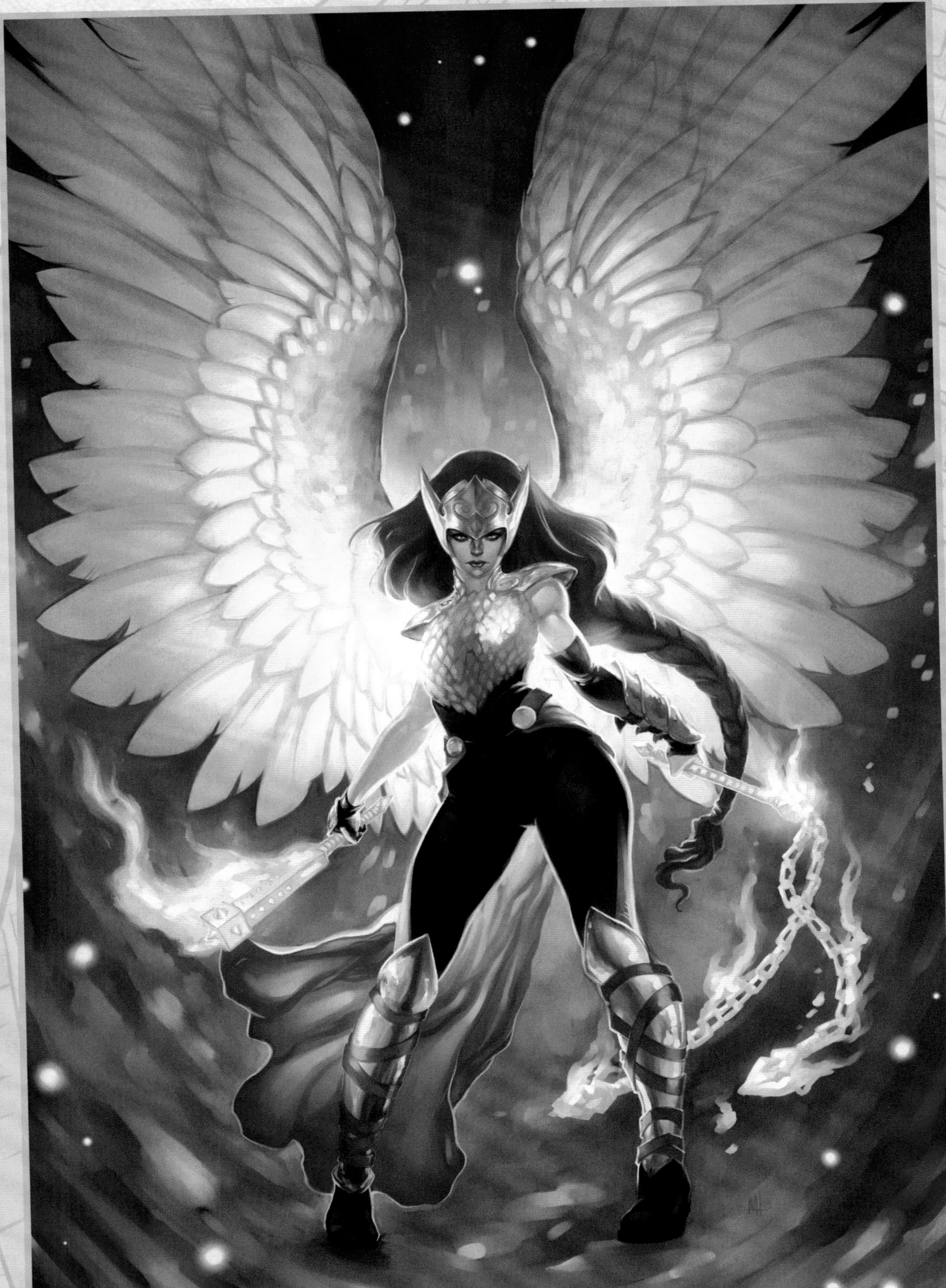

#1 VARIANT BY **MEGHAN HETRICK**

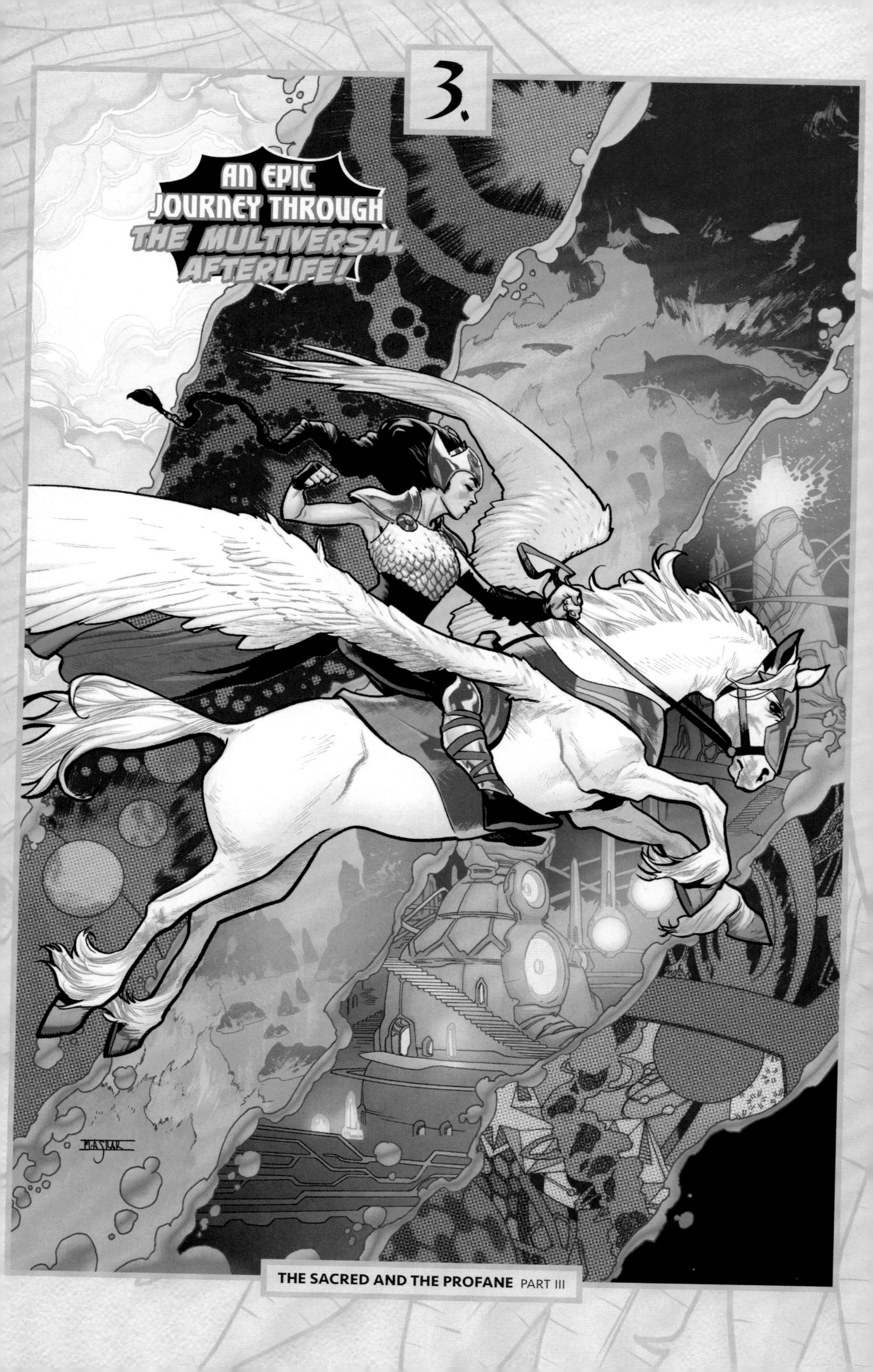
3.
AN EPIC JOURNEY THROUGH THE MULTIVERSAL AFTERLIFE!
THE SACRED AND THE PROFANE PART III

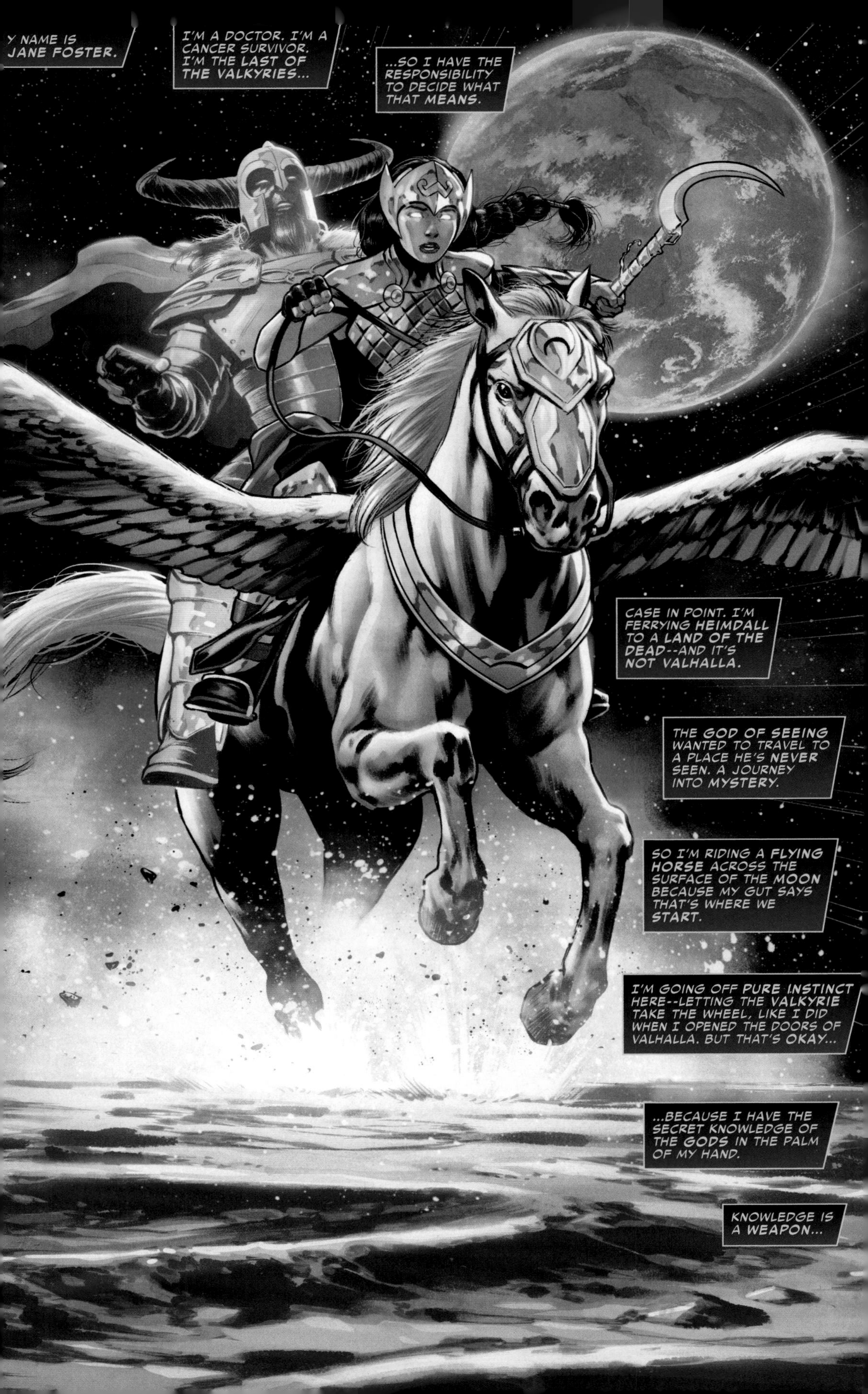
Y NAME IS JANE FOSTER.
I'M A DOCTOR. I'M A CANCER SURVIVOR. I'M THE LAST OF THE VALKYRIES...
...SO I HAVE THE RESPONSIBILITY TO DECIDE WHAT THAT MEANS.
CASE IN POINT. I'M FERRYING HEIMDALL TO A LAND OF THE DEAD--AND IT'S NOT VALHALLA.
THE GOD OF SEEING WANTED TO TRAVEL TO A PLACE HE'S NEVER SEEN. A JOURNEY INTO MYSTERY.
SO I'M RIDING A FLYING HORSE ACROSS THE SURFACE OF THE MOON BECAUSE MY GUT SAYS THAT'S WHERE WE START.
I'M GOING OFF PURE INSTINCT HERE--LETTING THE VALKYRIE TAKE THE WHEEL, LIKE I DID WHEN I OPENED THE DOORS OF VALHALLA. BUT THAT'S OKAY...
...BECAUSE I HAVE THE SECRET KNOWLEDGE OF THE GODS IN THE PALM OF MY HAND.
KNOWLEDGE IS A WEAPON...

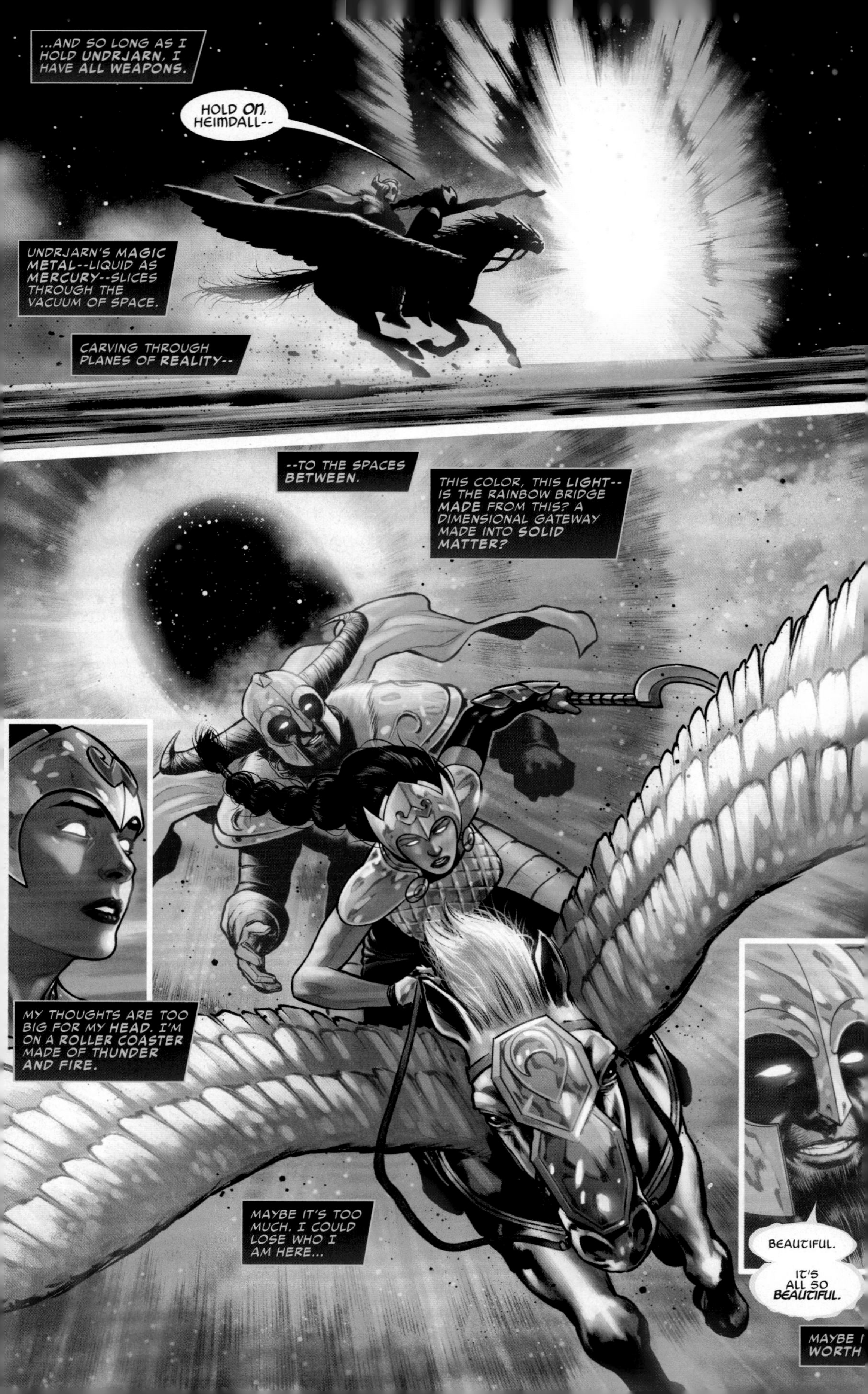
...AND SO LONG AS I HOLD UNDRJARN, I HAVE ALL WEAPONS.
HOLD ON, HEIMDALL--
UNDRJARN'S MAGIC METAL--LIQUID AS MERCURY--SLICES THROUGH THE VACUUM OF SPACE.
CARVING THROUGH PLANES OF REALITY--
--TO THE SPACES BETWEEN.
THIS COLOR, THIS LIGHT--IS THE RAINBOW BRIDGE MADE FROM THIS? A DIMENSIONAL GATEWAY MADE INTO SOLID MATTER?
MY THOUGHTS ARE TOO BIG FOR MY HEAD. I'M ON A ROLLER COASTER MADE OF THUNDER AND FIRE.
MAYBE IT'S TOO MUCH. I COULD LOSE WHO I AM HERE...
BEAUTIFUL.
IT'S ALL SO BEAUTIFUL.
MAYBE I WORTH

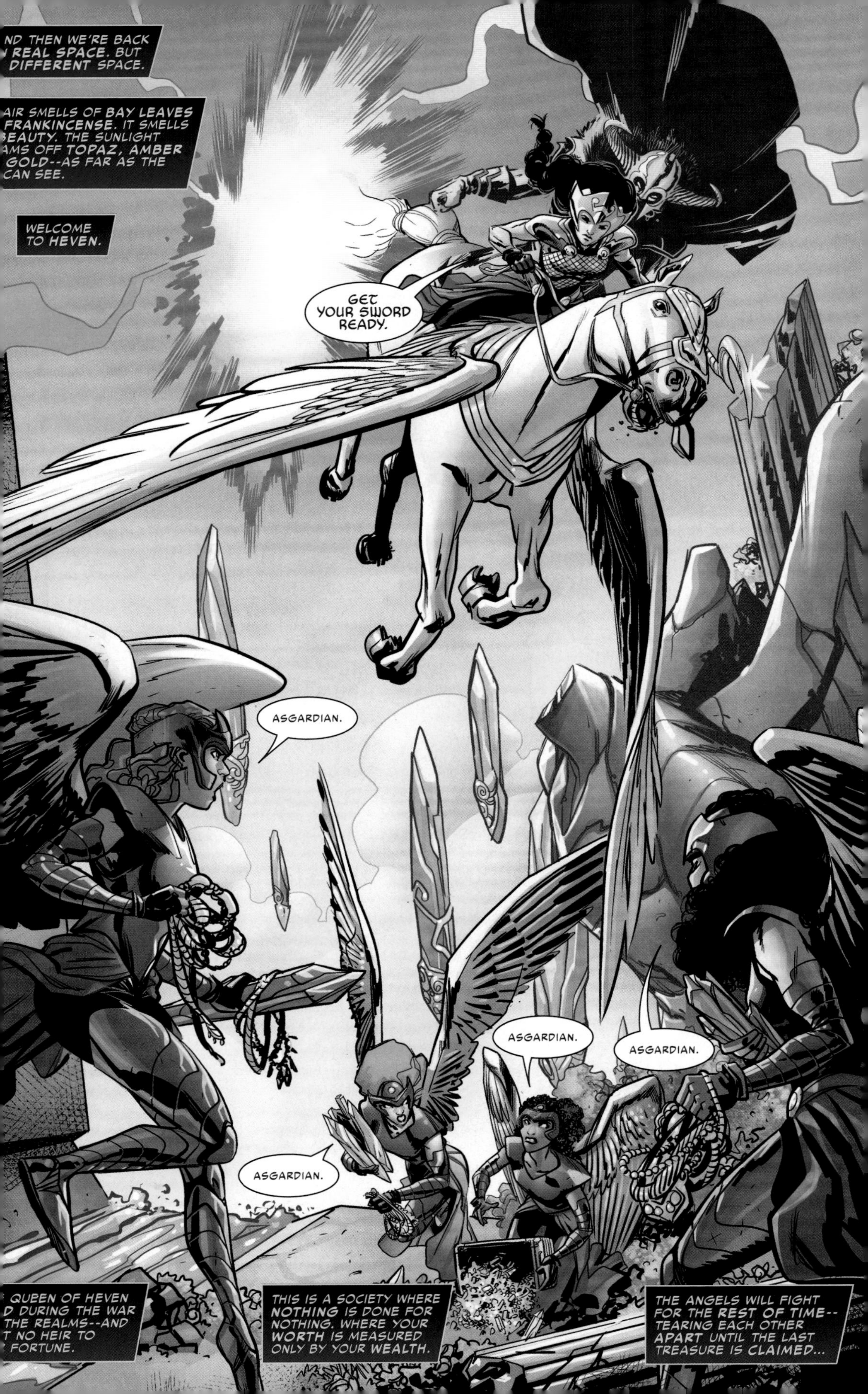
ND THEN WE'RE BACK
REAL SPACE. BUT
DIFFERENT SPACE.
AIR SMELLS OF BAY LEAVES
FRANKINCENSE. IT SMELLS
EAUTY. THE SUNLIGHT
AMS OFF TOPAZ, AMBER
GOLD--AS FAR AS THE
CAN SEE.
WELCOME TO HEVEN.
GET YOUR SWORD READY.
ASGARDIAN.
ASGARDIAN.
ASGARDIAN.
ASGARDIAN.
QUEEN OF HEVEN
D DURING THE WAR
THE REALMS--AND
T NO HEIR TO
FORTUNE.
THIS IS A SOCIETY WHERE NOTHING IS DONE FOR NOTHING. WHERE YOUR WORTH IS MEASURED ONLY BY YOUR WEALTH.
THE ANGELS WILL FIGHT FOR THE REST OF TIME-- TEARING EACH OTHER APART UNTIL THE LAST TREASURE IS CLAIMED...

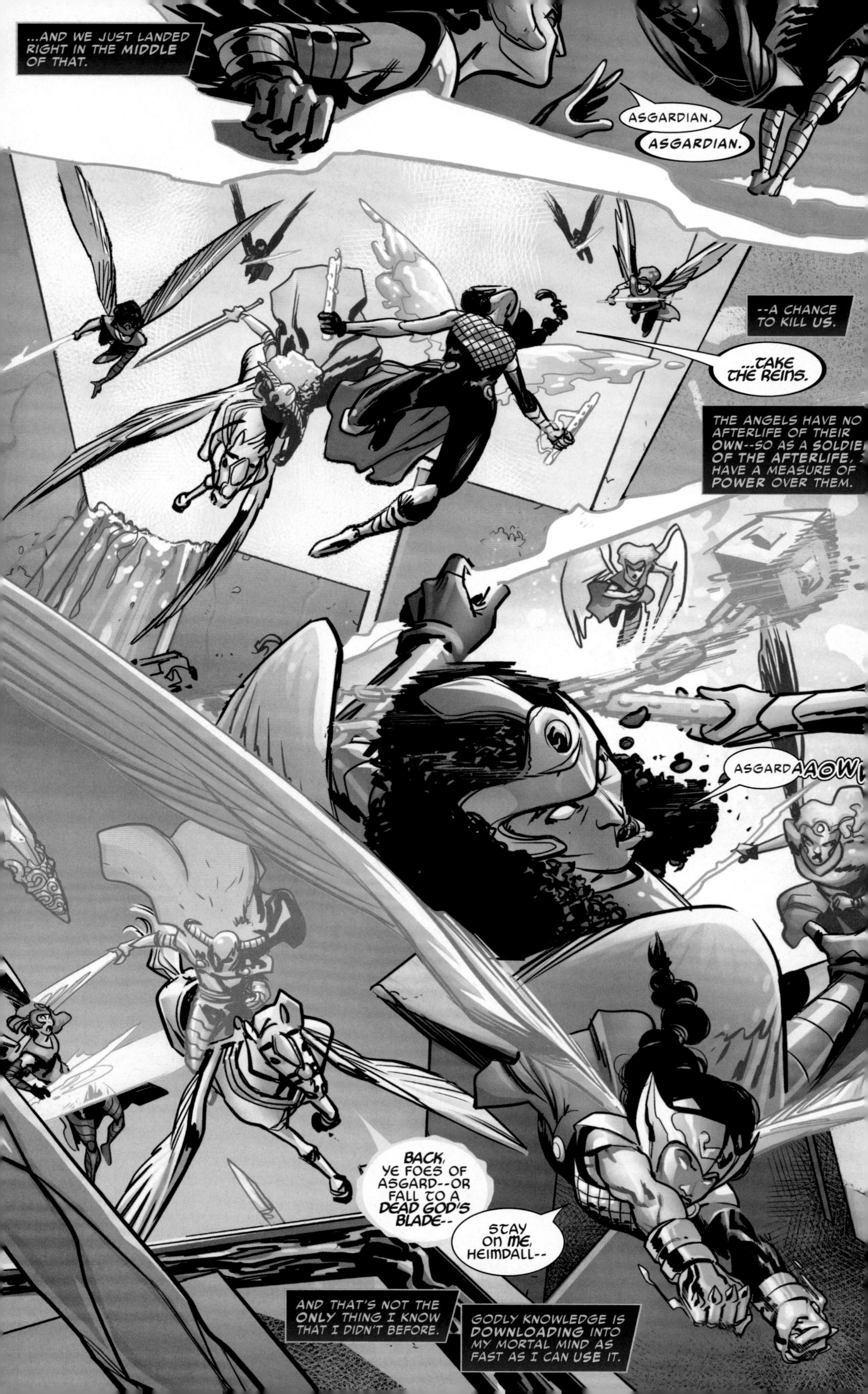
...AND WE JUST LANDED RIGHT IN THE MIDDLE OF THAT.
ASGARDIAN.
ASGARDIAN.
--A CHANCE TO KILL US.
...TAKE THE REINS.
THE ANGELS HAVE NO AFTERLIFE OF THEIR OWN--SO AS A SOLDIE OF THE AFTERLIFE, HAVE A MEASURE OF POWER OVER THEM.
ASGARDAAOW
BACK, YE FOES OF ASGARD--OR FALL TO A DEAD GOD'S BLADE--
STAY ON ME, HEIMDALL--
AND THAT'S NOT THE ONLY THING I KNOW THAT I DIDN'T BEFORE.
GODLY KNOWLEDGE IS DOWNLOADING INTO MY MORTAL MIND AS FAST AS I CAN USE IT.

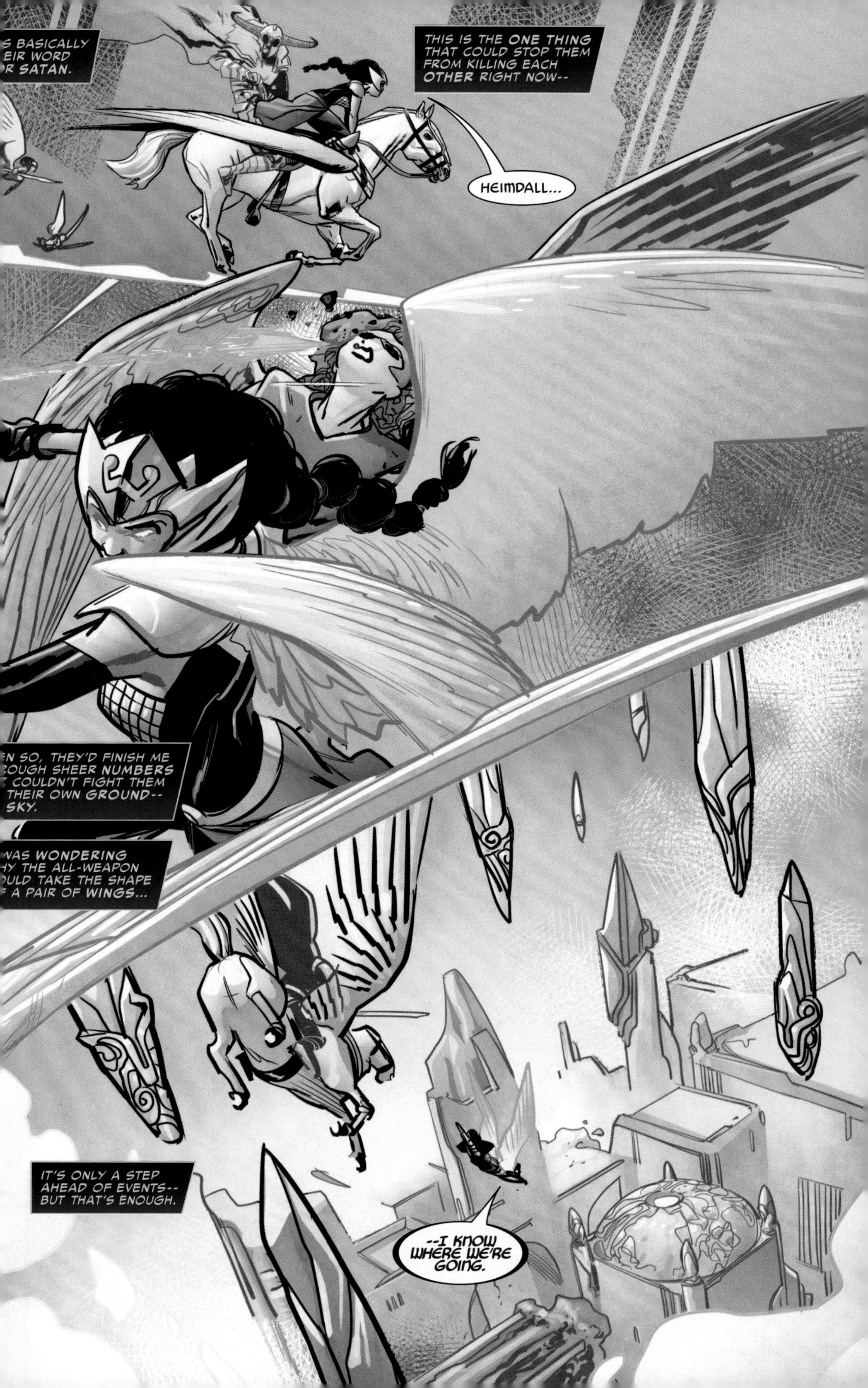
S BASICALLY EIR WORD R SATAN.
THIS IS THE ONE THING THAT COULD STOP THEM FROM KILLING EACH OTHER RIGHT NOW--
HEIMDALL...
N SO, THEY'D FINISH ME OUGH SHEER NUMBERS COULDN'T FIGHT THEM THEIR OWN GROUND-- SKY.
WAS WONDERING HY THE ALL-WEAPON OULD TAKE THE SHAPE A PAIR OF WINGS...
IT'S ONLY A STEP AHEAD OF EVENTS-- BUT THAT'S ENOUGH.
--I KNOW WHERE WE'RE GOING.

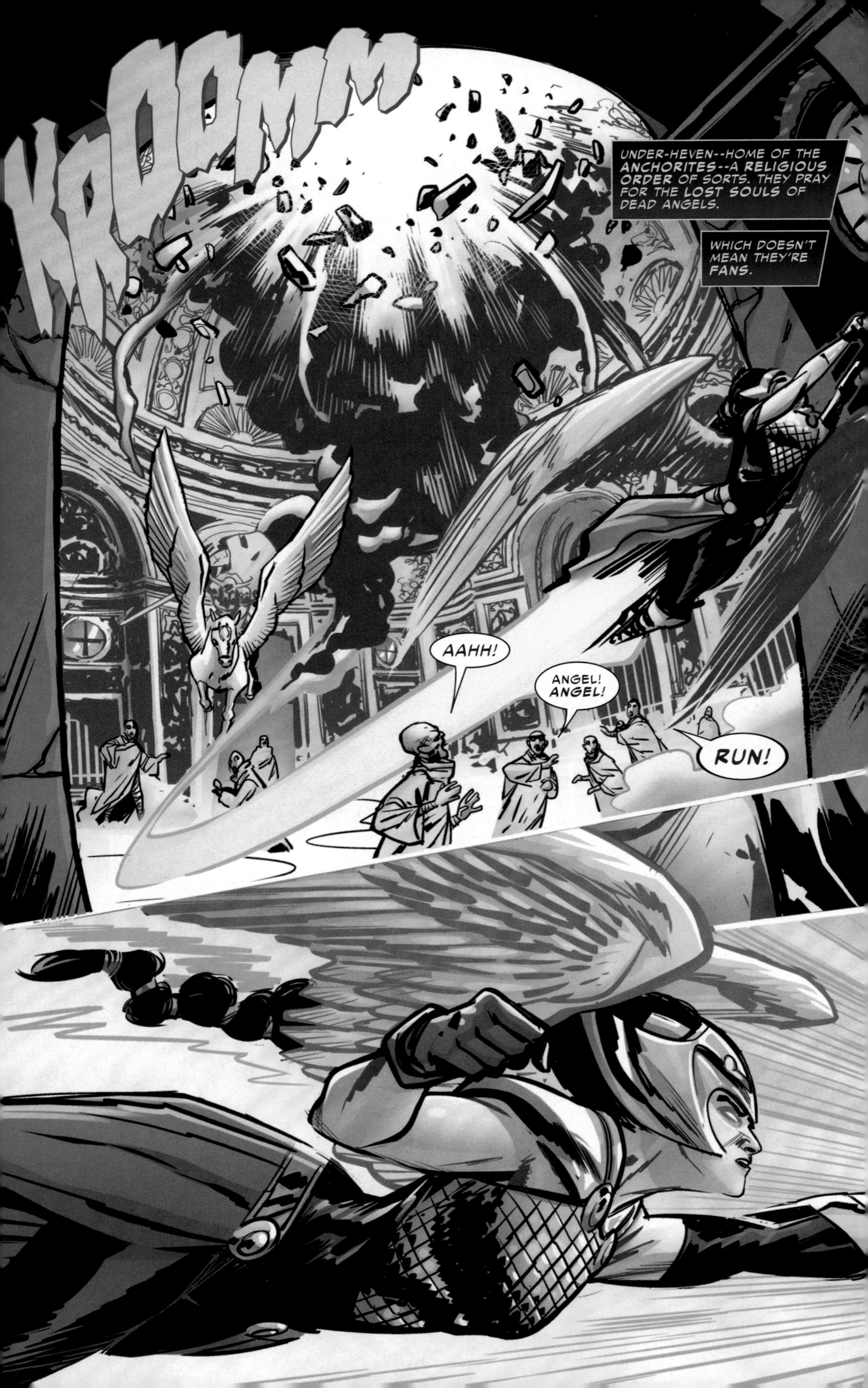
KROOMM
UNDER-HEVEN--HOME OF THE ANCHORITES--A RELIGIOUS ORDER OF SORTS. THEY PRAY FOR THE LOST SOULS OF DEAD ANGELS.
WHICH DOESN'T MEAN THEY'RE FANS.
AAHH!
ANGEL! ANGEL!
RUN!

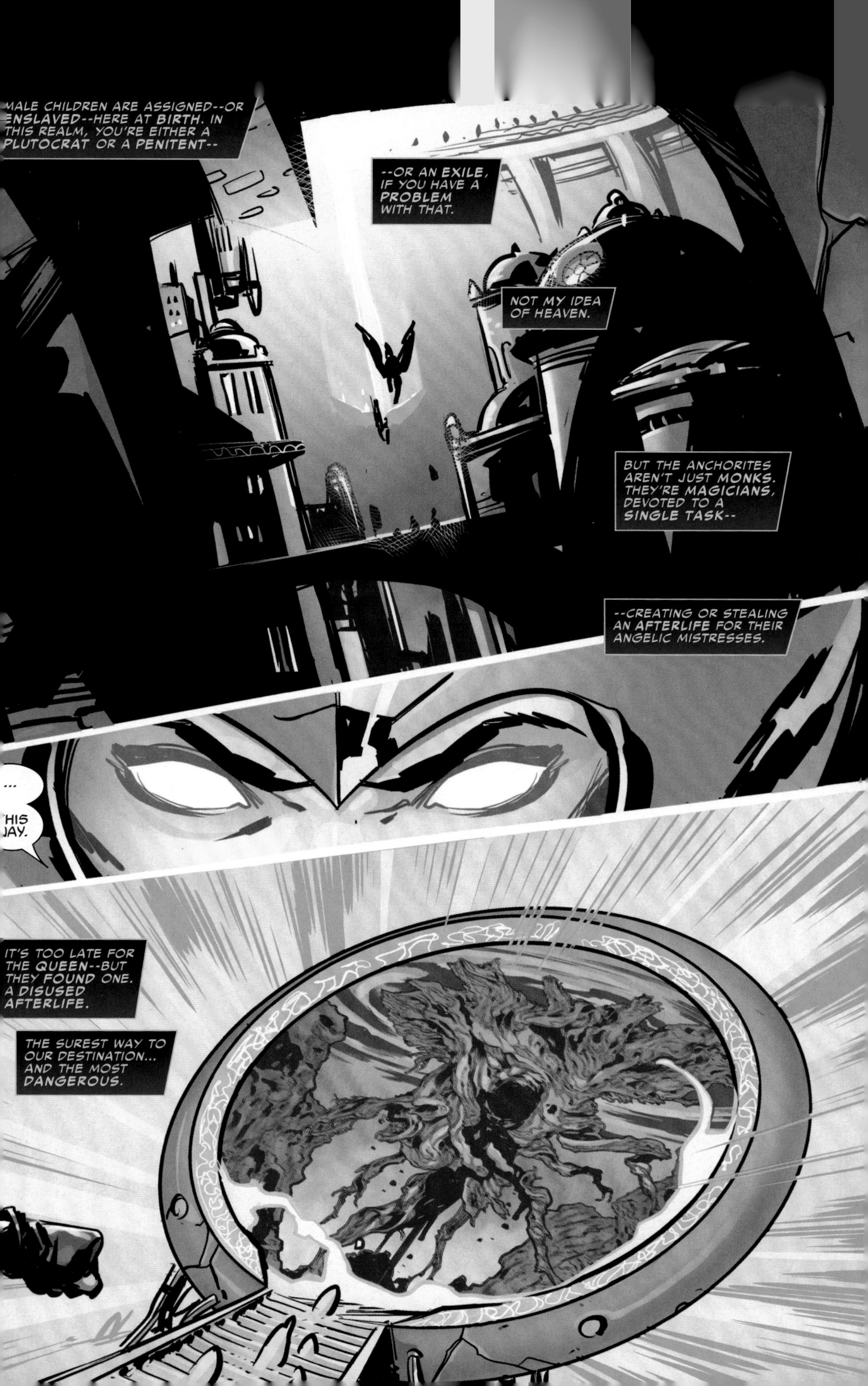
MALE CHILDREN ARE ASSIGNED--OR ENSLAVED--HERE AT BIRTH. IN THIS REALM, YOU'RE EITHER A PLUTOCRAT OR A PENITENT--
--OR AN EXILE, IF YOU HAVE A PROBLEM WITH THAT.
NOT MY IDEA OF HEAVEN.
BUT THE ANCHORITES AREN'T JUST MONKS. THEY'RE MAGICIANS, DEVOTED TO A SINGLE TASK--
--CREATING OR STEALING AN AFTERLIFE FOR THEIR ANGELIC MISTRESSES.
IT'S TOO LATE FOR THE QUEEN--BUT THEY FOUND ONE. A DISUSED AFTERLIFE.
THE SUREST WAY TO OUR DESTINATION... AND THE MOST DANGEROUS.

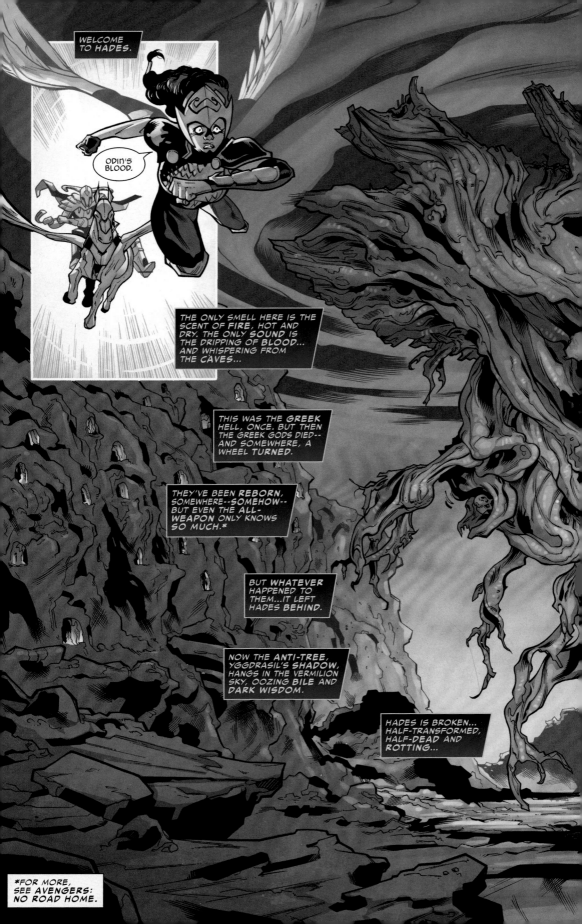

WELCOME TO HADES.

ODIN'S BLOOD.

THE ONLY SMELL HERE IS THE SCENT OF FIRE, HOT AND DRY. THE ONLY SOUND IS THE DRIPPING OF BLOOD... AND WHISPERING FROM THE CAVES...

THIS WAS THE GREEK HELL, ONCE. BUT THEN THE GREEK GODS DIED-- AND SOMEWHERE, A WHEEL TURNED.

THEY'VE BEEN REBORN, SOMEWHERE--SOMEHOW-- BUT EVEN THE ALL-WEAPON ONLY KNOWS SO MUCH.*

BUT WHATEVER HAPPENED TO THEM...IT LEFT HADES BEHIND.

NOW THE ANTI-TREE, YGGDRASIL'S SHADOW, HANGS IN THE VERMILION SKY, OOZING BILE AND DARK WISDOM.

HADES IS BROKEN... HALF-TRANSFORMED, HALF-DEAD AND ROTTING...

*FOR MORE, SEE AVENGERS: NO ROAD HOME.

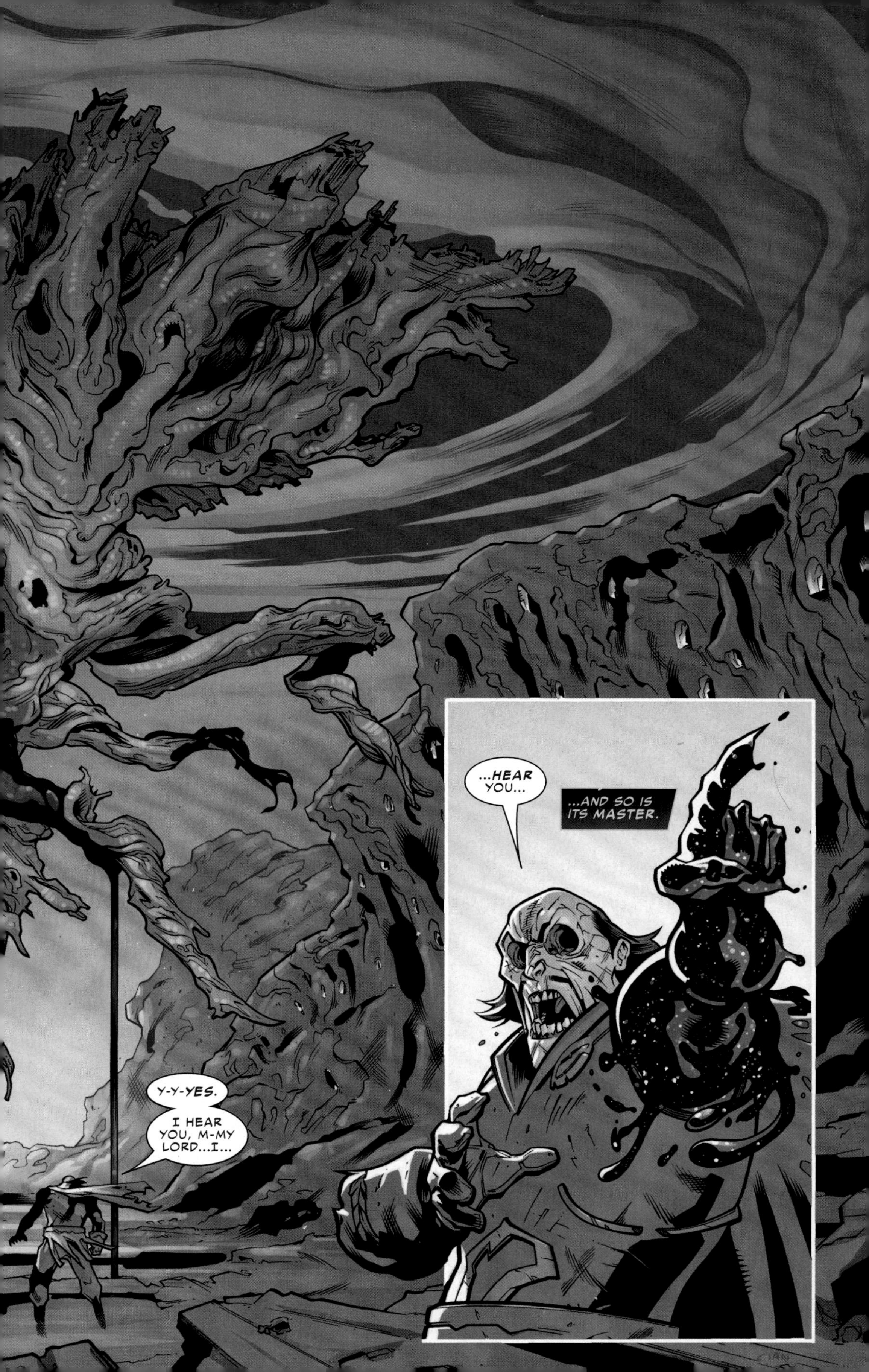
Y-Y-YES.
I HEAR YOU, M-MY LORD...I...
...HEAR YOU...
...AND SO IS ITS MASTER.

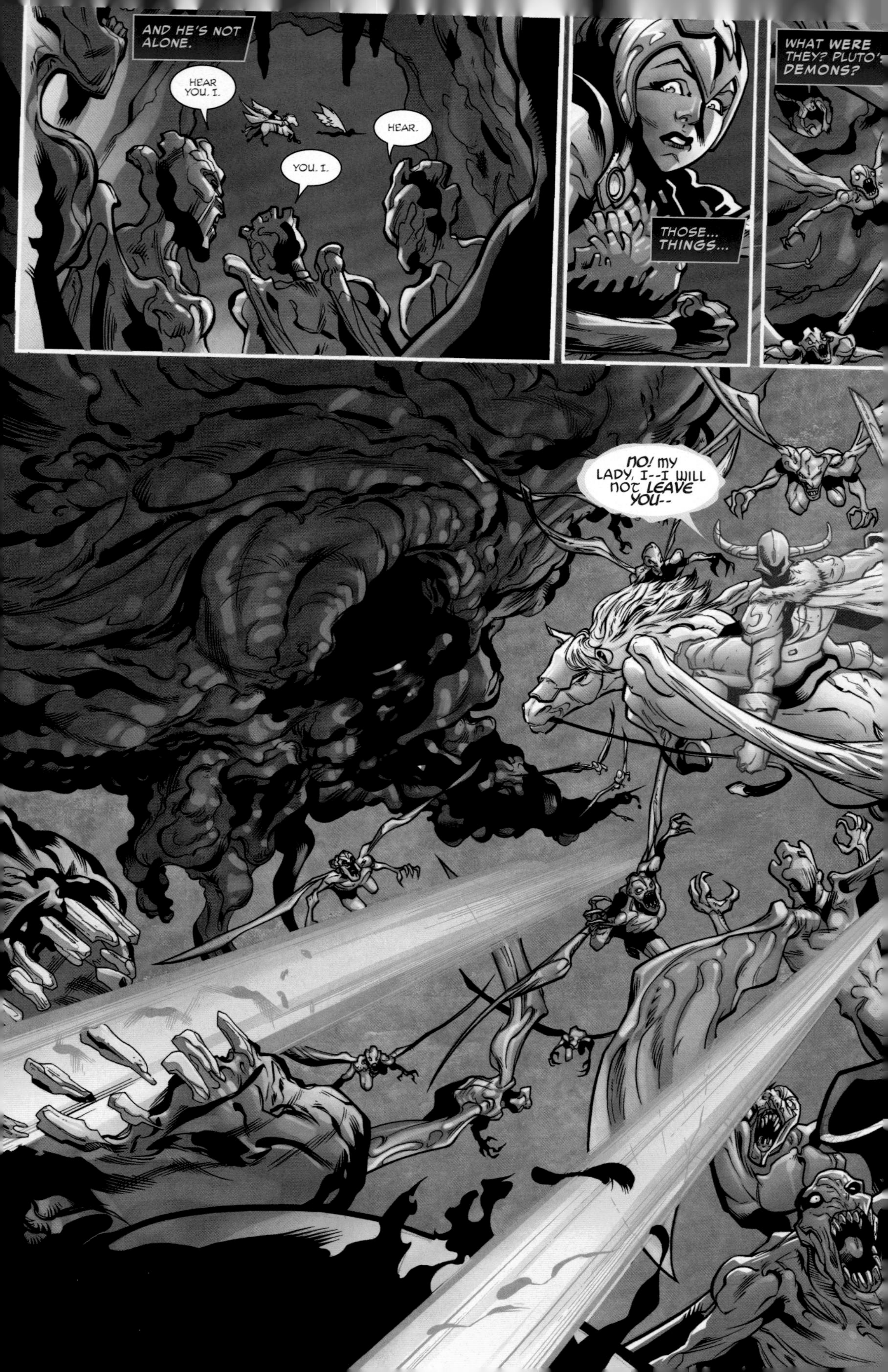
AND HE'S NOT ALONE.
HEAR YOU. I.
YOU. I.
HEAR.
THOSE... THINGS...
WHAT WERE THEY? PLUTO'S DEMONS?
NO! MY LADY, I--I WILL NOT LEAVE YOU--

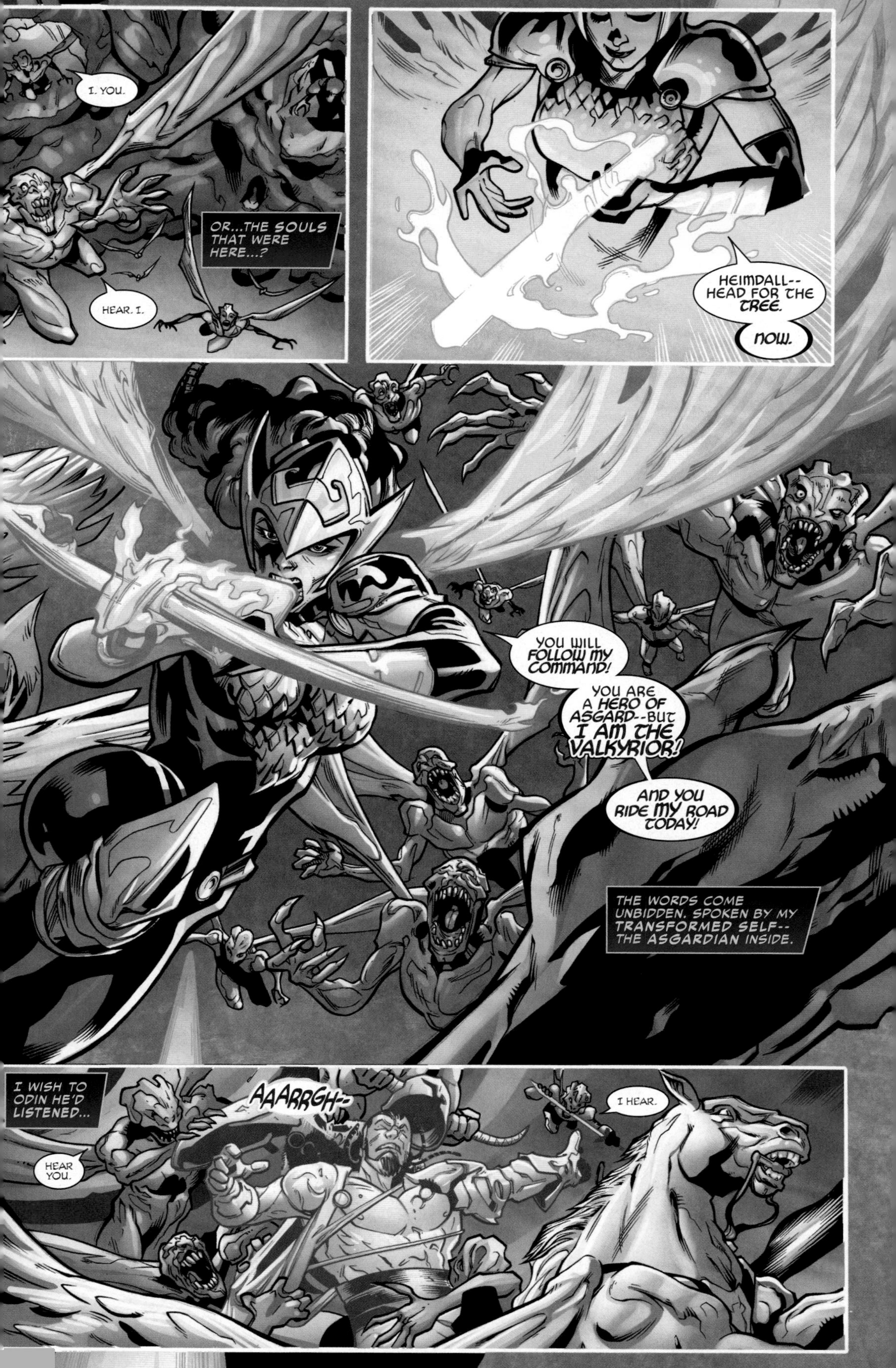
I. YOU.
OR...THE SOULS THAT WERE HERE...?
HEAR. I.
HEIMDALL-- HEAD FOR THE TREE.
NOW.
YOU WILL FOLLOW MY COMMAND!
YOU ARE A HERO OF ASGARD--BUT I AM THE VALKYRIOR!
AND YOU RIDE MY ROAD TODAY!
THE WORDS COME UNBIDDEN. SPOKEN BY MY TRANSFORMED SELF-- THE ASGARDIAN INSIDE.
I WISH TO ODIN HE'D LISTENED...
AAARRGH--
I HEAR.
HEAR YOU.

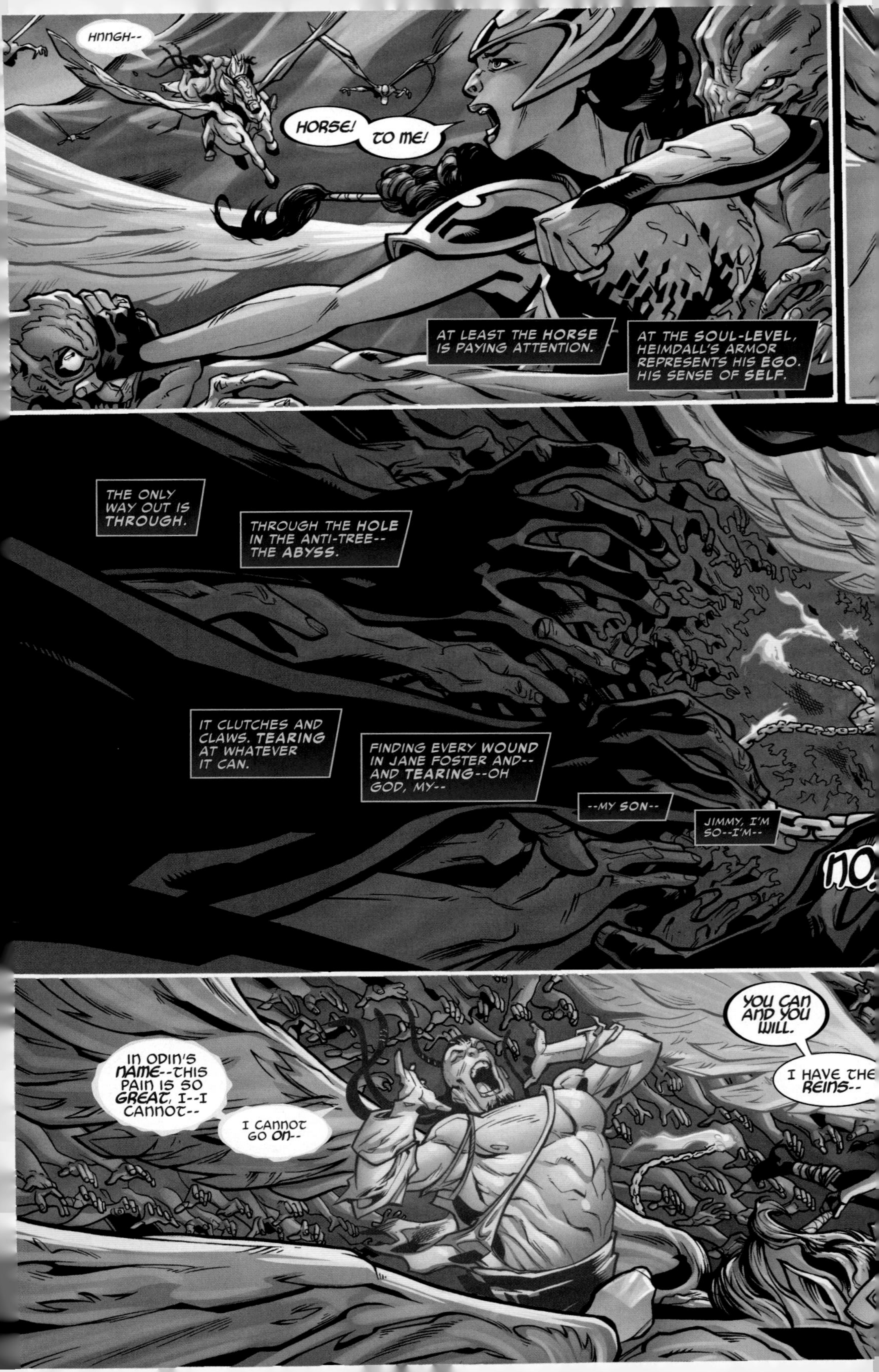
HNNGH--
HORSE!
TO ME!
AT LEAST THE HORSE IS PAYING ATTENTION.
AT THE SOUL-LEVEL, HEIMDALL'S ARMOR REPRESENTS HIS EGO. HIS SENSE OF SELF.
THE ONLY WAY OUT IS THROUGH.
THROUGH THE HOLE IN THE ANTI-TREE-- THE ABYSS.
IT CLUTCHES AND CLAWS. TEARING AT WHATEVER IT CAN.
FINDING EVERY WOUND IN JANE FOSTER AND-- AND TEARING--OH GOD, MY--
--MY SON--
JIMMY, I'M SO--I'M--
NO
IN ODIN'S NAME--THIS PAIN IS SO GREAT, I--I CANNOT--
I CANNOT GO ON--
YOU CAN AND YOU WILL.
I HAVE THE REINS--

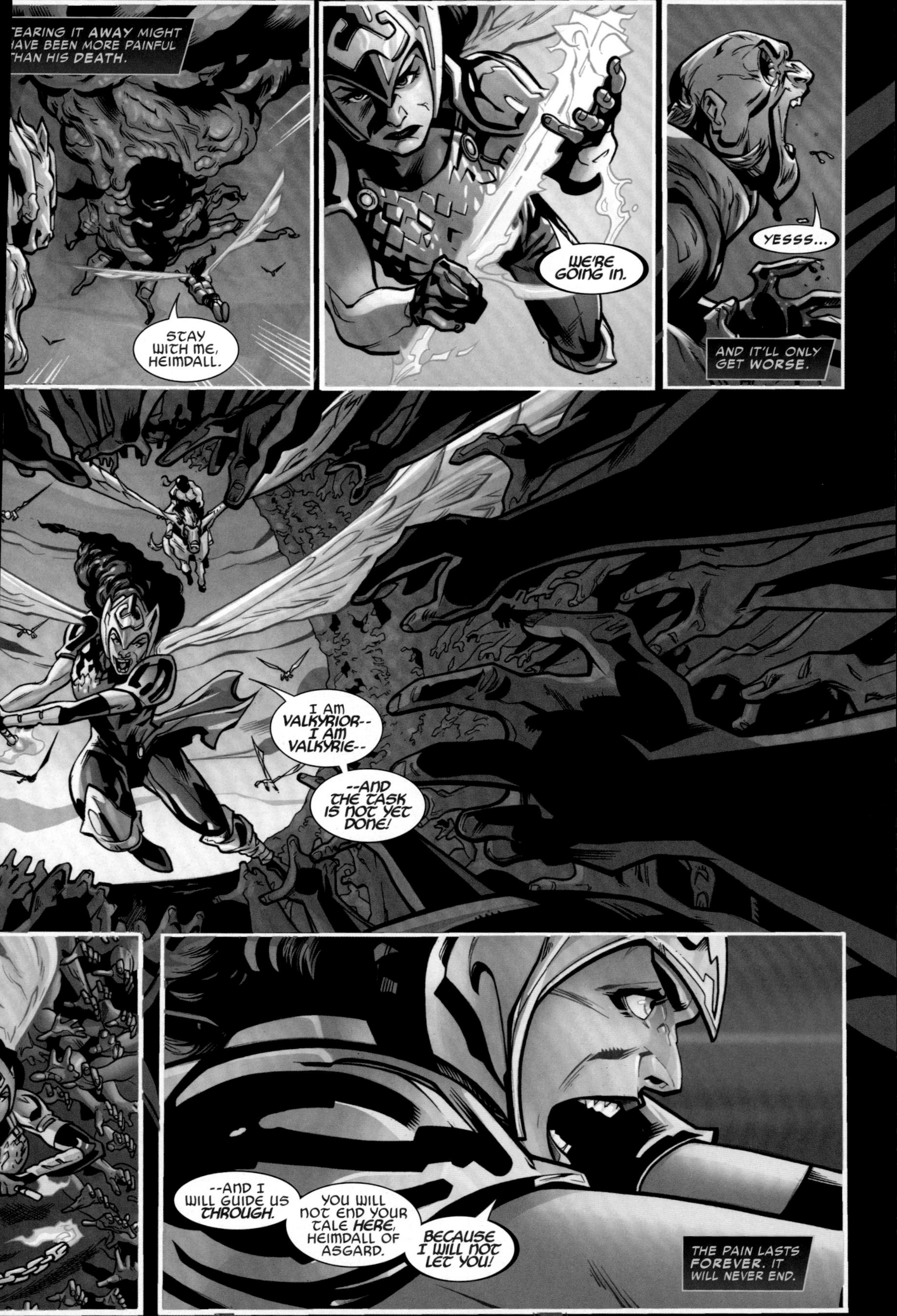
TEARING IT AWAY MIGHT HAVE BEEN MORE PAINFUL THAN HIS DEATH.
STAY WITH ME, HEIMDALL.
WE'RE GOING IN.
YESSS...
AND IT'LL ONLY GET WORSE.
I AM VALKYRIOR-- I AM VALKYRIE--
--AND THE TASK IS NOT YET DONE!
--AND I WILL GUIDE US THROUGH.
YOU WILL NOT END YOUR TALE HERE, HEIMDALL OF ASGARD.
BECAUSE I WILL NOT LET YOU!
THE PAIN LASTS FOREVER. IT WILL NEVER END.

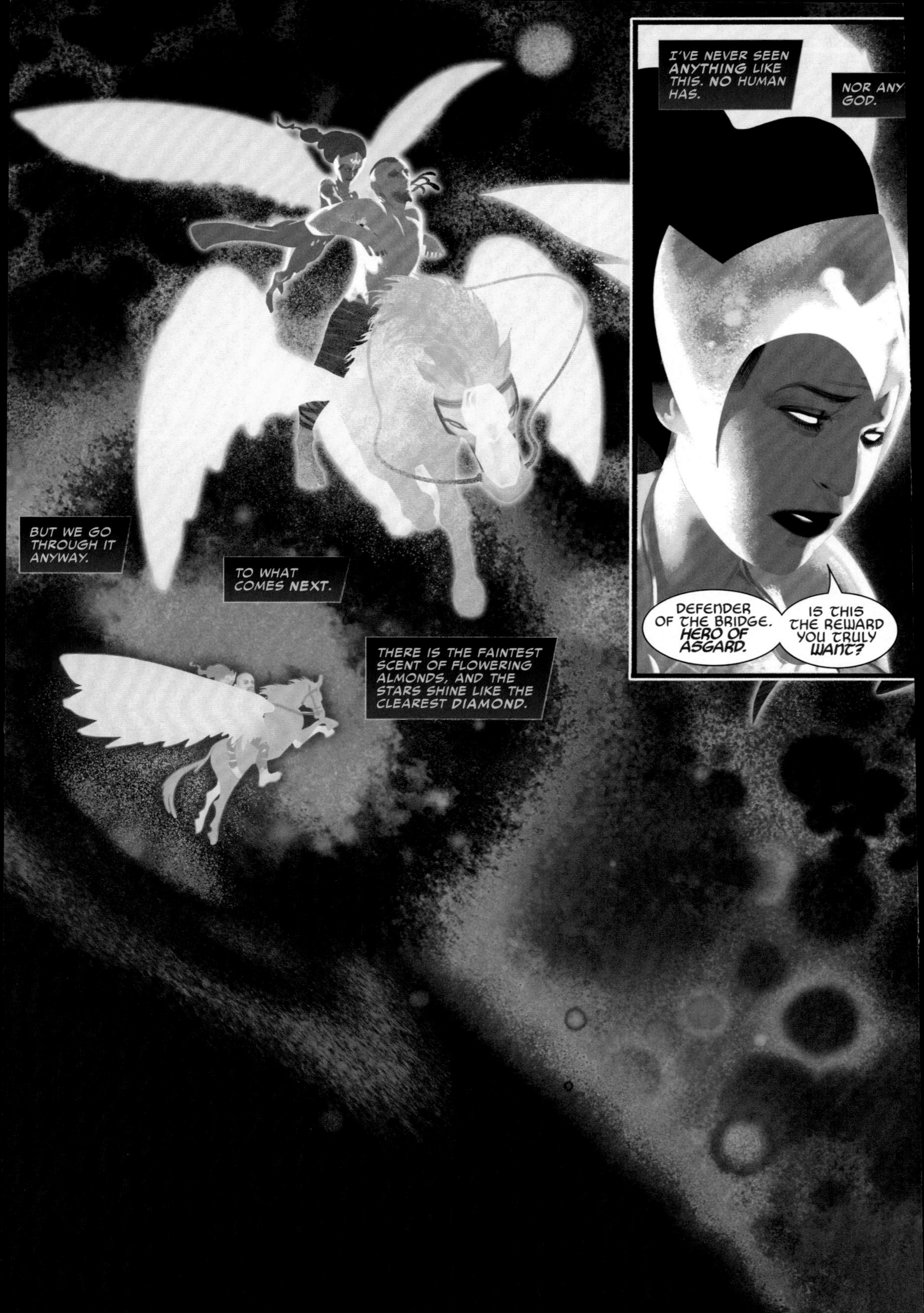
I'VE NEVER SEEN ANYTHING LIKE THIS. NO HUMAN HAS.
NOR ANY GOD.
DEFENDER OF THE BRIDGE. HERO OF ASGARD.
IS THIS THE REWARD YOU TRULY WANT?
BUT WE GO THROUGH IT ANYWAY.
TO WHAT COMES NEXT.
THERE IS THE FAINTEST SCENT OF FLOWERING ALMONDS, AND THE STARS SHINE LIKE THE CLEAREST DIAMOND.

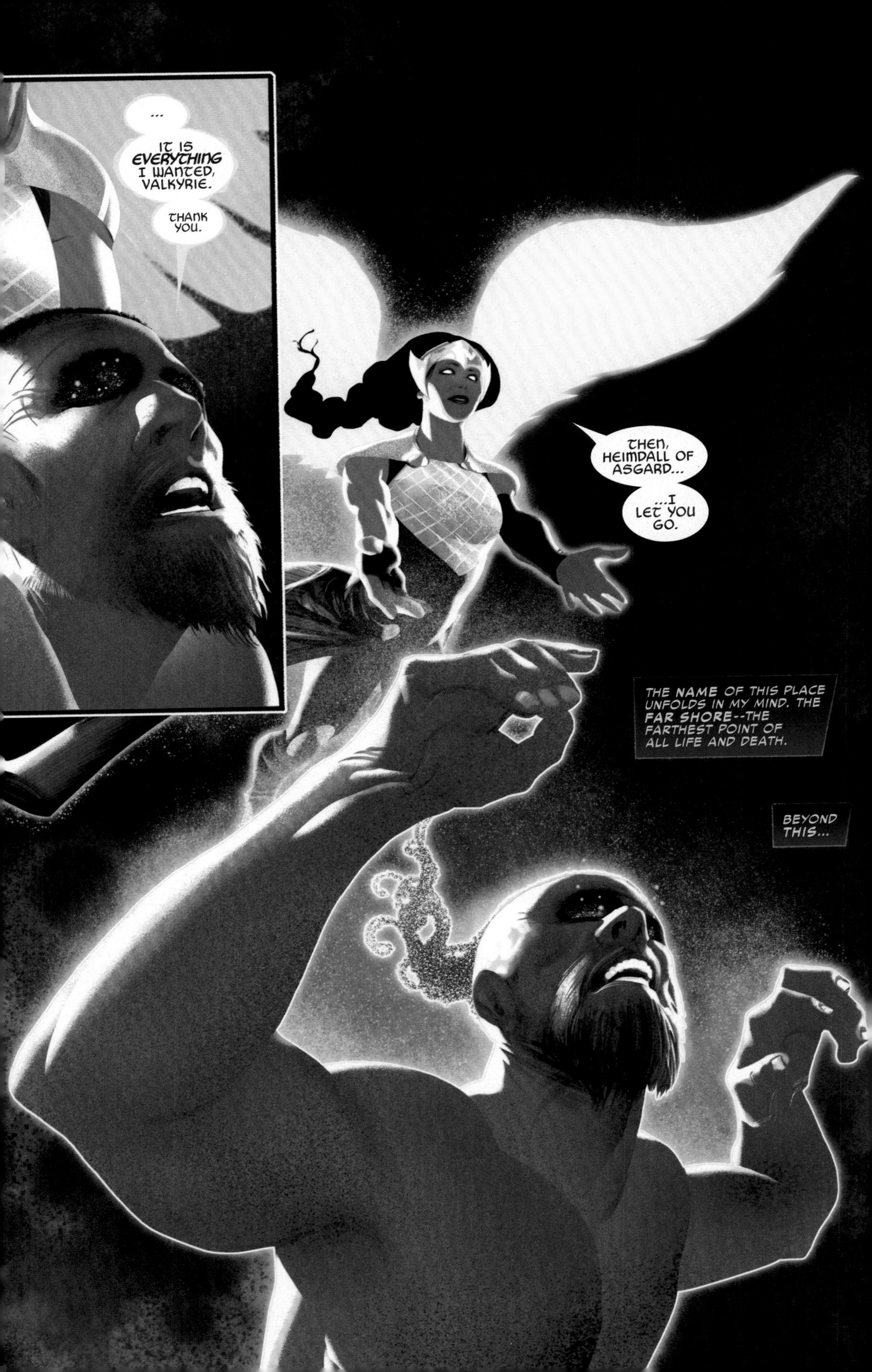
...
IT IS EVERYTHING I WANTED, VALKYRIE.
THANK YOU.
THEN, HEIMDALL OF ASGARD...
...I LET YOU GO.
THE NAME OF THIS PLACE UNFOLDS IN MY MIND. THE FAR SHORE--THE FARTHEST POINT OF ALL LIFE AND DEATH.
BEYOND THIS...

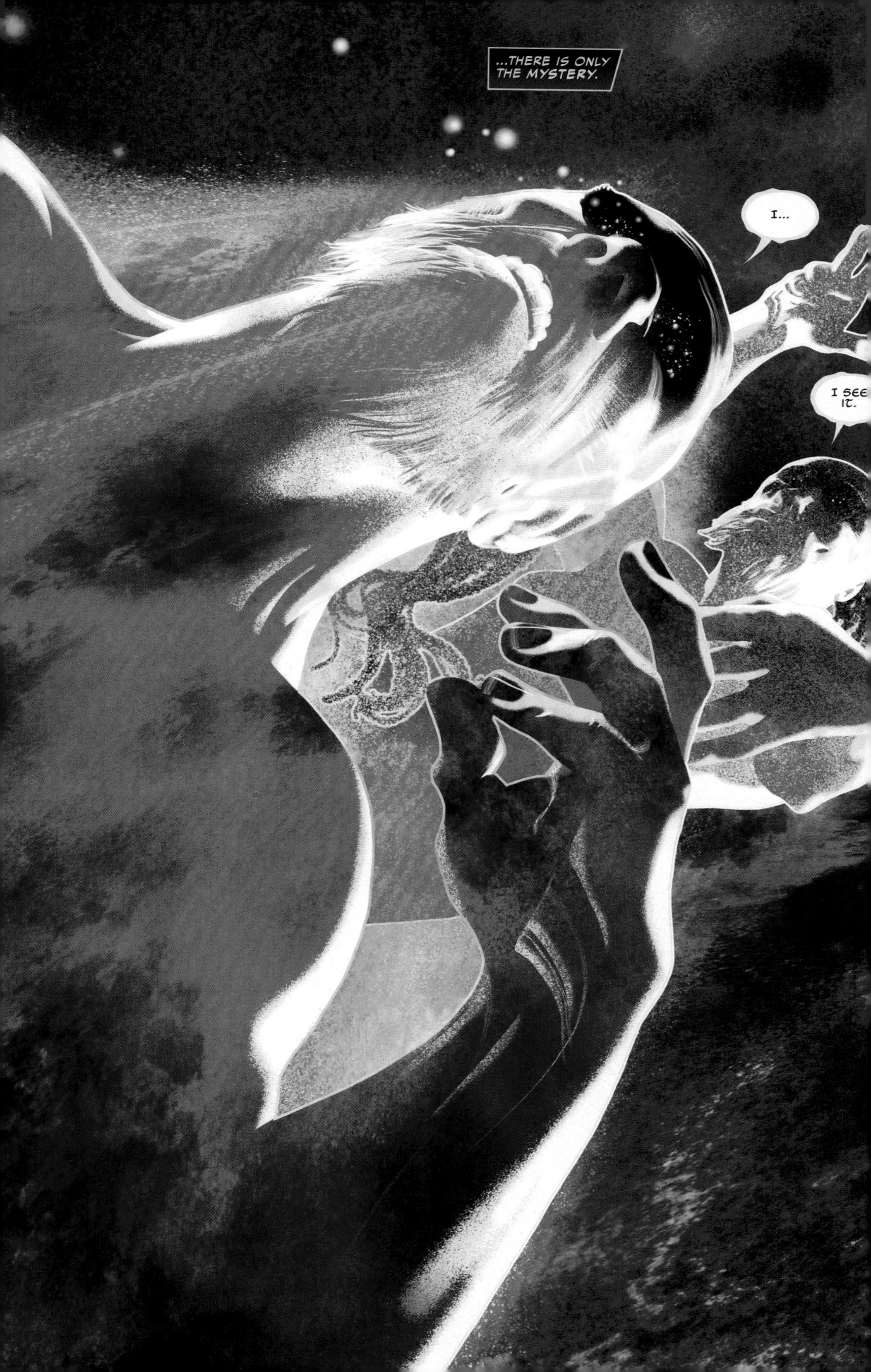
...THERE IS ONLY THE MYSTERY.
I...
I SEE IT.

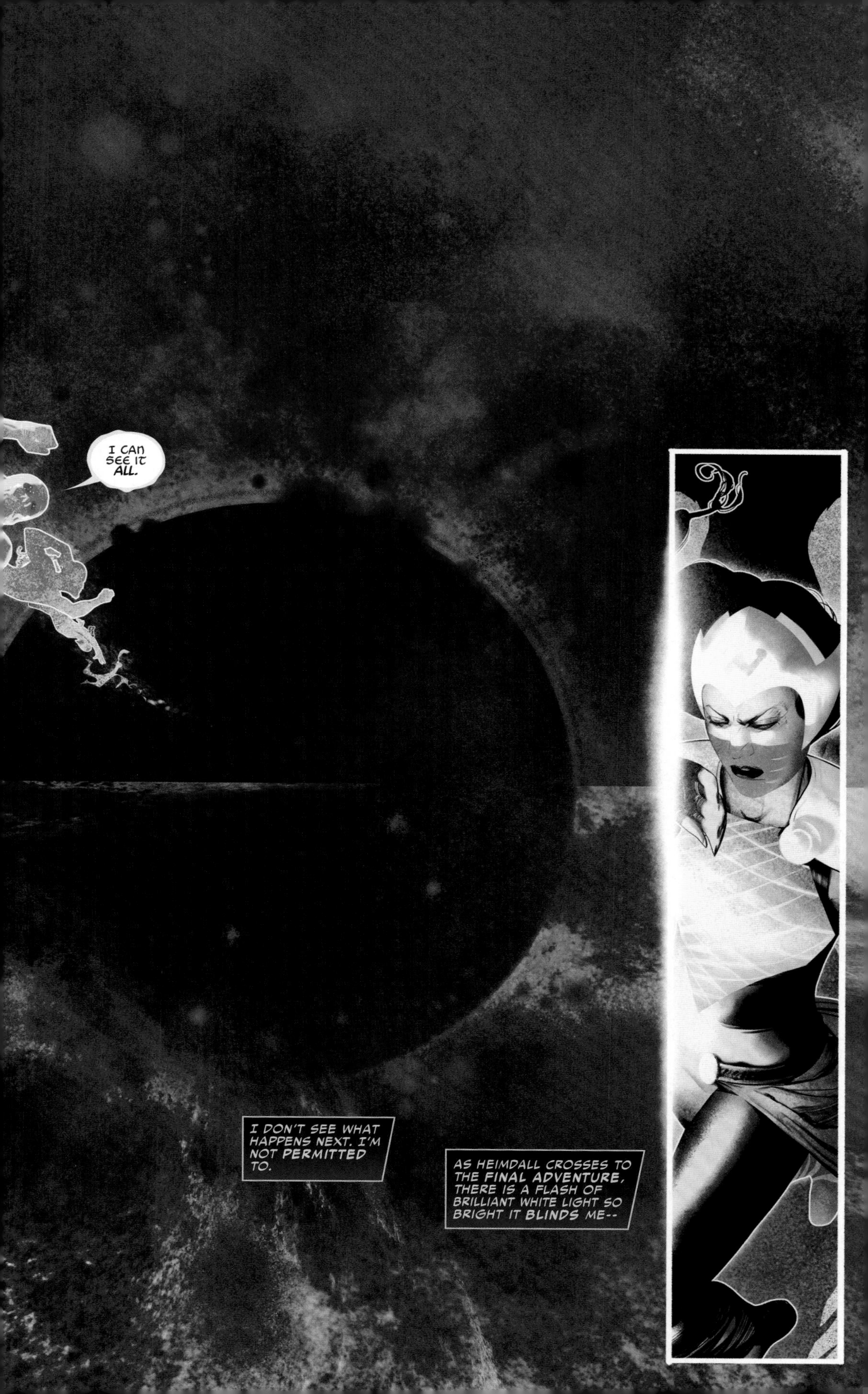

I CAN SEE IT ALL.
I DON'T SEE WHAT HAPPENS NEXT. I'M NOT PERMITTED TO.
AS HEIMDALL CROSSES TO THE FINAL ADVENTURE, THERE IS A FLASH OF BRILLIANT WHITE LIGHT SO BRIGHT IT BLINDS ME--

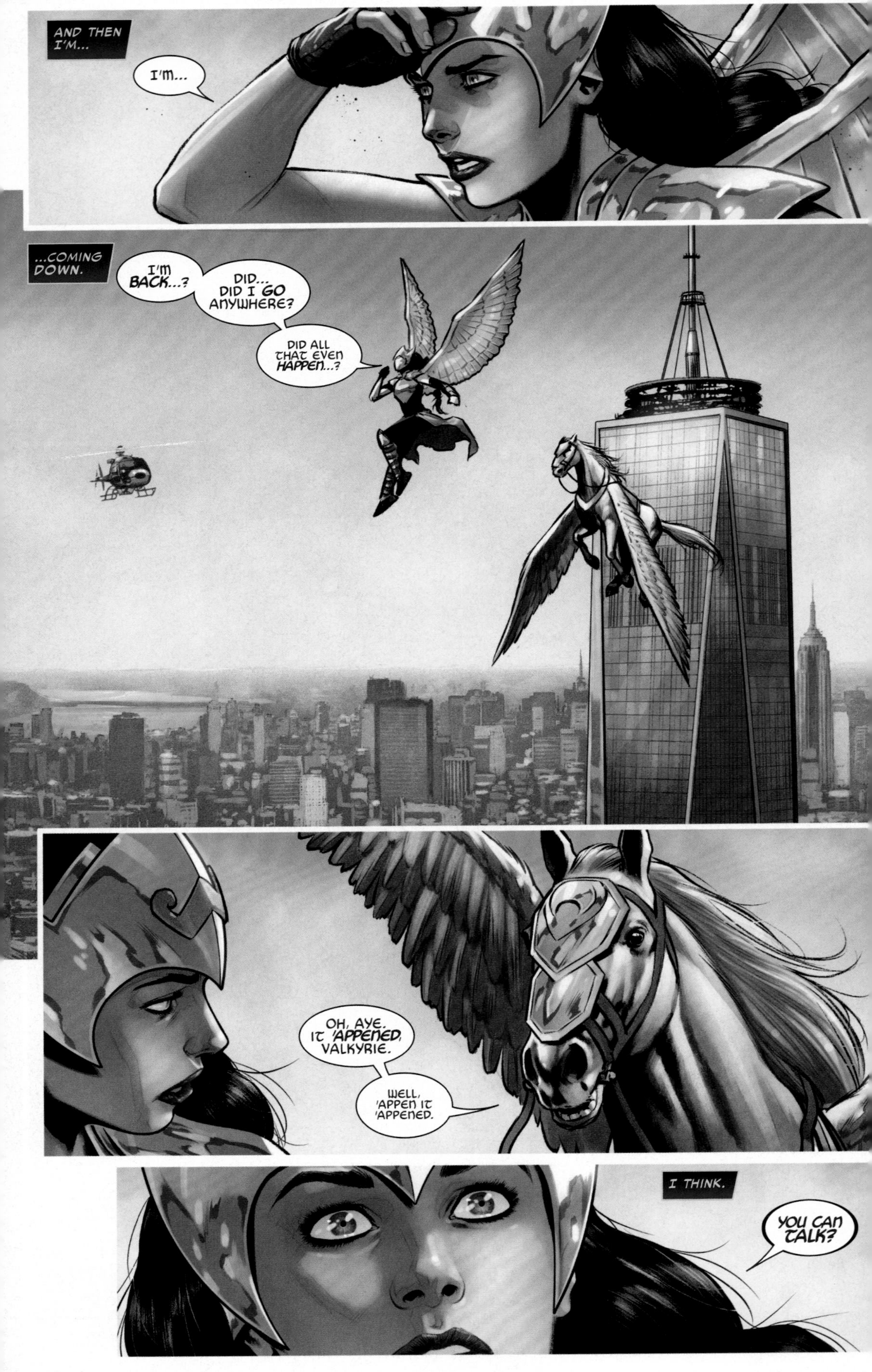
AND THEN I'M...
I'M...
...COMING DOWN.
I'M BACK...?
DID... DID I GO ANYWHERE?
DID ALL THAT EVEN HAPPEN...?
OH, AYE. IT 'APPENED, VALKYRIE.
WELL, 'APPEN IT 'APPENED.
I THINK.
YOU CAN TALK?

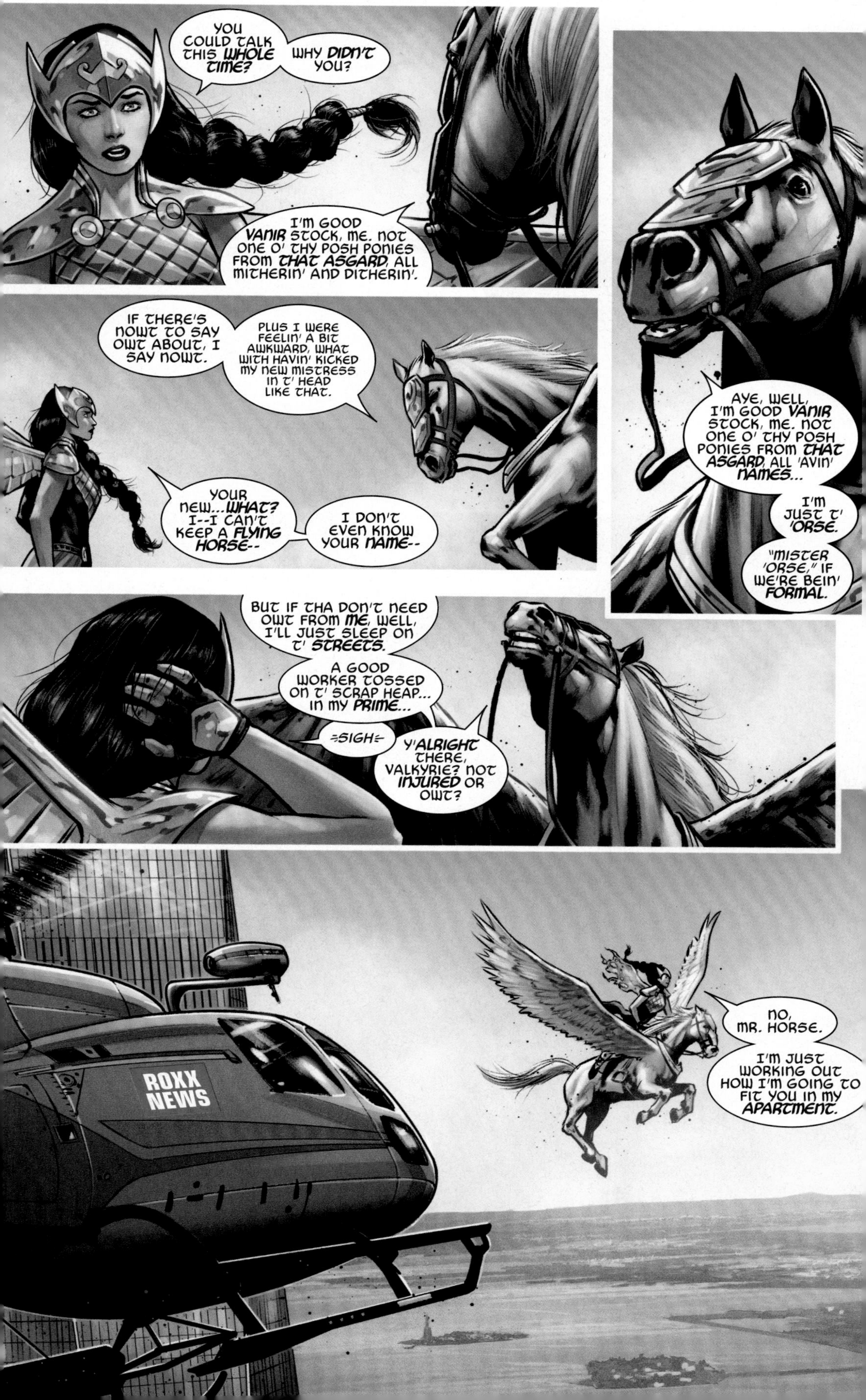
YOU COULD TALK THIS WHOLE TIME?
WHY DIDN'T YOU?
I'M GOOD VANIR STOCK, ME. NOT ONE O' THY POSH PONIES FROM THAT ASGARD, ALL MITHERIN' AND DITHERIN'.
AYE, WELL, I'M GOOD VANIR STOCK, ME. NOT ONE O' THY POSH PONIES FROM THAT ASGARD, ALL 'AVIN' NAMES...
I'M JUST T' 'ORSE.
"MISTER 'ORSE," IF WE'RE BEIN' FORMAL.
IF THERE'S NOWT TO SAY OWT ABOUT, I SAY NOWT.
PLUS I WERE FEELIN' A BIT AWKWARD, WHAT WITH HAVIN' KICKED MY NEW MISTRESS IN T' HEAD LIKE THAT.
YOUR NEW...WHAT? I--I CAN'T KEEP A FLYING HORSE--
I DON'T EVEN KNOW YOUR NAME--
BUT IF THA DON'T NEED OWT FROM ME, WELL, I'LL JUST SLEEP ON T' STREETS.
A GOOD WORKER TOSSED ON T' SCRAP HEAP... IN MY PRIME...
=SIGH=
Y'ALRIGHT THERE, VALKYRIE? NOT INJURED OR OWT?
ROXX NEWS
NO, MR. HORSE.
I'M JUST WORKING OUT HOW I'M GOING TO FIT YOU IN MY APARTMENT.

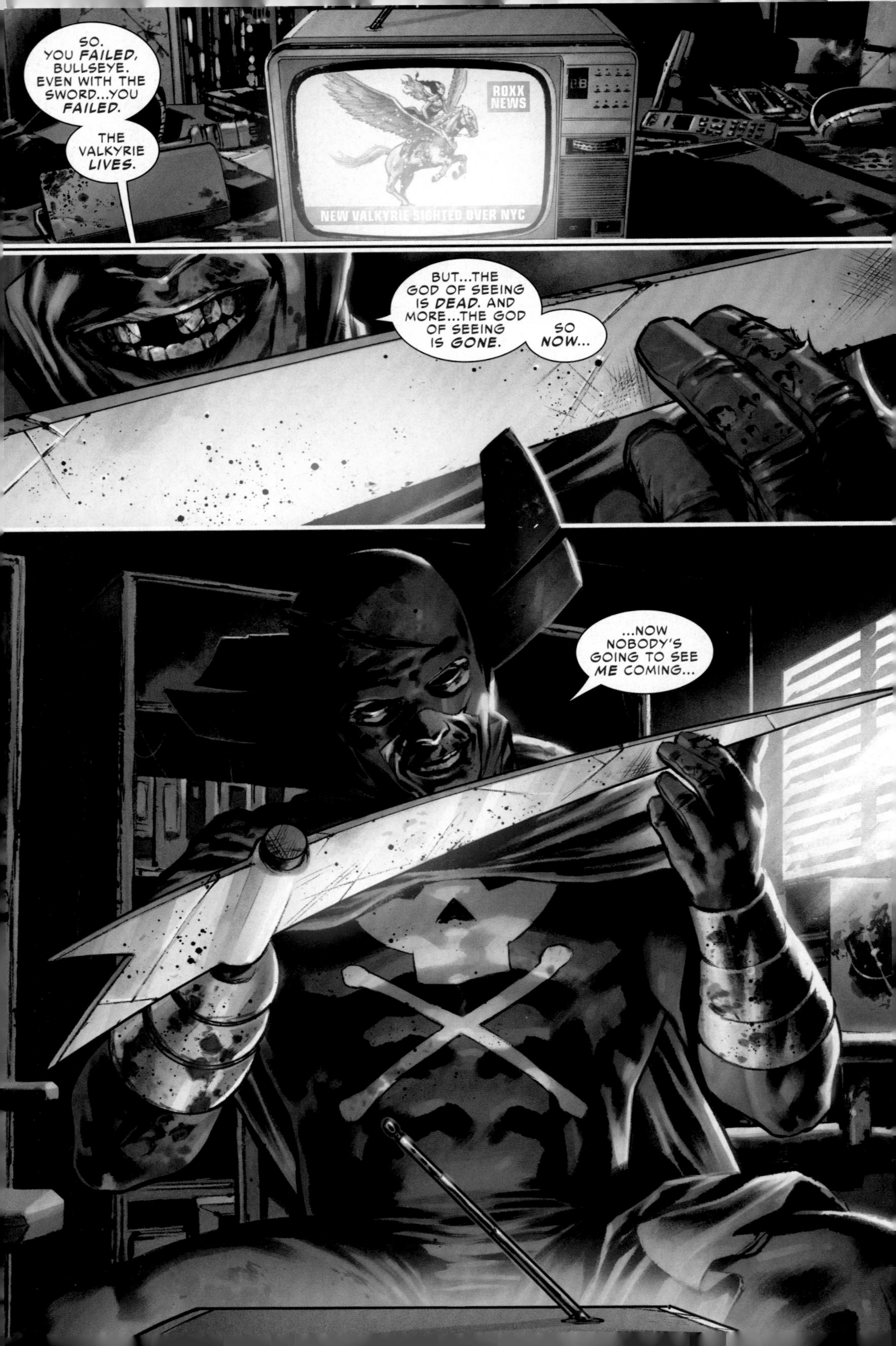
SO. YOU FAILED, BULLSEYE. EVEN WITH THE SWORD...YOU FAILED.
THE VALKYRIE LIVES.
ROXX NEWS
NEW VALKYRIE SIGHTED OVER NYC
BUT...THE GOD OF SEEING IS DEAD. AND MORE...THE GOD OF SEEING IS GONE.
SO NOW...
...NOW NOBODY'S GOING TO SEE ME COMING...

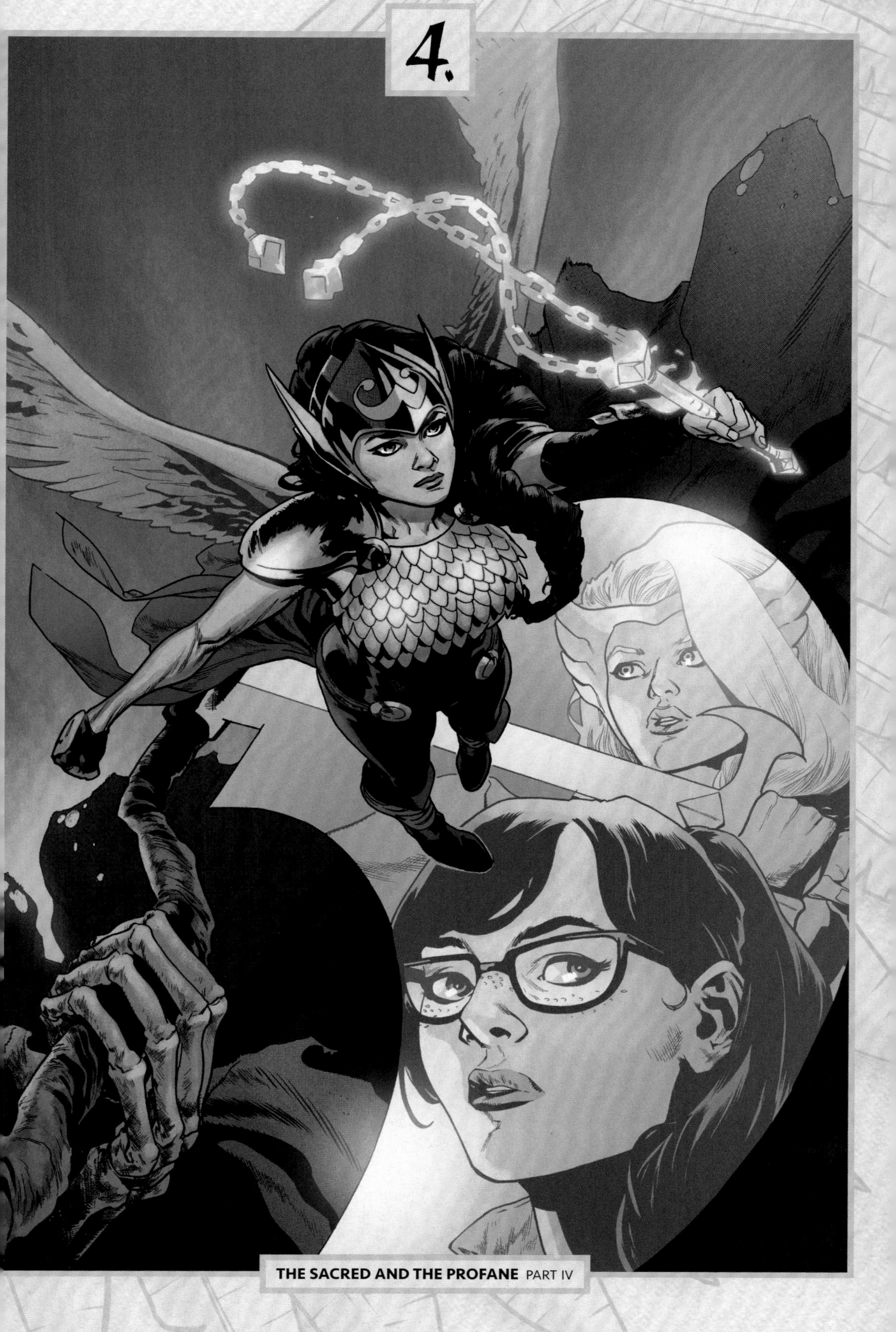
4.
THE SACRED AND THE PROFANE PART IV

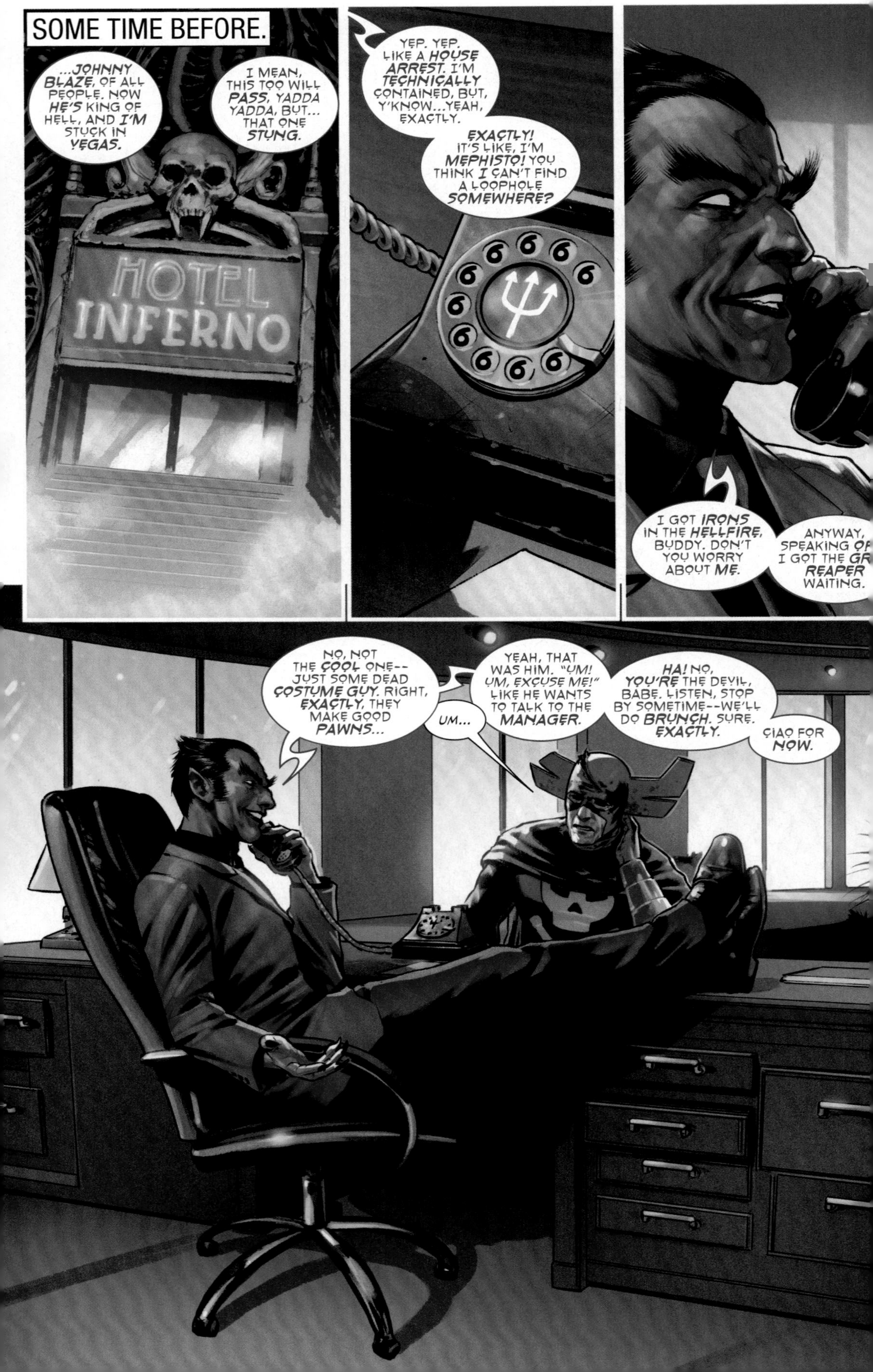
SOME TIME BEFORE.
...JOHNNY BLAZE, OF ALL PEOPLE. NOW HE'S KING OF HELL, AND I'M STUCK IN VEGAS.
I MEAN, THIS TOO WILL PASS, YADDA YADDA, BUT... THAT ONE STUNG.
HOTEL INFERNO
YEP. YEP. LIKE A HOUSE ARREST. I'M TECHNICALLY CONTAINED, BUT, Y'KNOW...YEAH, EXACTLY.
EXACTLY! IT'S LIKE, I'M MEPHISTO! YOU THINK I CAN'T FIND A LOOPHOLE SOMEWHERE?
I GOT IRONS IN THE HELLFIRE, BUDDY. DON'T YOU WORRY ABOUT ME.
ANYWAY, SPEAKING OF I GOT THE GR REAPER WAITING.
NO, NOT THE COOL ONE-- JUST SOME DEAD COSTUME GUY. RIGHT, EXACTLY, THEY MAKE GOOD PAWNS...
UM...
YEAH, THAT WAS HIM. "UM! UM, EXCUSE ME!" LIKE HE WANTS TO TALK TO THE MANAGER.
HA! NO, YOU'RE THE DEVIL, BABE. LISTEN, STOP BY SOMETIME--WE'LL DO BRUNCH. SURE. EXACTLY.
CIAO FOR NOW.

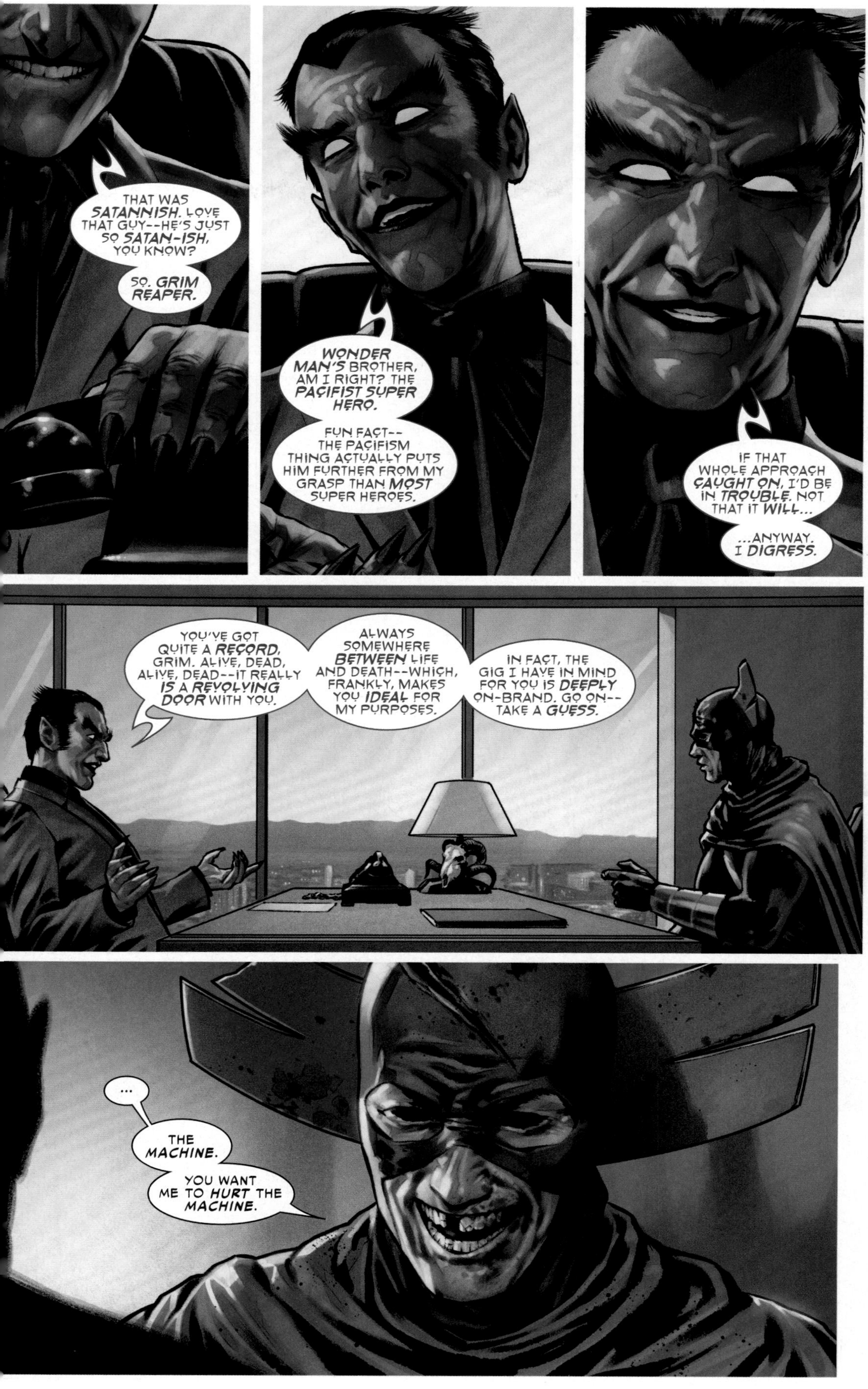
THAT WAS SATANNISH. LOVE THAT GUY--HE'S JUST SO SATAN-ISH, YOU KNOW?
SO. GRIM REAPER.
WONDER MAN'S BROTHER, AM I RIGHT? THE PACIFIST SUPER HERO.
FUN FACT-- THE PACIFISM THING ACTUALLY PUTS HIM FURTHER FROM MY GRASP THAN MOST SUPER HEROES.
IF THAT WHOLE APPROACH CAUGHT ON, I'D BE IN TROUBLE. NOT THAT IT WILL...
...ANYWAY. I DIGRESS.
YOU'VE GOT QUITE A RECORD, GRIM. ALIVE, DEAD, ALIVE, DEAD--IT REALLY IS A REVOLVING DOOR WITH YOU.
ALWAYS SOMEWHERE BETWEEN LIFE AND DEATH--WHICH, FRANKLY, MAKES YOU IDEAL FOR MY PURPOSES.
IN FACT, THE GIG I HAVE IN MIND FOR YOU IS DEEPLY ON-BRAND. GO ON-- TAKE A GUESS.
...
THE MACHINE.
YOU WANT ME TO HURT THE MACHINE.

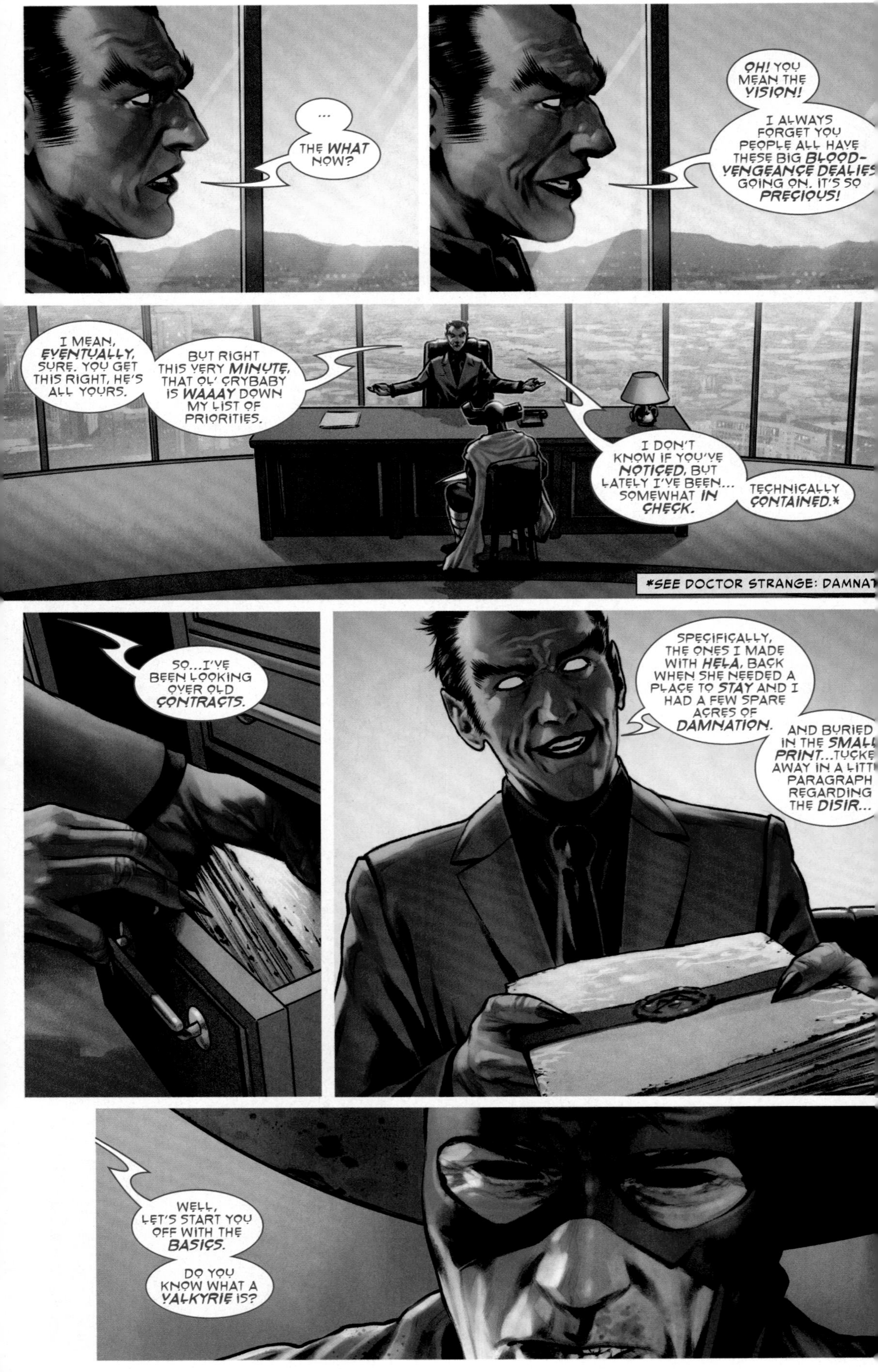
...
THE WHAT NOW?
OH! YOU MEAN THE VISION!
I ALWAYS FORGET YOU PEOPLE ALL HAVE THESE BIG BLOOD-VENGEANCE DEALIES GOING ON. IT'S SO PRECIOUS!
I MEAN, EVENTUALLY, SURE. YOU GET THIS RIGHT, HE'S ALL YOURS.
BUT RIGHT THIS VERY MINUTE, THAT OL' CRYBABY IS WAAAY DOWN MY LIST OF PRIORITIES.
I DON'T KNOW IF YOU'VE NOTICED, BUT LATELY I'VE BEEN... SOMEWHAT IN CHECK.
TECHNICALLY CONTAINED.*
*SEE DOCTOR STRANGE: DAMNAT
SO...I'VE BEEN LOOKING OVER OLD CONTRACTS.
SPECIFICALLY, THE ONES I MADE WITH HELA, BACK WHEN SHE NEEDED A PLACE TO STAY AND I HAD A FEW SPARE ACRES OF DAMNATION.
AND BURIED IN THE SMALL PRINT...TUCKE AWAY IN A LITT PARAGRAPH REGARDING THE DISIR...
WELL, LET'S START YOU OFF WITH THE BASICS.
DO YOU KNOW WHAT A VALKYRIE IS?

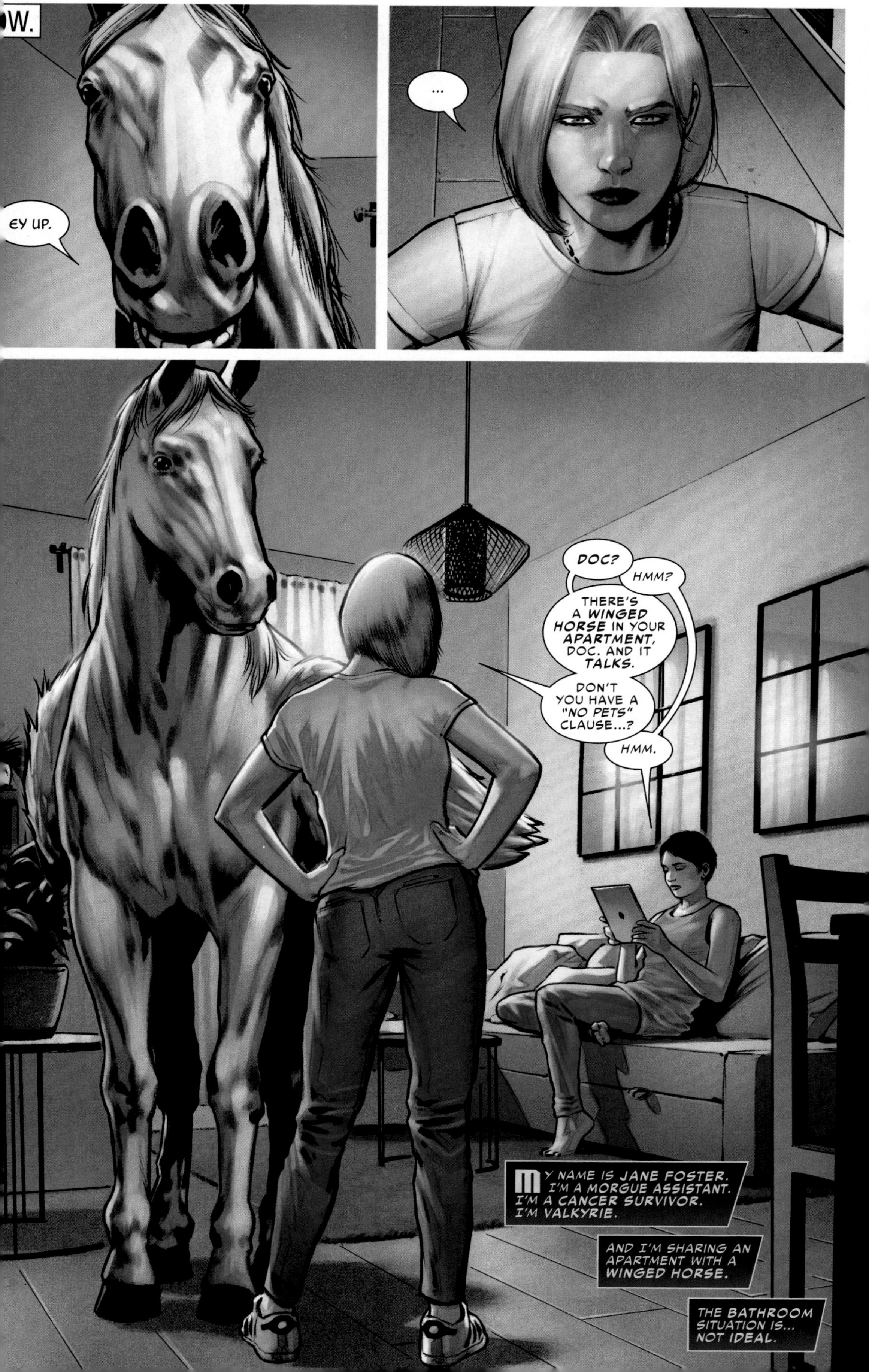

W.
EY UP.
...
DOC?
HMM?
THERE'S A WINGED HORSE IN YOUR APARTMENT, DOC. AND IT TALKS.
DON'T YOU HAVE A "NO PETS" CLAUSE...?
HMM.
MY NAME IS JANE FOSTER. I'M A MORGUE ASSISTANT. I'M A CANCER SURVIVOR. I'M VALKYRIE.
AND I'M SHARING AN APARTMENT WITH A WINGED HORSE.
THE BATHROOM SITUATION IS... NOT IDEAL.

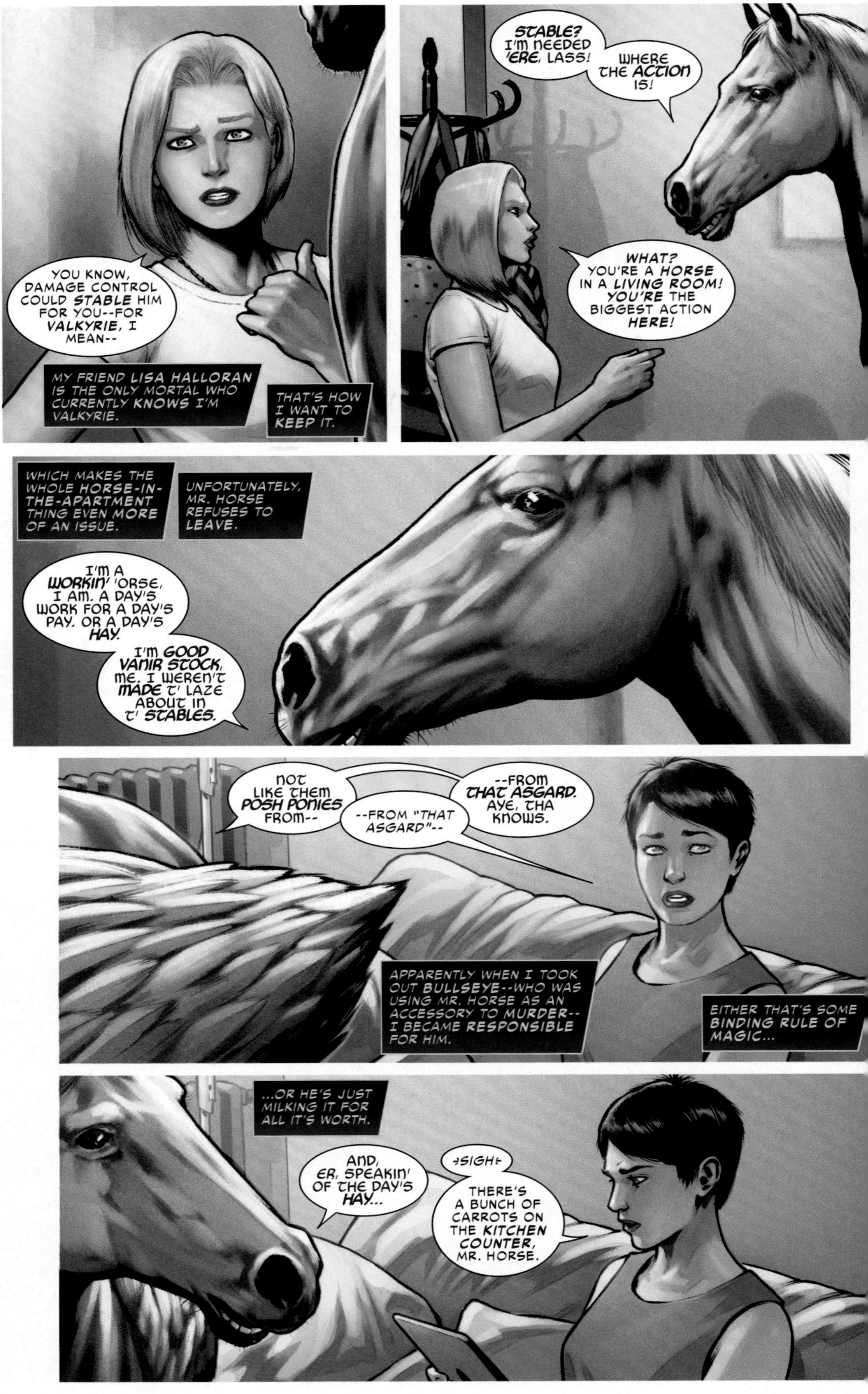
YOU KNOW, DAMAGE CONTROL COULD STABLE HIM FOR YOU--FOR VALKYRIE, I MEAN--
MY FRIEND LISA HALLORAN IS THE ONLY MORTAL WHO CURRENTLY KNOWS I'M VALKYRIE.
THAT'S HOW I WANT TO KEEP IT.
STABLE? I'M NEEDED 'ERE, LASS!
WHERE THE ACTION IS!
WHAT? YOU'RE A HORSE IN A LIVING ROOM! YOU'RE THE BIGGEST ACTION HERE!
WHICH MAKES THE WHOLE HORSE-IN-THE-APARTMENT THING EVEN MORE OF AN ISSUE.
UNFORTUNATELY, MR. HORSE REFUSES TO LEAVE.
I'M A WORKIN' 'ORSE, I AM. A DAY'S WORK FOR A DAY'S PAY. OR A DAY'S HAY.
I'M GOOD VANIR STOCK, ME. I WEREN'T MADE T' LAZE ABOUT IN T' STABLES.
NOT LIKE THEM POSH PONIES FROM--
--FROM "THAT ASGARD"--
--FROM THAT ASGARD. AYE, THA KNOWS.
APPARENTLY WHEN I TOOK OUT BULLSEYE--WHO WAS USING MR. HORSE AS AN ACCESSORY TO MURDER--I BECAME RESPONSIBLE FOR HIM.
EITHER THAT'S SOME BINDING RULE OF MAGIC...
...OR HE'S JUST MILKING IT FOR ALL IT'S WORTH.
AND, ER, SPEAKIN' OF THE DAY'S HAY...
-SIGH-
THERE'S A BUNCH OF CARROTS ON THE KITCHEN COUNTER, MR. HORSE.

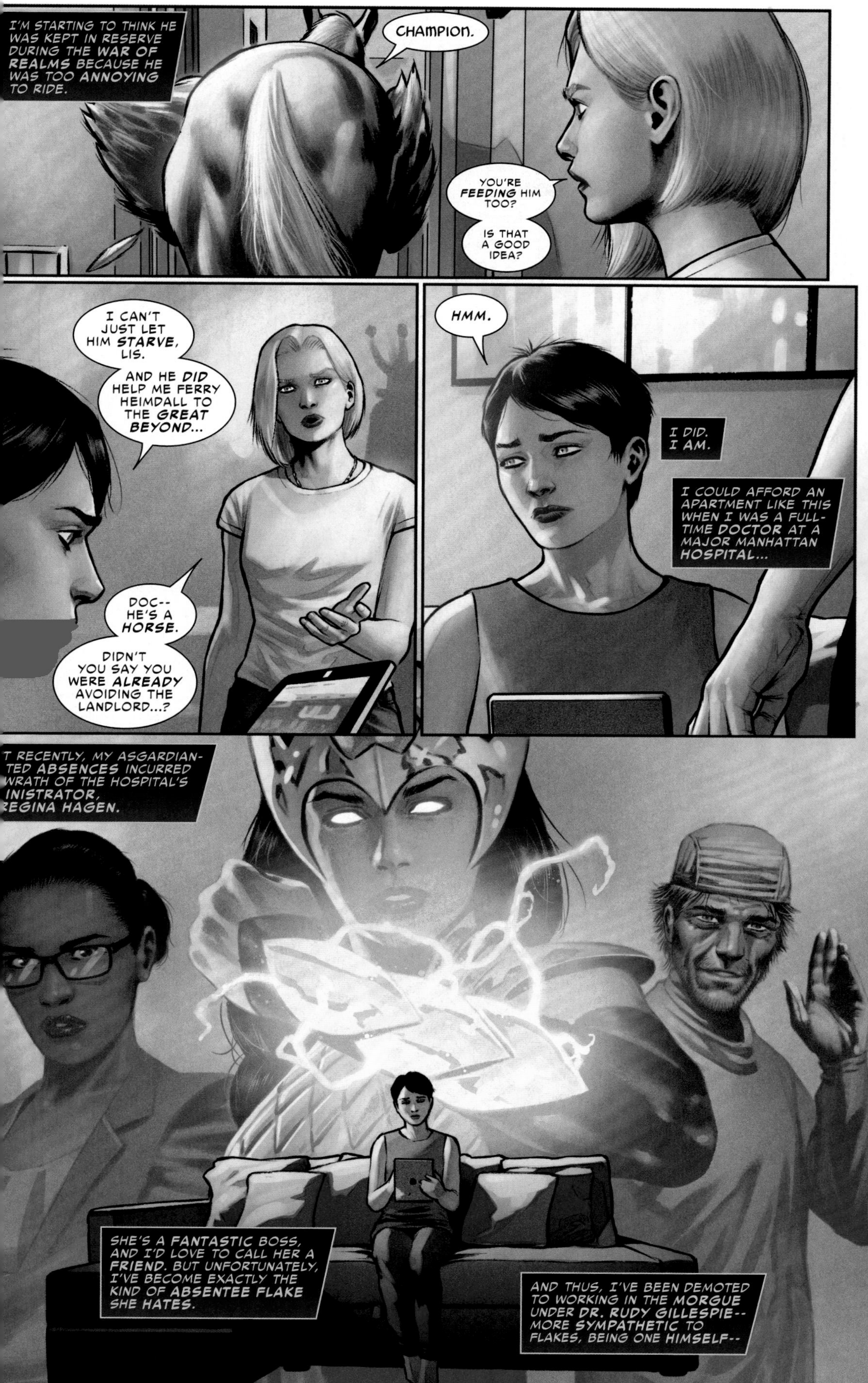
I'M STARTING TO THINK HE WAS KEPT IN RESERVE DURING THE WAR OF REALMS BECAUSE HE WAS TOO ANNOYING TO RIDE.
CHAMPION.
YOU'RE FEEDING HIM TOO?
IS THAT A GOOD IDEA?
I CAN'T JUST LET HIM STARVE, LIS.
AND HE DID HELP ME FERRY HEIMDALL TO THE GREAT BEYOND...
DOC-- HE'S A HORSE.
DIDN'T YOU SAY YOU WERE ALREADY AVOIDING THE LANDLORD...?
HMM.
I DID. I AM.
I COULD AFFORD AN APARTMENT LIKE THIS WHEN I WAS A FULL-TIME DOCTOR AT A MAJOR MANHATTAN HOSPITAL...
T RECENTLY, MY ASGARDIAN-TED ABSENCES INCURRED WRATH OF THE HOSPITAL'S INISTRATOR, EGINA HAGEN.
SHE'S A FANTASTIC BOSS, AND I'D LOVE TO CALL HER A FRIEND. BUT UNFORTUNATELY, I'VE BECOME EXACTLY THE KIND OF ABSENTEE FLAKE SHE HATES.
AND THUS, I'VE BEEN DEMOTED TO WORKING IN THE MORGUE UNDER DR. RUDY GILLESPIE-- MORE SYMPATHETIC TO FLAKES, BEING ONE HIMSELF--

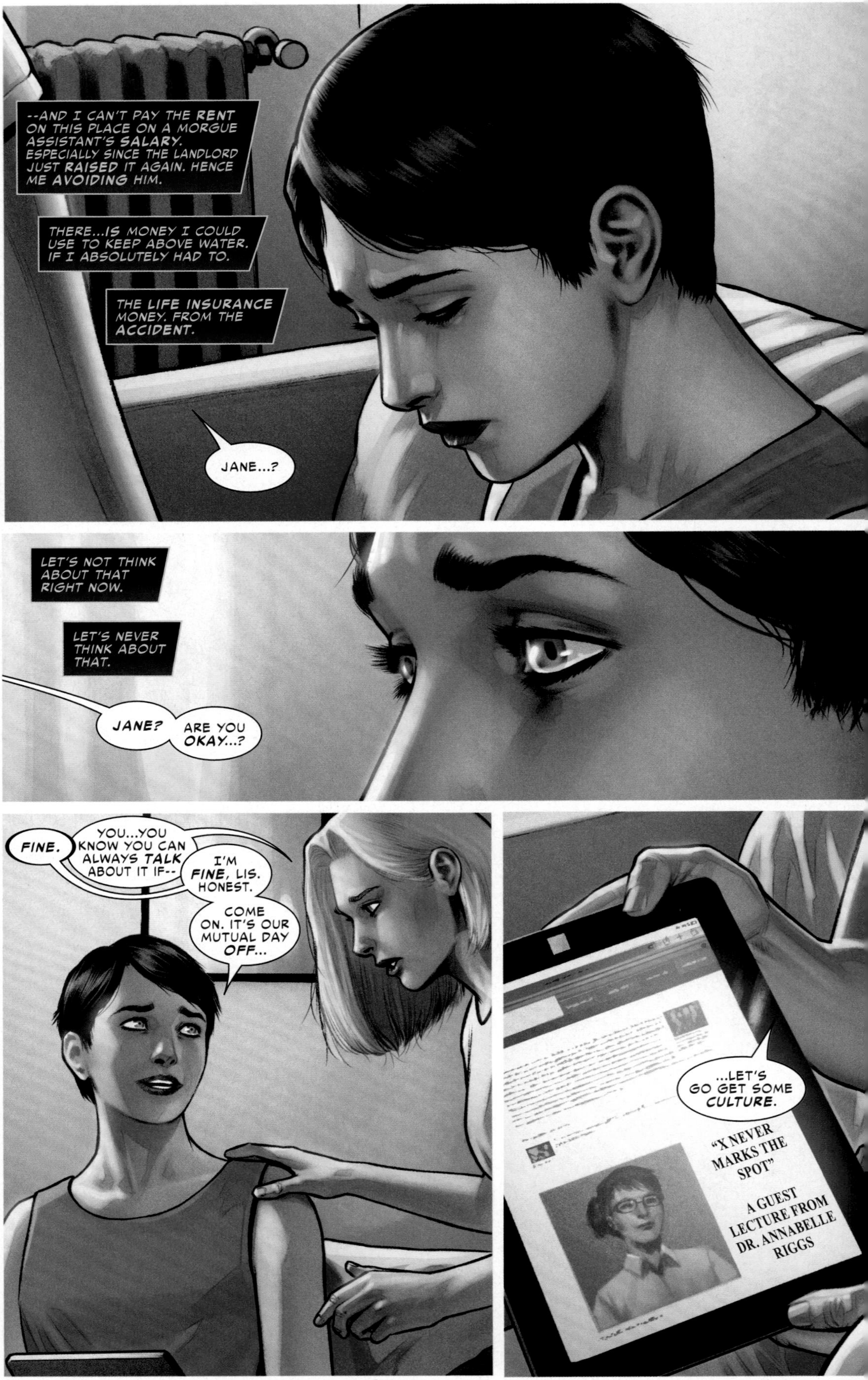

--AND I CAN'T PAY THE RENT ON THIS PLACE ON A MORGUE ASSISTANT'S SALARY. ESPECIALLY SINCE THE LANDLORD JUST RAISED IT AGAIN. HENCE ME AVOIDING HIM.
THERE...IS MONEY I COULD USE TO KEEP ABOVE WATER. IF I ABSOLUTELY HAD TO.
THE LIFE INSURANCE MONEY. FROM THE ACCIDENT.
JANE...?
LET'S NOT THINK ABOUT THAT RIGHT NOW.
LET'S NEVER THINK ABOUT THAT.
JANE?
ARE YOU OKAY...?
FINE.
YOU...YOU KNOW YOU CAN ALWAYS TALK ABOUT IT IF--
I'M FINE, LIS. HONEST.
COME ON. IT'S OUR MUTUAL DAY OFF...
...LET'S GO GET SOME CULTURE.
"X NEVER MARKS THE SPOT"
A GUEST LECTURE FROM DR. ANNABELLE RIGGS

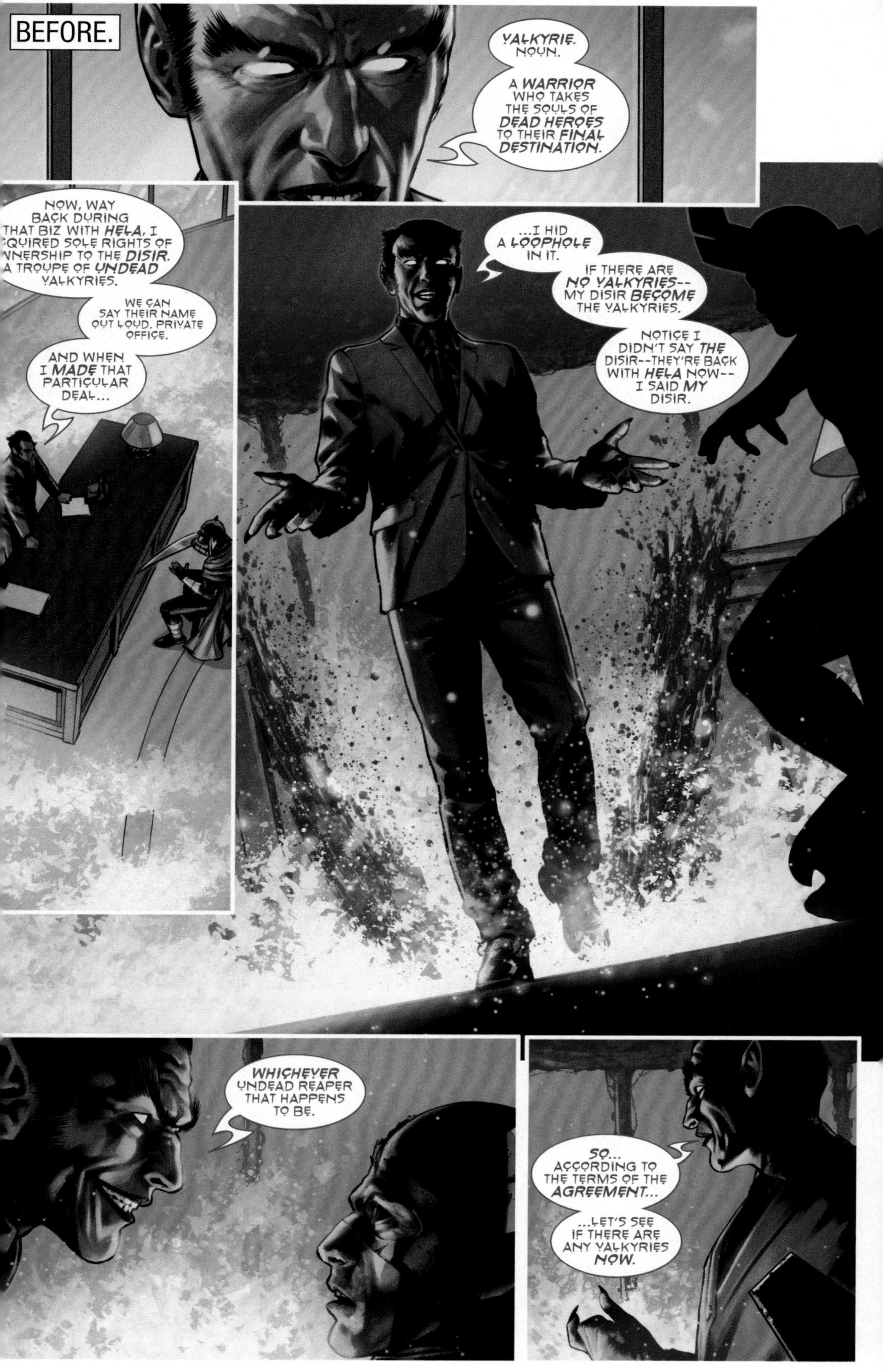
BEFORE.
YALKYRIE. NOUN.
A WARRIOR WHO TAKES THE SOULS OF DEAD HEROES TO THEIR FINAL DESTINATION.
NOW, WAY BACK DURING THAT BIZ WITH HELA, I CQUIRED SOLE RIGHTS OF NNERSHIP TO THE DISIR. A TROUPE OF UNDEAD VALKYRIES.
WE CAN SAY THEIR NAME OUT LOUD. PRIVATE OFFICE.
AND WHEN I MADE THAT PARTICULAR DEAL...
...I HID A LOOPHOLE IN IT.
IF THERE ARE NO VALKYRIES-- MY DISIR BECOME THE VALKYRIES.
NOTICE I DIDN'T SAY THE DISIR--THEY'RE BACK WITH HELA NOW-- I SAID MY DISIR.
WHICHEVER UNDEAD REAPER THAT HAPPENS TO BE.
SO... ACCORDING TO THE TERMS OF THE AGREEMENT...
...LET'S SEE IF THERE ARE ANY VALKYRIES NOW.

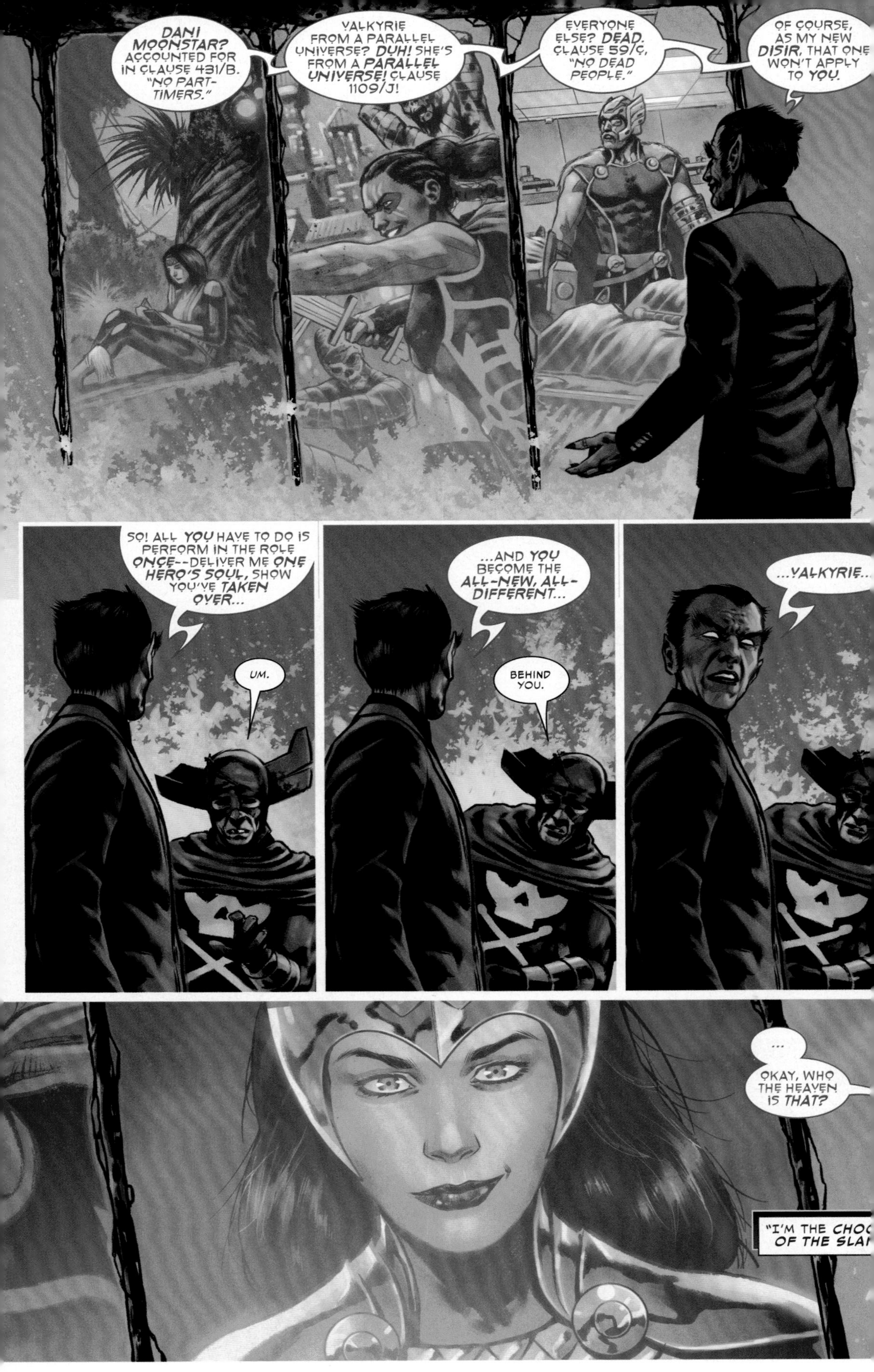
DANI MOONSTAR? ACCOUNTED FOR IN CLAUSE 431/B. "NO PART-TIMERS."
VALKYRIE FROM A PARALLEL UNIVERSE? DUH! SHE'S FROM A PARALLEL UNIVERSE! CLAUSE 1109/J!
EVERYONE ELSE? DEAD. CLAUSE 59/C, "NO DEAD PEOPLE."
OF COURSE, AS MY NEW DISIR, THAT ONE WON'T APPLY TO YOU.
SO! ALL YOU HAVE TO DO IS PERFORM IN THE ROLE ONCE--DELIVER ME ONE HERO'S SOUL, SHOW YOU'VE TAKEN OVER...
UM.
...AND YOU BECOME THE ALL-NEW, ALL-DIFFERENT...
BEHIND YOU.
...VALKYRIE...
...
OKAY, WHO THE HEAVEN IS THAT?
"I'M THE CHOO
OF THE SLAI

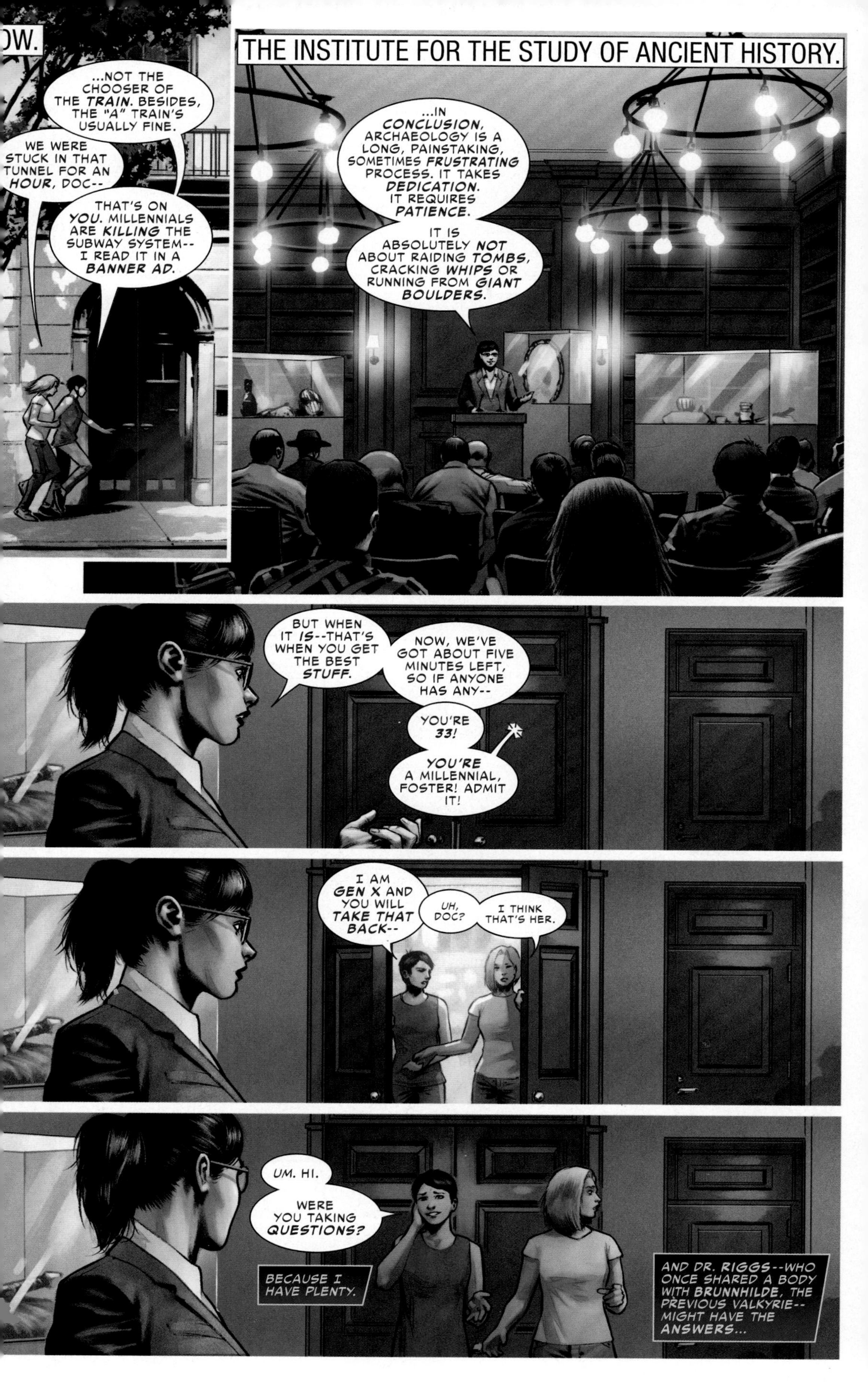

OW.
...NOT THE CHOOSER OF THE TRAIN. BESIDES, THE "A" TRAIN'S USUALLY FINE.
WE WERE STUCK IN THAT TUNNEL FOR AN HOUR, DOC--
THAT'S ON YOU. MILLENNIALS ARE KILLING THE SUBWAY SYSTEM-- I READ IT IN A BANNER AD.
THE INSTITUTE FOR THE STUDY OF ANCIENT HISTORY.
...IN CONCLUSION, ARCHAEOLOGY IS A LONG, PAINSTAKING, SOMETIMES FRUSTRATING PROCESS. IT TAKES DEDICATION. IT REQUIRES PATIENCE.
IT IS ABSOLUTELY NOT ABOUT RAIDING TOMBS, CRACKING WHIPS OR RUNNING FROM GIANT BOULDERS.
BUT WHEN IT IS--THAT'S WHEN YOU GET THE BEST STUFF.
NOW, WE'VE GOT ABOUT FIVE MINUTES LEFT, SO IF ANYONE HAS ANY--
YOU'RE 33!
YOU'RE A MILLENNIAL, FOSTER! ADMIT IT!
I AM GEN X AND YOU WILL TAKE THAT BACK--
UH, DOC?
I THINK THAT'S HER.
UM. HI.
WERE YOU TAKING QUESTIONS?
BECAUSE I HAVE PLENTY.
AND DR. RIGGS--WHO ONCE SHARED A BODY WITH BRUNNHILDE, THE PREVIOUS VALKYRIE--MIGHT HAVE THE ANSWERS...

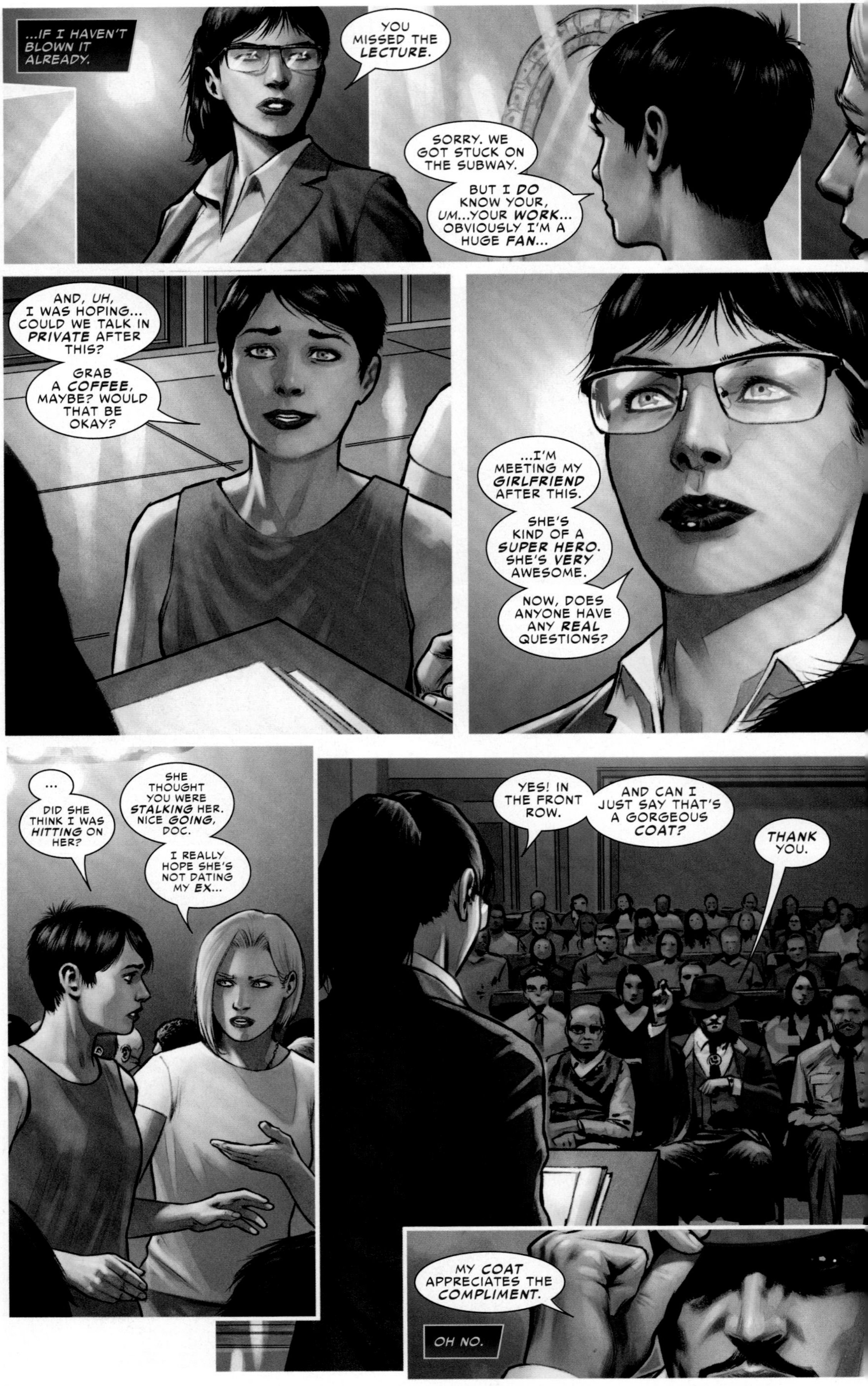

...IF I HAVEN'T BLOWN IT ALREADY.
YOU MISSED THE LECTURE.
SORRY. WE GOT STUCK ON THE SUBWAY.
BUT I DO KNOW YOUR, UM...YOUR WORK... OBVIOUSLY I'M A HUGE FAN...
AND, UH, I WAS HOPING... COULD WE TALK IN PRIVATE AFTER THIS?
GRAB A COFFEE, MAYBE? WOULD THAT BE OKAY?
...I'M MEETING MY GIRLFRIEND AFTER THIS.
SHE'S KIND OF A SUPER HERO. SHE'S VERY AWESOME.
NOW, DOES ANYONE HAVE ANY REAL QUESTIONS?
...
DID SHE THINK I WAS HITTING ON HER?
SHE THOUGHT YOU WERE STALKING HER. NICE GOING, DOC.
I REALLY HOPE SHE'S NOT DATING MY EX...
YES! IN THE FRONT ROW.
AND CAN I JUST SAY THAT'S A GORGEOUS COAT?
THANK YOU.
MY COAT APPRECIATES THE COMPLIMENT.
OH NO.

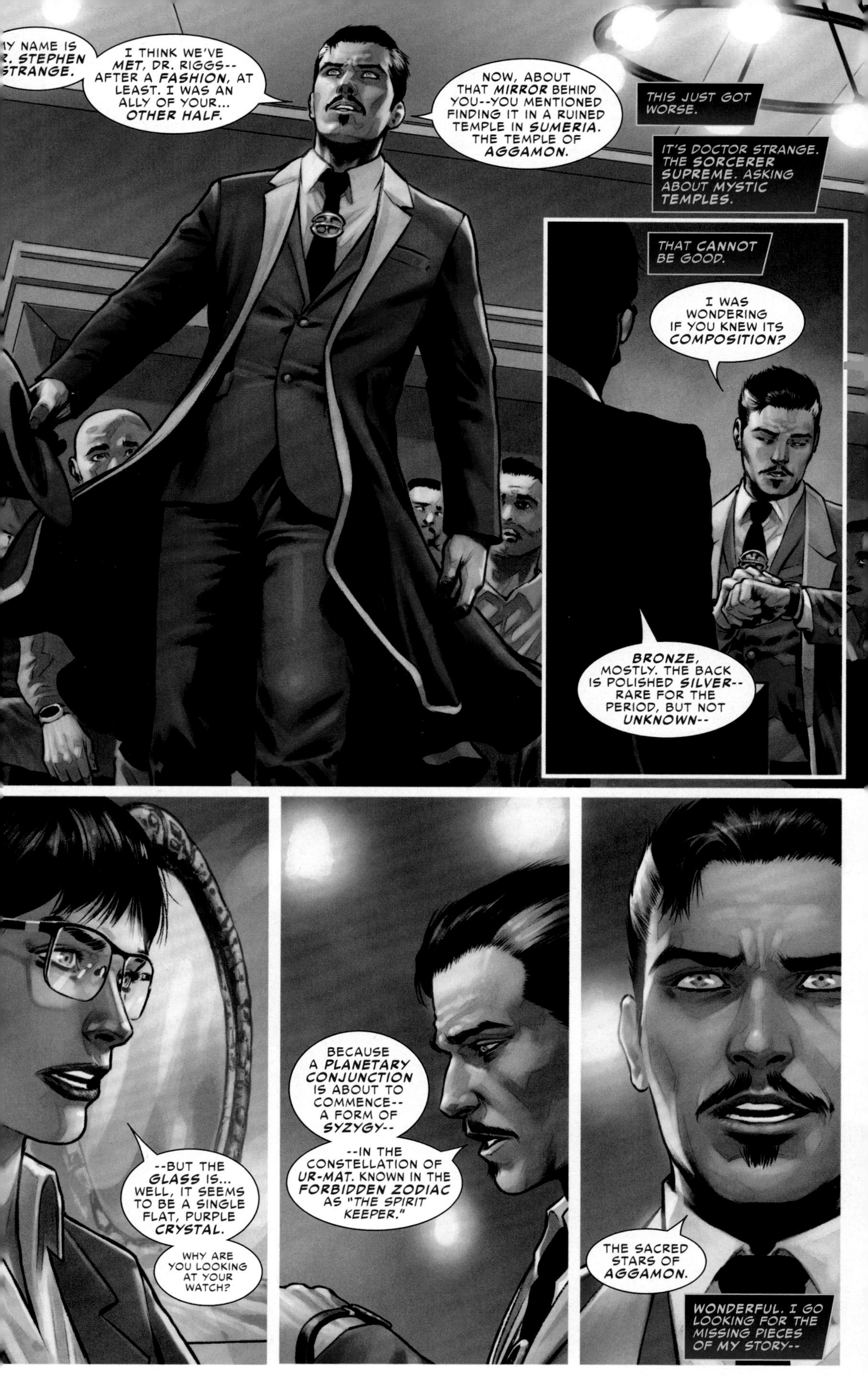
MY NAME IS R. STEPHEN STRANGE.
I THINK WE'VE MET, DR. RIGGS-- AFTER A FASHION, AT LEAST. I WAS AN ALLY OF YOUR... OTHER HALF.
NOW, ABOUT THAT MIRROR BEHIND YOU--YOU MENTIONED FINDING IT IN A RUINED TEMPLE IN SUMERIA. THE TEMPLE OF AGGAMON.
THIS JUST GOT WORSE.
IT'S DOCTOR STRANGE. THE SORCERER SUPREME. ASKING ABOUT MYSTIC TEMPLES.
THAT CANNOT BE GOOD.
I WAS WONDERING IF YOU KNEW ITS COMPOSITION?
BRONZE, MOSTLY. THE BACK IS POLISHED SILVER-- RARE FOR THE PERIOD, BUT NOT UNKNOWN--
--BUT THE GLASS IS... WELL, IT SEEMS TO BE A SINGLE FLAT, PURPLE CRYSTAL.
WHY ARE YOU LOOKING AT YOUR WATCH?
BECAUSE A PLANETARY CONJUNCTION IS ABOUT TO COMMENCE-- A FORM OF SYZYGY--
--IN THE CONSTELLATION OF UR-MAT. KNOWN IN THE FORBIDDEN ZODIAC AS "THE SPIRIT KEEPER."
THE SACRED STARS OF AGGAMON.
WONDERFUL. I GO LOOKING FOR THE MISSING PIECES OF MY STORY--

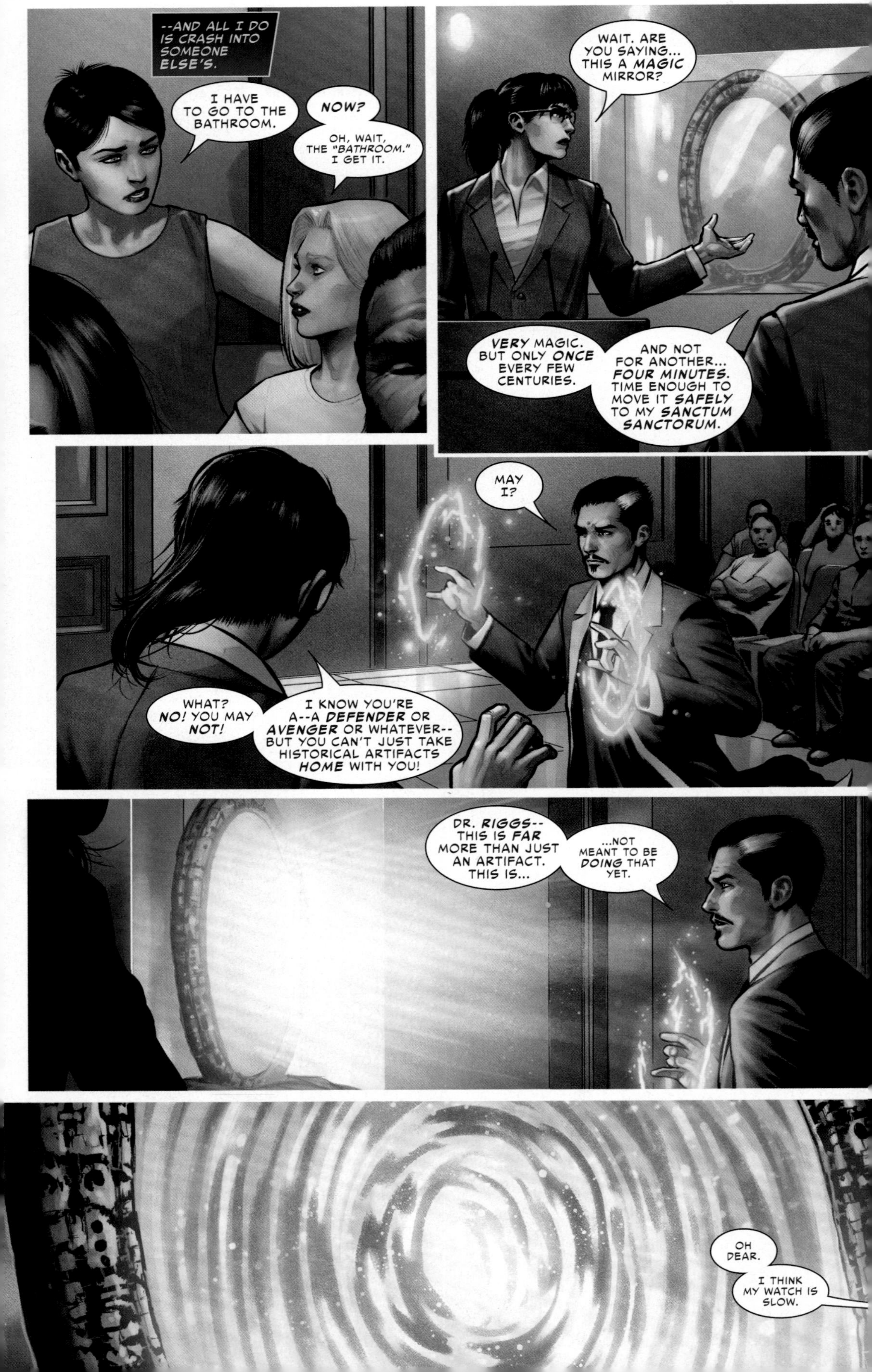
--AND ALL I DO IS CRASH INTO SOMEONE ELSE'S.
I HAVE TO GO TO THE BATHROOM.
NOW?
OH, WAIT, THE "BATHROOM." I GET IT.
WAIT. ARE YOU SAYING... THIS A MAGIC MIRROR?
VERY MAGIC. BUT ONLY ONCE EVERY FEW CENTURIES.
AND NOT FOR ANOTHER... FOUR MINUTES. TIME ENOUGH TO MOVE IT SAFELY TO MY SANCTUM SANCTORUM.
MAY I?
WHAT? NO! YOU MAY NOT!
I KNOW YOU'RE A--A DEFENDER OR AVENGER OR WHATEVER--BUT YOU CAN'T JUST TAKE HISTORICAL ARTIFACTS HOME WITH YOU!
DR. RIGGS--THIS IS FAR MORE THAN JUST AN ARTIFACT. THIS IS...
...NOT MEANT TO BE DOING THAT YET.
OH DEAR.
I THINK MY WATCH IS SLOW.

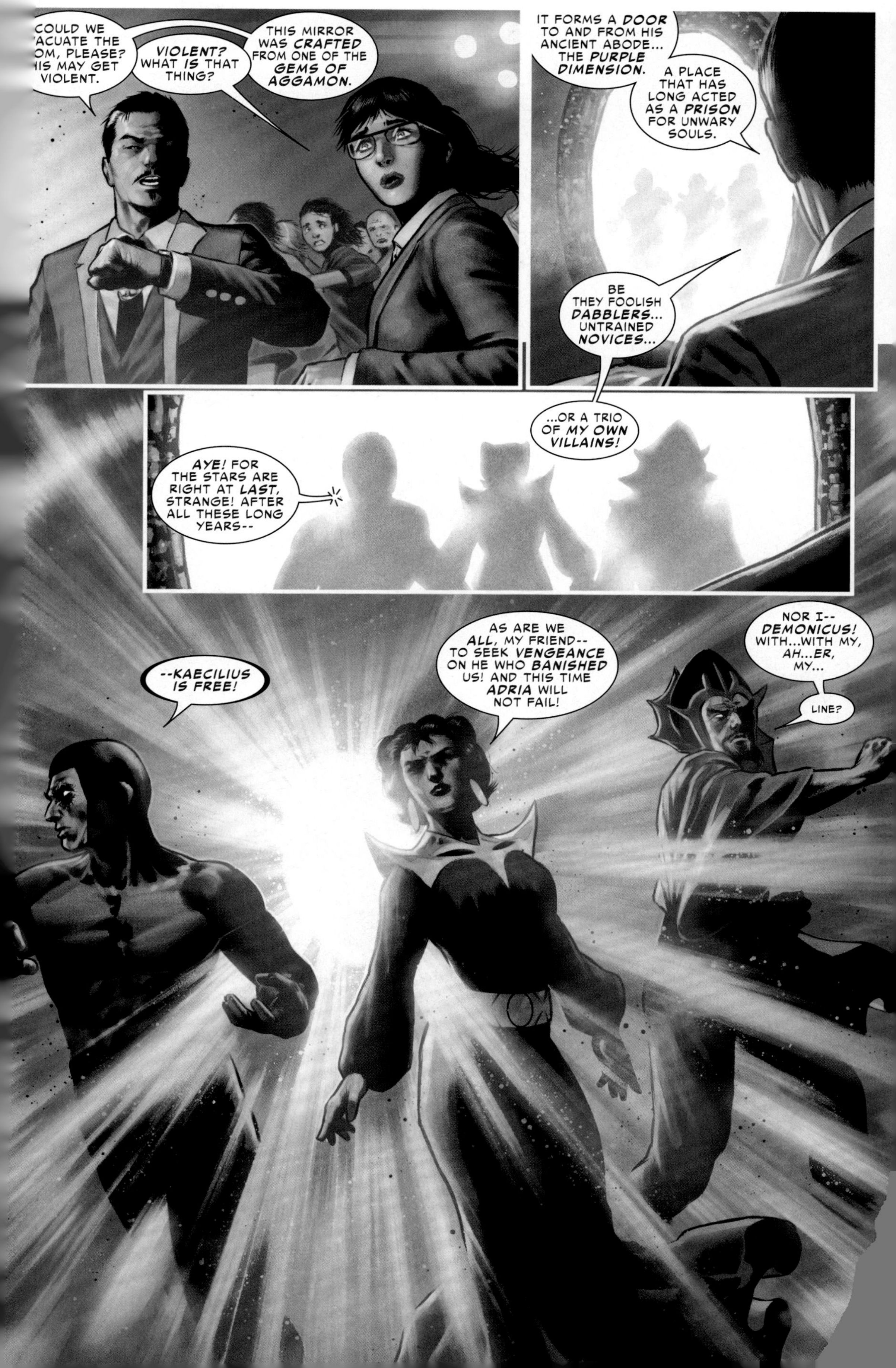
COULD WE EVACUATE THE ROOM, PLEASE? THIS MAY GET VIOLENT.
VIOLENT? WHAT IS THAT THING?
THIS MIRROR WAS CRAFTED FROM ONE OF THE GEMS OF AGGAMON.
IT FORMS A DOOR TO AND FROM HIS ANCIENT ABODE... THE PURPLE DIMENSION.
A PLACE THAT HAS LONG ACTED AS A PRISON FOR UNWARY SOULS.
BE THEY FOOLISH DABBLERS... UNTRAINED NOVICES...
...OR A TRIO OF MY OWN VILLAINS!
AYE! FOR THE STARS ARE RIGHT AT LAST, STRANGE! AFTER ALL THESE LONG YEARS--
--KAECILIUS IS FREE!
AS ARE WE ALL, MY FRIEND-- TO SEEK VENGEANCE ON HE WHO BANISHED US! AND THIS TIME ADRIA WILL NOT FAIL!
NOR I-- DEMONICUS! WITH...WITH MY, AH...ER, MY...
LINE?

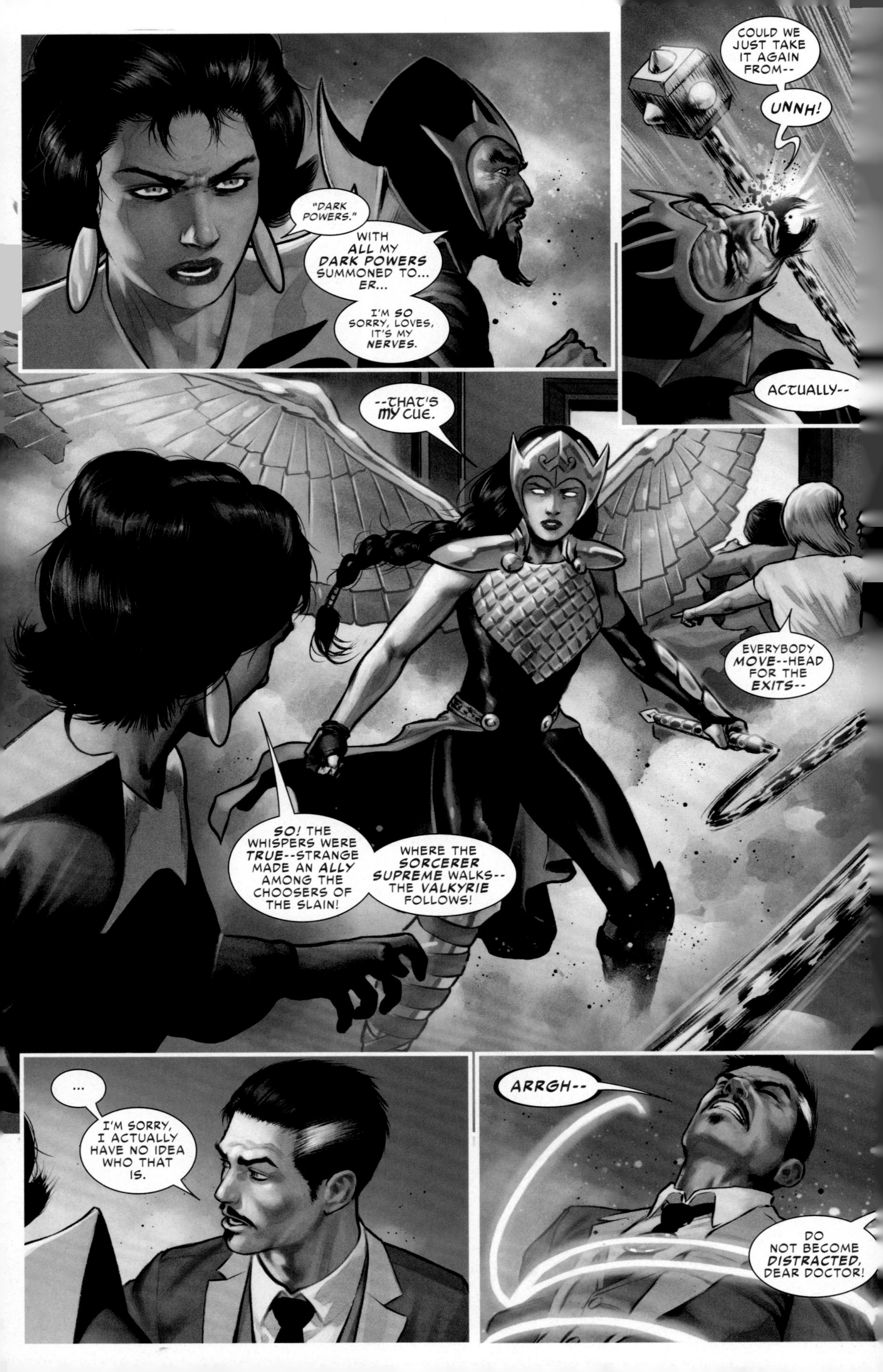
"DARK POWERS."
WITH ALL MY DARK POWERS SUMMONED TO... ER...
I'M SO SORRY, LOVES, IT'S MY NERVES.
COULD WE JUST TAKE IT AGAIN FROM--
UNNH!
ACTUALLY--
--THAT'S MY CUE.
EVERYBODY MOVE--HEAD FOR THE EXITS--
SO! THE WHISPERS WERE TRUE--STRANGE MADE AN ALLY AMONG THE CHOOSERS OF THE SLAIN!
WHERE THE SORCERER SUPREME WALKS--THE VALKYRIE FOLLOWS!
...
I'M SORRY, I ACTUALLY HAVE NO IDEA WHO THAT IS.
ARRGH--
DO NOT BECOME DISTRACTED, DEAR DOCTOR!

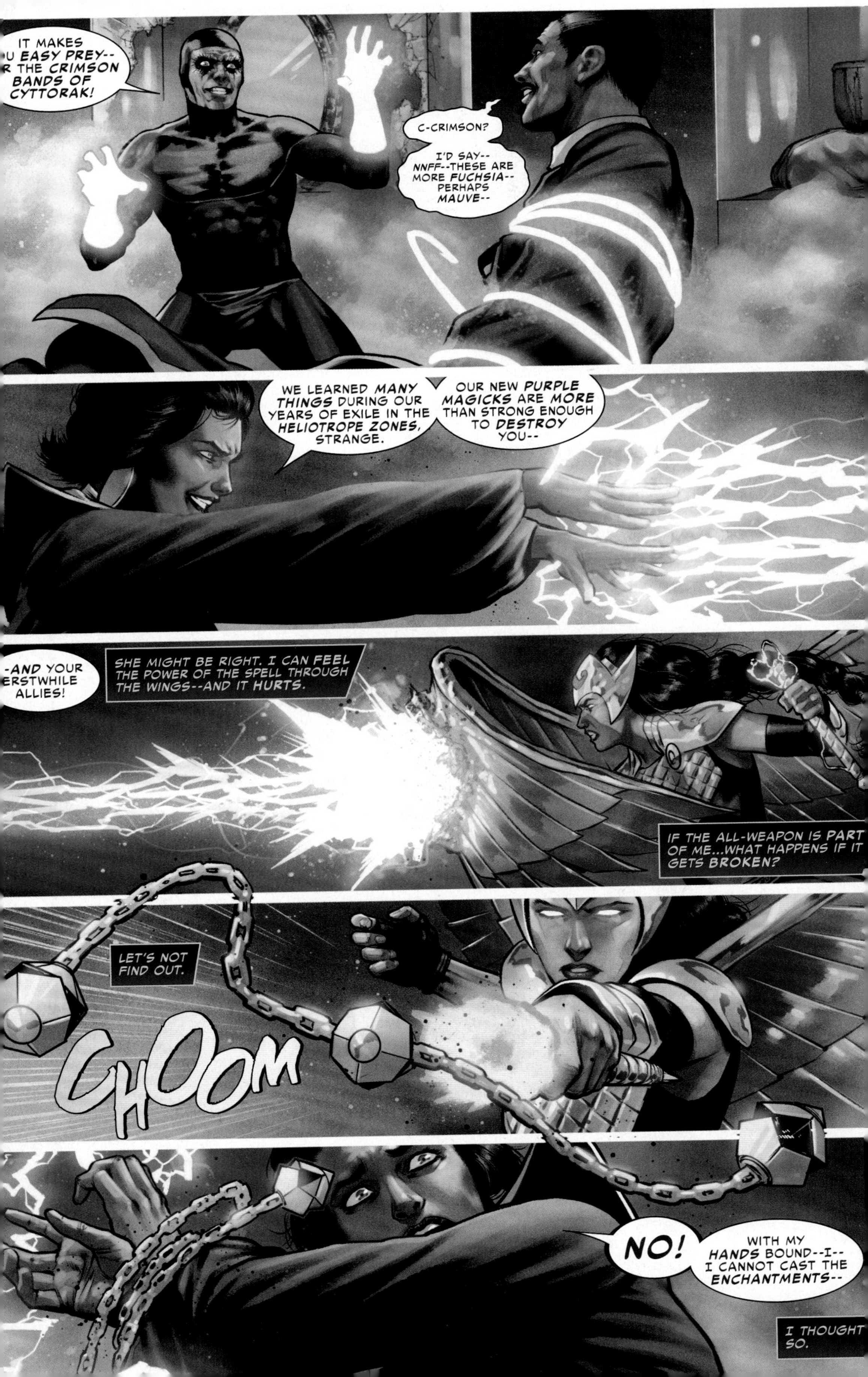
IT MAKES
U EASY PREY--
R THE CRIMSON
BANDS OF
CYTTORAK!
C-CRIMSON?
I'D SAY--
NNFF--THESE ARE
MORE FUCHSIA--
PERHAPS
MAUVE--
WE LEARNED MANY THINGS DURING OUR YEARS OF EXILE IN THE HELIOTROPE ZONES, STRANGE.
OUR NEW PURPLE MAGICKS ARE MORE THAN STRONG ENOUGH TO DESTROY YOU--
-AND YOUR ERSTWHILE ALLIES!
SHE MIGHT BE RIGHT. I CAN FEEL THE POWER OF THE SPELL THROUGH THE WINGS--AND IT HURTS.
IF THE ALL-WEAPON IS PART OF ME...WHAT HAPPENS IF IT GETS BROKEN?
LET'S NOT FIND OUT.
CHOOM
NO!
WITH MY HANDS BOUND--I--
I CANNOT CAST THE ENCHANTMENTS--
I THOUGHT SO.

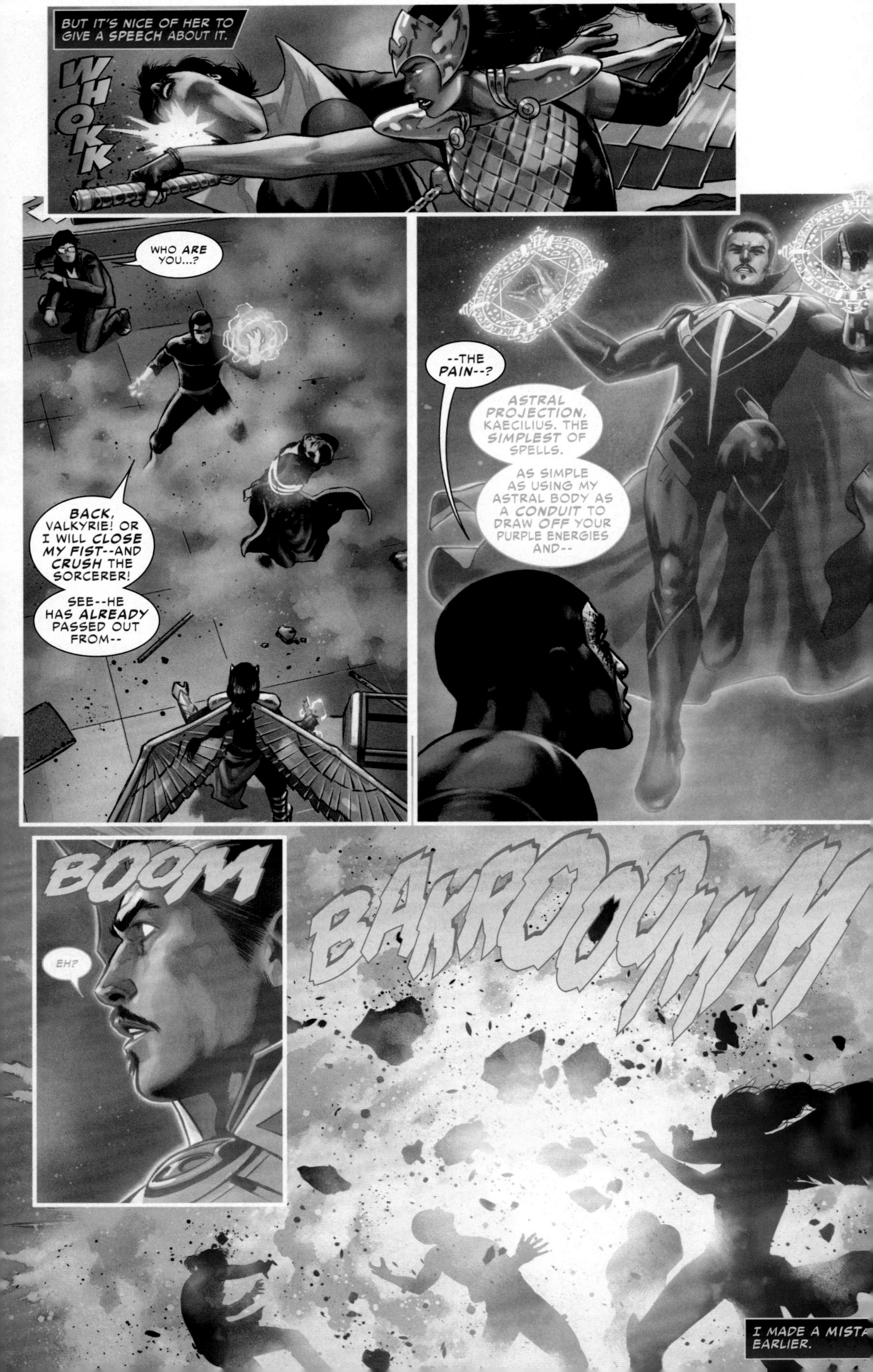
BUT IT'S NICE OF HER TO GIVE A SPEECH ABOUT IT.
WHOKK
WHO ARE YOU...?
BACK, VALKYRIE! OR I WILL CLOSE MY FIST--AND CRUSH THE SORCERER!
SEE--HE HAS ALREADY PASSED OUT FROM--
--THE PAIN--?
ASTRAL PROJECTION, KAECILIUS. THE SIMPLEST OF SPELLS.
AS SIMPLE AS USING MY ASTRAL BODY AS A CONDUIT TO DRAW OFF YOUR PURPLE ENERGIES AND--
BOOM
EH?
BAKROOOMM
I MADE A MISTA
EARLIER.

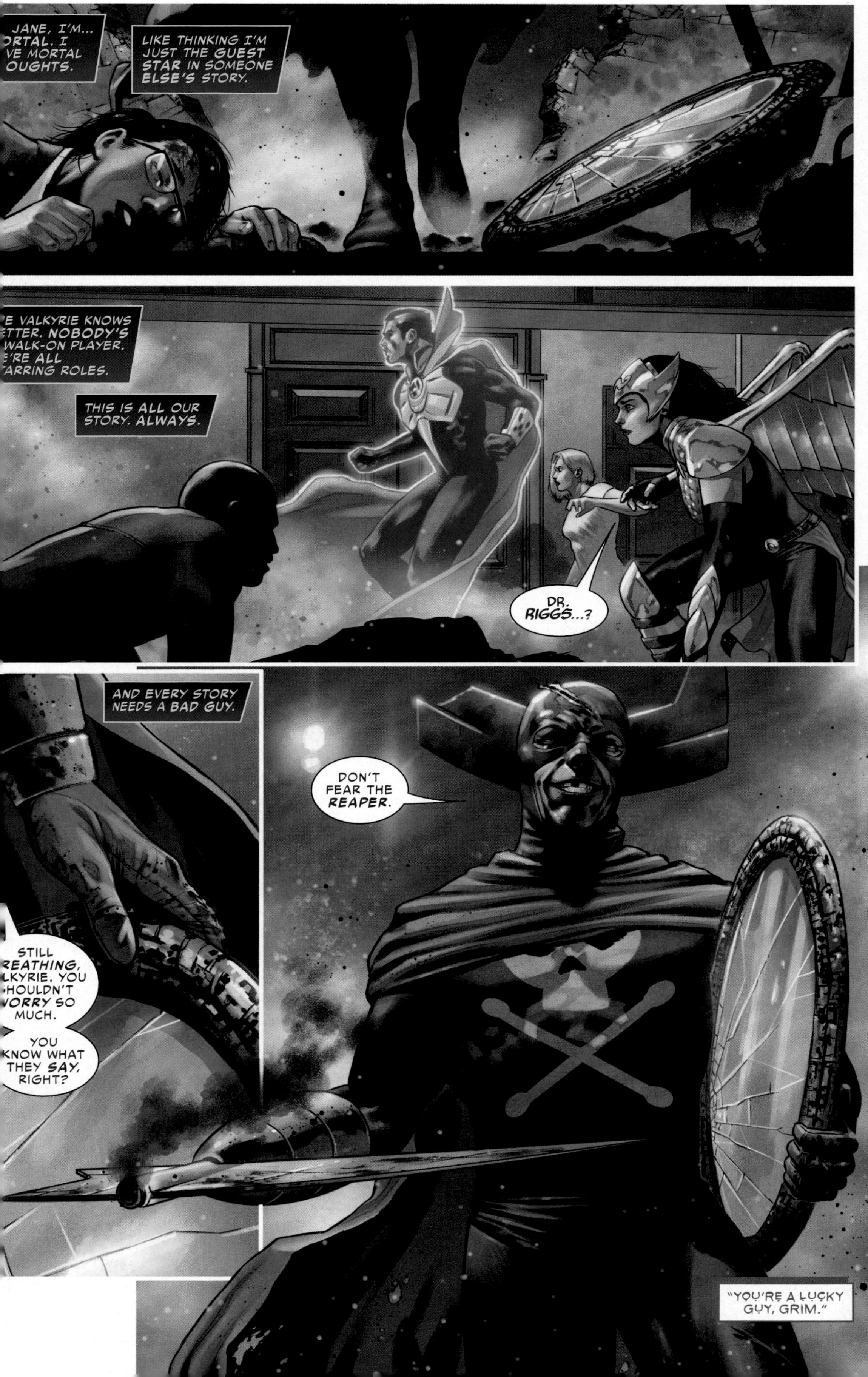

JANE, I'M... ORTAL. I VE MORTAL OUGHTS.
LIKE THINKING I'M JUST THE GUEST STAR IN SOMEONE ELSE'S STORY.
E VALKYRIE KNOWS TTER. NOBODY'S WALK-ON PLAYER. E'RE ALL ARRING ROLES.
THIS IS ALL OUR STORY. ALWAYS.
DR. RIGGS...?
AND EVERY STORY NEEDS A BAD GUY.
DON'T FEAR THE REAPER.
STILL REATHING, LKYRIE. YOU HOULDN'T ORRY SO MUCH.
YOU KNOW WHAT THEY SAY, RIGHT?
"YOU'RE A LUCKY GUY, GRIM."

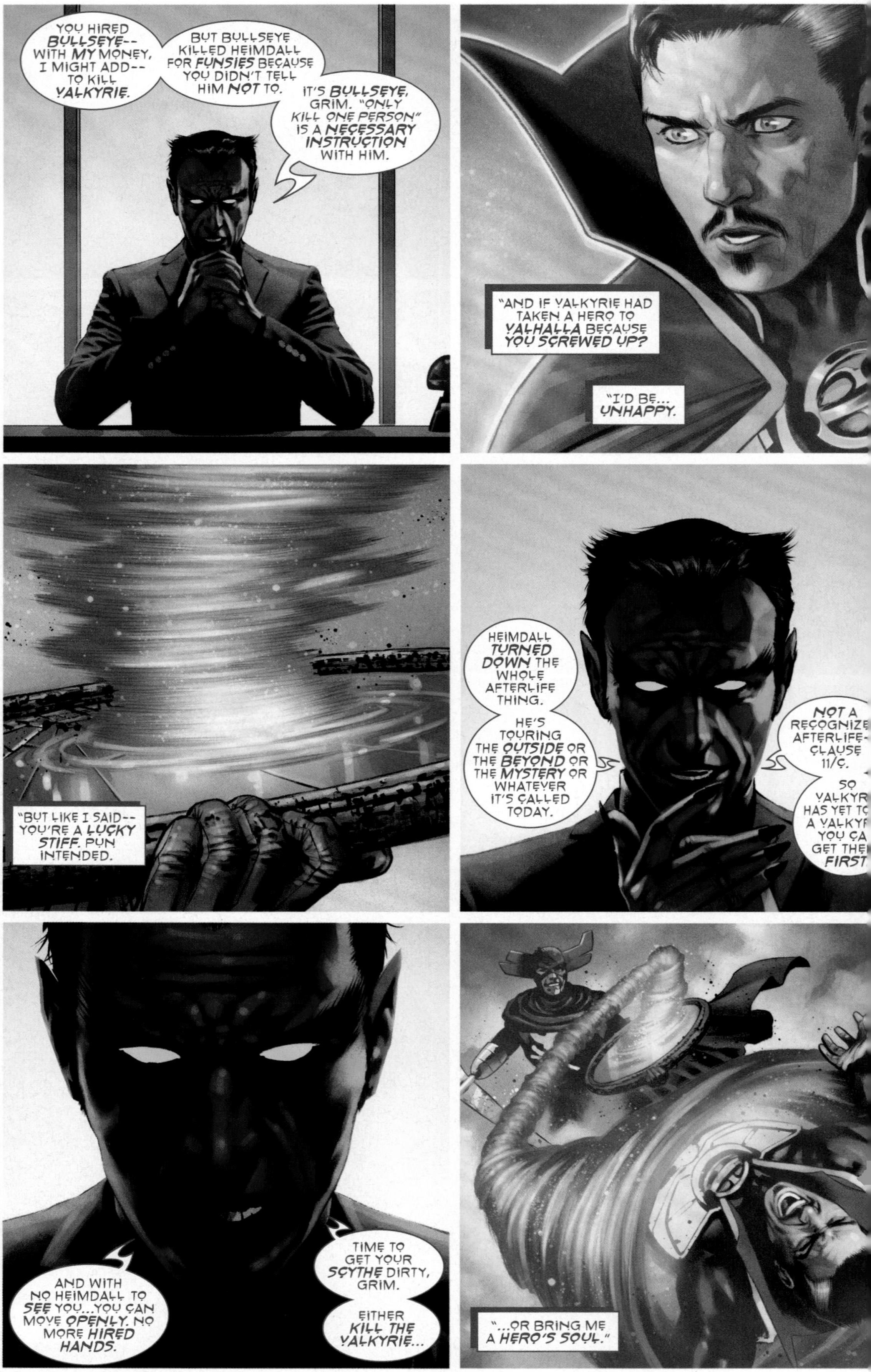
YOU HIRED BULLSEYE-- WITH MY MONEY, I MIGHT ADD-- TO KILL VALKYRIE.
BUT BULLSEYE KILLED HEIMDALL FOR FUNSIES BECAUSE YOU DIDN'T TELL HIM NOT TO.
IT'S BULLSEYE, GRIM. "ONLY KILL ONE PERSON" IS A NECESSARY INSTRUCTION WITH HIM.
"AND IF VALKYRIE HAD TAKEN A HERO TO VALHALLA BECAUSE YOU SCREWED UP?
"I'D BE... UNHAPPY.
"BUT LIKE I SAID-- YOU'RE A LUCKY STIFF. PUN INTENDED.
HEIMDALL TURNED DOWN THE WHOLE AFTERLIFE THING.
HE'S TOURING THE OUTSIDE OR THE BEYOND OR THE MYSTERY OR WHATEVER IT'S CALLED TODAY.
NOT A RECOGNIZE AFTERLIFE-CLAUSE 11/C.
SO VALKYR HAS YET TO A VALKYR YOU CA GET THE FIRST
AND WITH NO HEIMDALL TO SEE YOU...YOU CAN MOVE OPENLY. NO MORE HIRED HANDS.
TIME TO GET YOUR SCYTHE DIRTY, GRIM.
EITHER KILL THE VALKYRIE...
"...OR BRING ME A HERO'S SOUL."

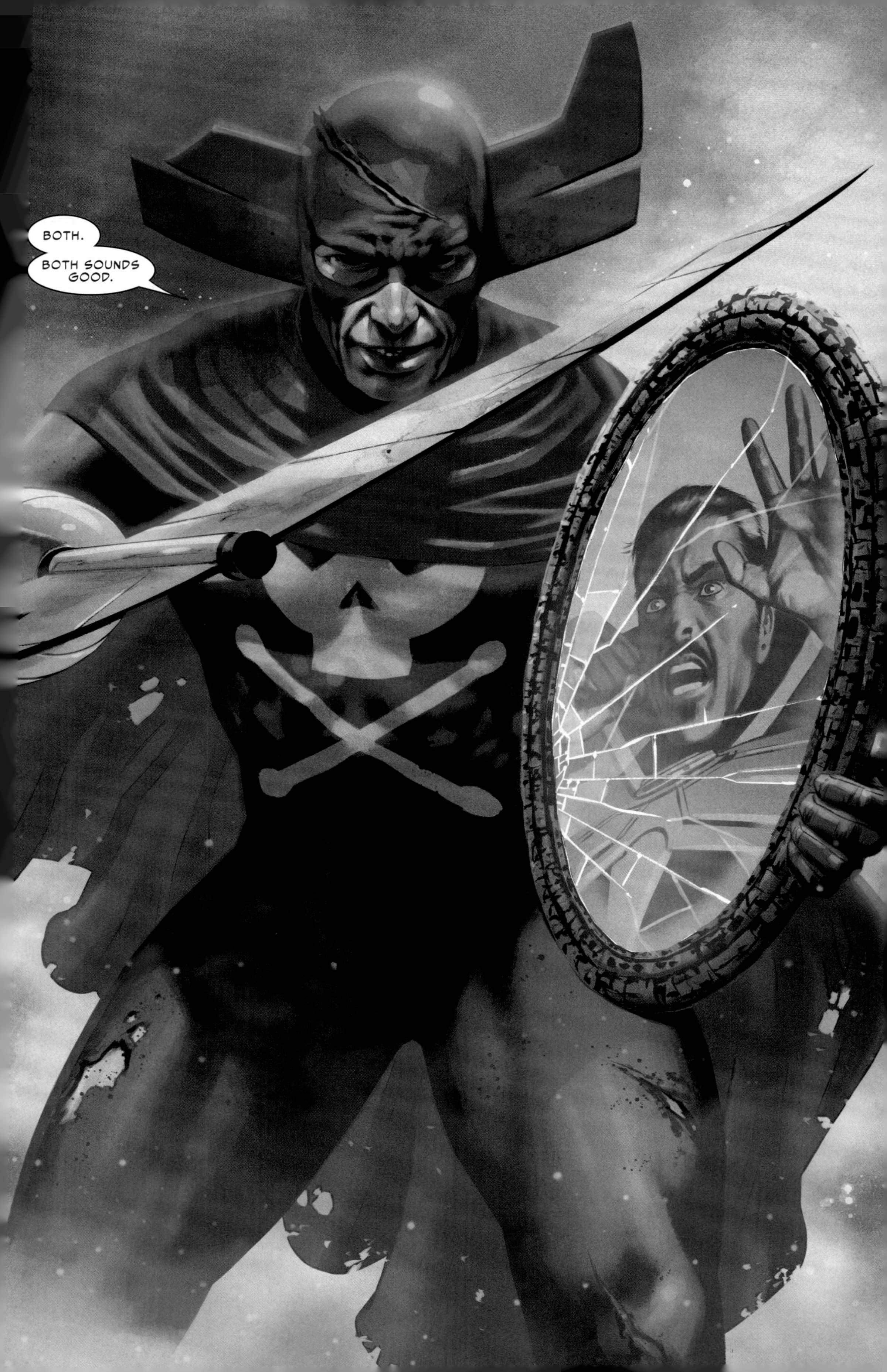
BOTH.
BOTH SOUNDS GOOD.

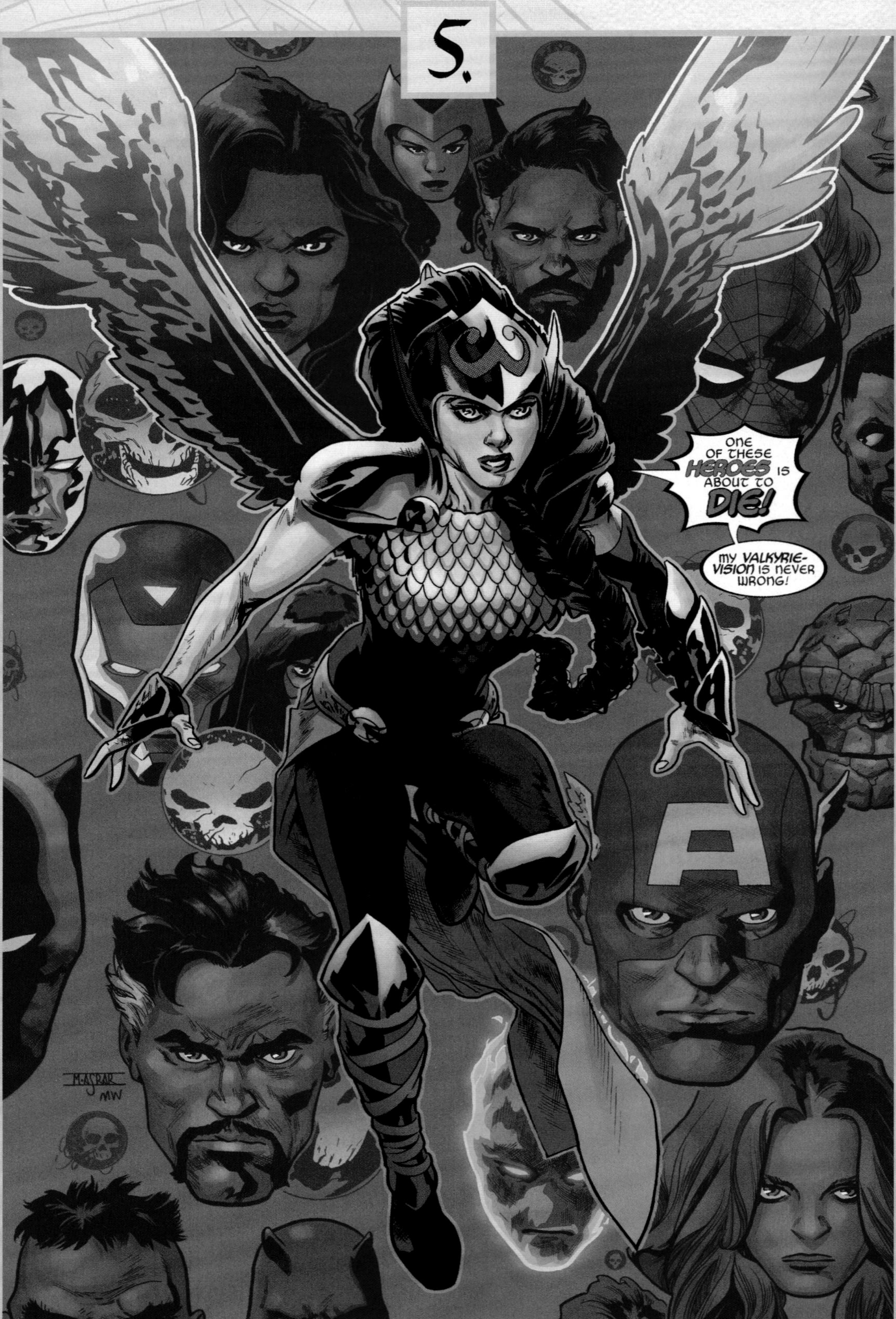
5.
ONE OF THESE HEROES IS ABOUT TO DIE!
MY VALKYRIE-VISION IS NEVER WRONG!
M-ASRAR MW

THE SACRED AND THE PROFANE CONCLUSION

MY NAME IS JANE FOSTER.

I'M A DOCTOR. I'M A CANCER SURVIVOR. I'M A VALKYRIE--THE ONLY ONE CURRENTLY IN BUSINESS.

THAT'S APPARENTLY A BONE OF CONTENTION.

HIS NAME IS STEPHEN STRANGE.

HE'S A DOCTOR TOO. HE'S ALSO THE SORCERER SUPREME OF THIS DIMENSION.

HE'S TRAPPED IN HIS ASTRAL FORM INSIDE A MAGIC PURPLE MIRROR. IT'S ALL A LITTLE BIT PROG ROCK.

AND HE'S ALSO IN A COMA ON THE FLOOR WITH A DEATH THE SIZE OF A BEACH BALL HANGING OVER HIS HEAD.

MY DIAGNOSIS--UNLESS WE GET HIS SOUL OUT OF THE MIRROR, THE BODY WON'T LAST MUCH LONGER.

SO THERE'S A TICKING CLOCK.

HIS NAME I DON'T KNOW.

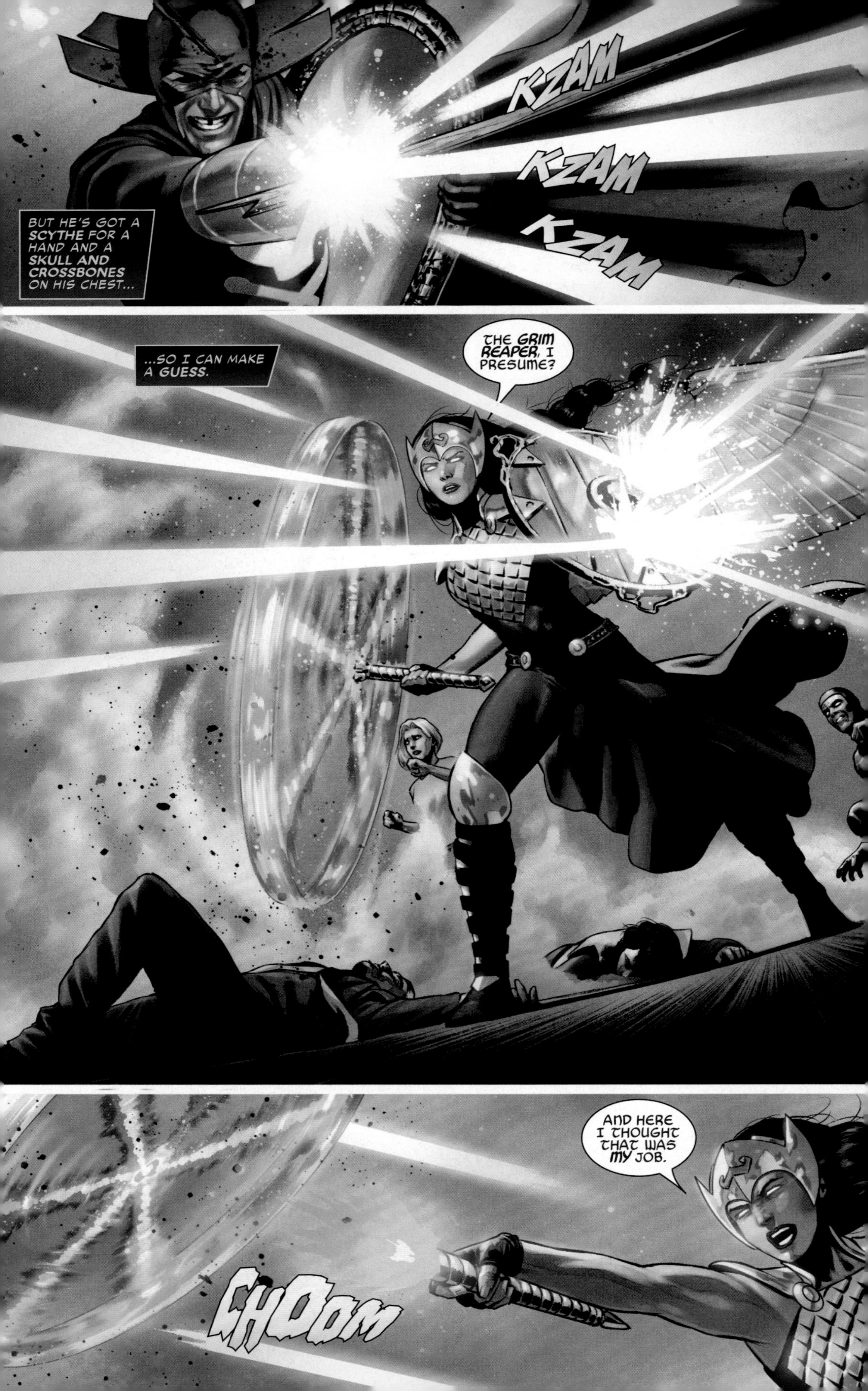
KZAM
KZAM
KZAM
BUT HE'S GOT A SCYTHE FOR A HAND AND A SKULL AND CROSSBONES ON HIS CHEST...
...SO I CAN MAKE A GUESS.
THE GRIM REAPER, I PRESUME?
AND HERE I THOUGHT THAT WAS MY JOB.
CHOOM

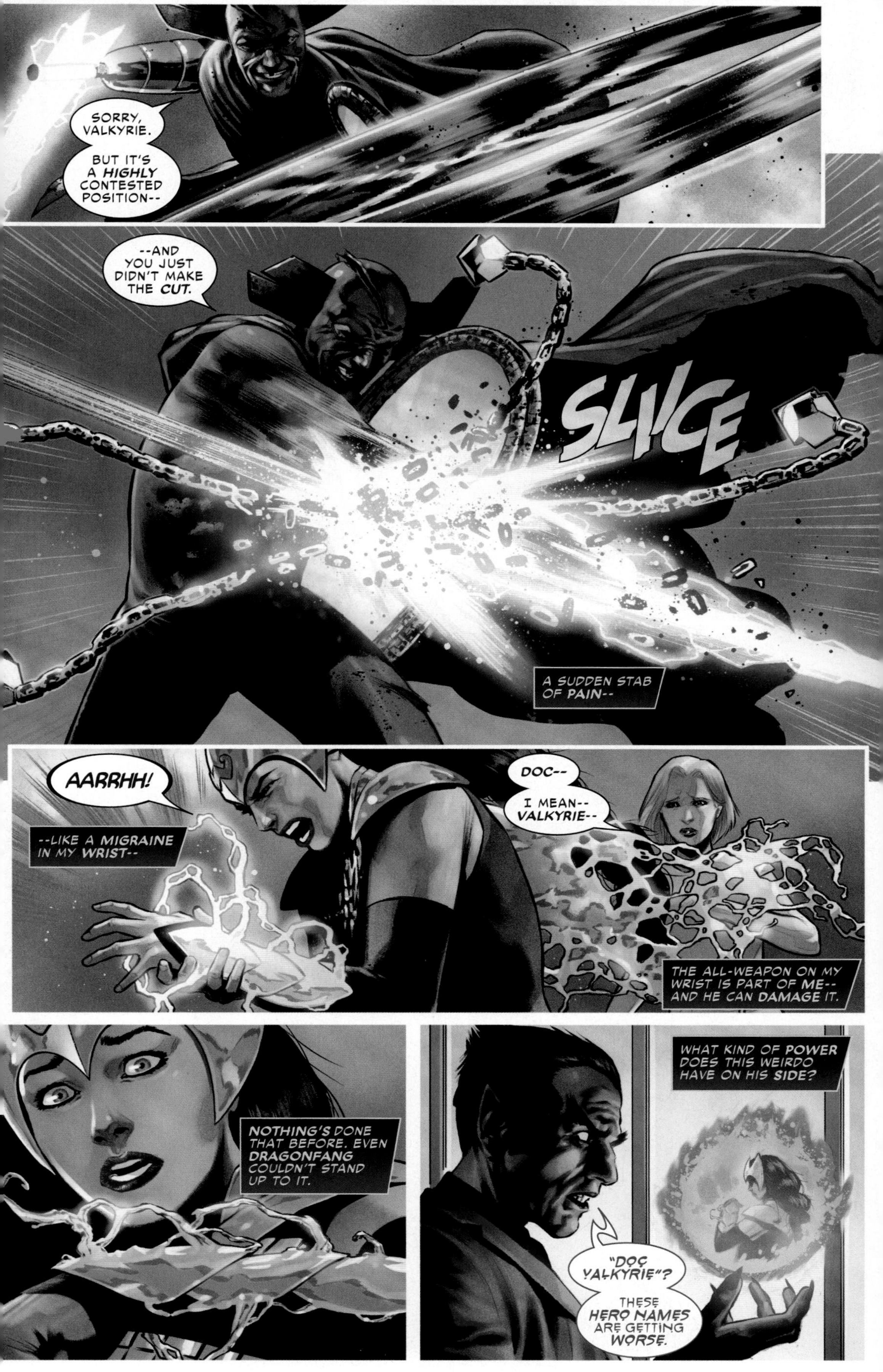
SORRY, VALKYRIE.
BUT IT'S A HIGHLY CONTESTED POSITION--
--AND YOU JUST DIDN'T MAKE THE CUT.
SLICE
A SUDDEN STAB OF PAIN--
AARRHH!
--LIKE A MIGRAINE IN MY WRIST--
DOC--
I MEAN-- VALKYRIE--
THE ALL-WEAPON ON MY WRIST IS PART OF ME-- AND HE CAN DAMAGE IT.
NOTHING'S DONE THAT BEFORE. EVEN DRAGONFANG COULDN'T STAND UP TO IT.
WHAT KIND OF POWER DOES THIS WEIRDO HAVE ON HIS SIDE?
"DOC VALKYRIE"?
THESE HERO NAMES ARE GETTING WORSE.

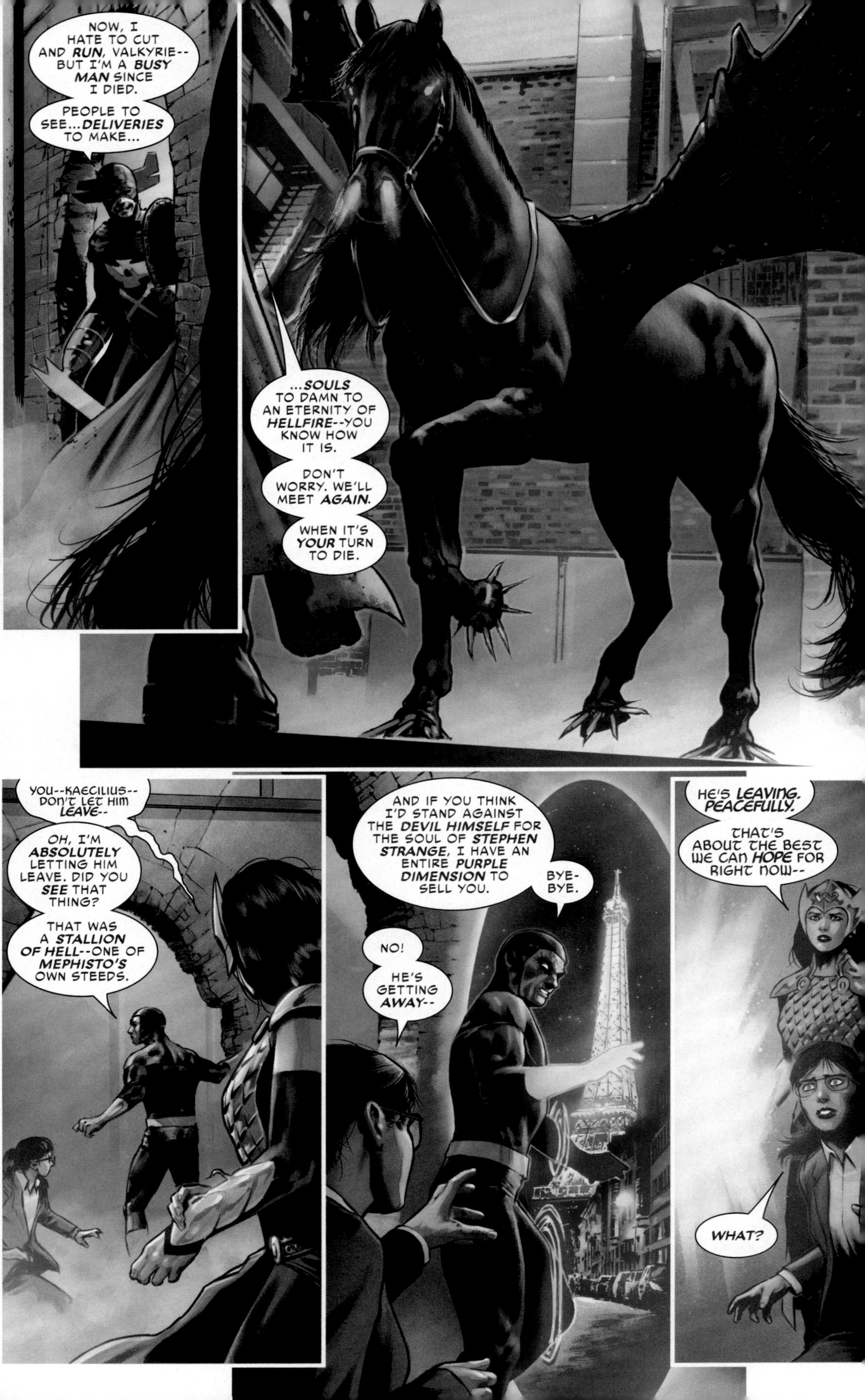
NOW, I HATE TO CUT AND RUN, VALKYRIE-- BUT I'M A BUSY MAN SINCE I DIED.
PEOPLE TO SEE...DELIVERIES TO MAKE...
...SOULS TO DAMN TO AN ETERNITY OF HELLFIRE--YOU KNOW HOW IT IS.
DON'T WORRY. WE'LL MEET AGAIN.
WHEN IT'S YOUR TURN TO DIE.
YOU--KAECILIUS-- DON'T LET HIM LEAVE--
OH, I'M ABSOLUTELY LETTING HIM LEAVE. DID YOU SEE THAT THING?
THAT WAS A STALLION OF HELL--ONE OF MEPHISTO'S OWN STEEDS.
AND IF YOU THINK I'D STAND AGAINST THE DEVIL HIMSELF FOR THE SOUL OF STEPHEN STRANGE, I HAVE AN ENTIRE PURPLE DIMENSION TO SELL YOU.
BYE-BYE.
NO!
HE'S GETTING AWAY--
HE'S LEAVING. PEACEFULLY.
THAT'S ABOUT THE BEST WE CAN HOPE FOR RIGHT NOW--
WHAT?

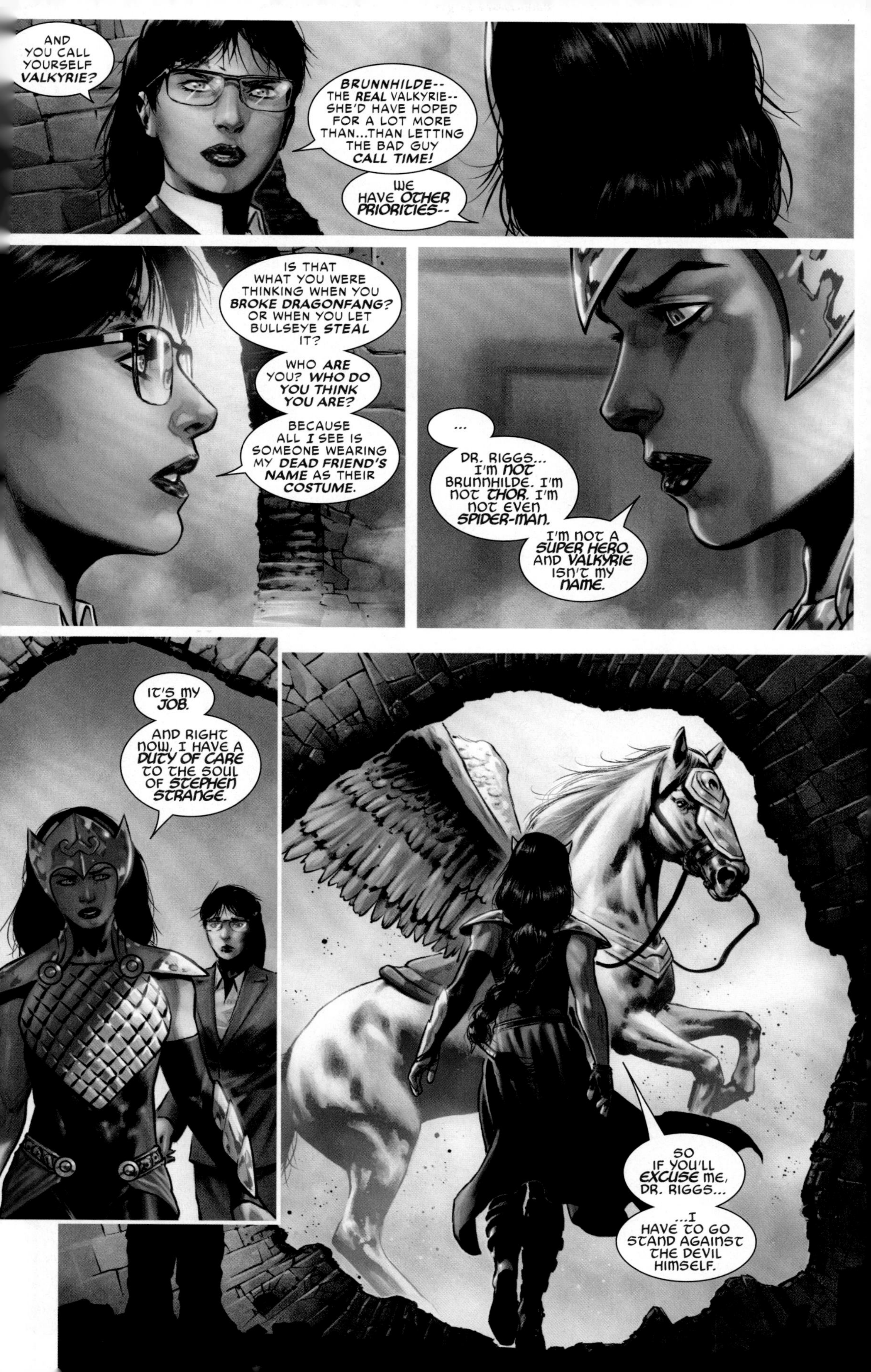
AND YOU CALL YOURSELF VALKYRIE?
BRUNNHILDE-- THE REAL VALKYRIE-- SHE'D HAVE HOPED FOR A LOT MORE THAN...THAN LETTING THE BAD GUY CALL TIME!
WE HAVE OTHER PRIORITIES--
IS THAT WHAT YOU WERE THINKING WHEN YOU BROKE DRAGONFANG? OR WHEN YOU LET BULLSEYE STEAL IT?
WHO ARE YOU? WHO DO YOU THINK YOU ARE?
BECAUSE ALL I SEE IS SOMEONE WEARING MY DEAD FRIEND'S NAME AS THEIR COSTUME.
...
DR. RIGGS... I'M NOT BRUNNHILDE. I'M NOT THOR. I'M NOT EVEN SPIDER-MAN.
I'M NOT A SUPER HERO. AND VALKYRIE ISN'T MY NAME.
IT'S MY JOB.
AND RIGHT NOW, I HAVE A DUTY OF CARE TO THE SOUL OF STEPHEN STRANGE.
SO IF YOU'LL EXCUSE ME, DR. RIGGS...
...I HAVE TO GO STAND AGAINST THE DEVIL HIMSELF.

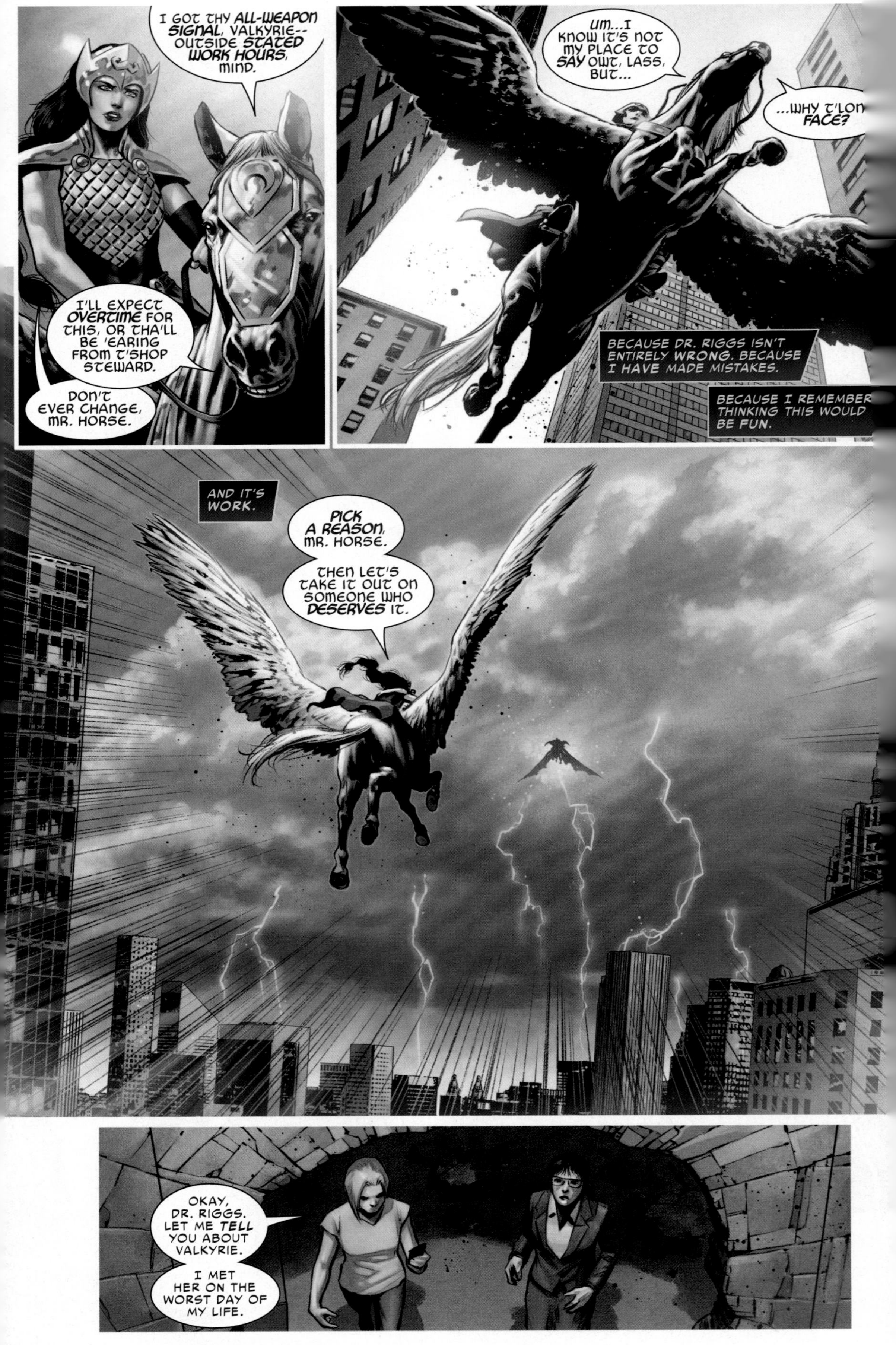

I GOT THY ALL-WEAPON SIGNAL, VALKYRIE-- OUTSIDE STATED WORK HOURS, MIND.
I'LL EXPECT OVERTIME FOR THIS, OR THA'LL BE 'EARING FROM T'SHOP STEWARD.
DON'T EVER CHANGE, MR. HORSE.
UM...I KNOW IT'S NOT MY PLACE TO SAY OWT, LASS, BUT...
...WHY T'LON FACE?
BECAUSE DR. RIGGS ISN'T ENTIRELY WRONG. BECAUSE I HAVE MADE MISTAKES.
BECAUSE I REMEMBER THINKING THIS WOULD BE FUN.
AND IT'S WORK.
PICK A REASON, MR. HORSE.
THEN LET'S TAKE IT OUT ON SOMEONE WHO DESERVES IT.
OKAY, DR. RIGGS. LET ME TELL YOU ABOUT VALKYRIE.
I MET HER ON THE WORST DAY OF MY LIFE.

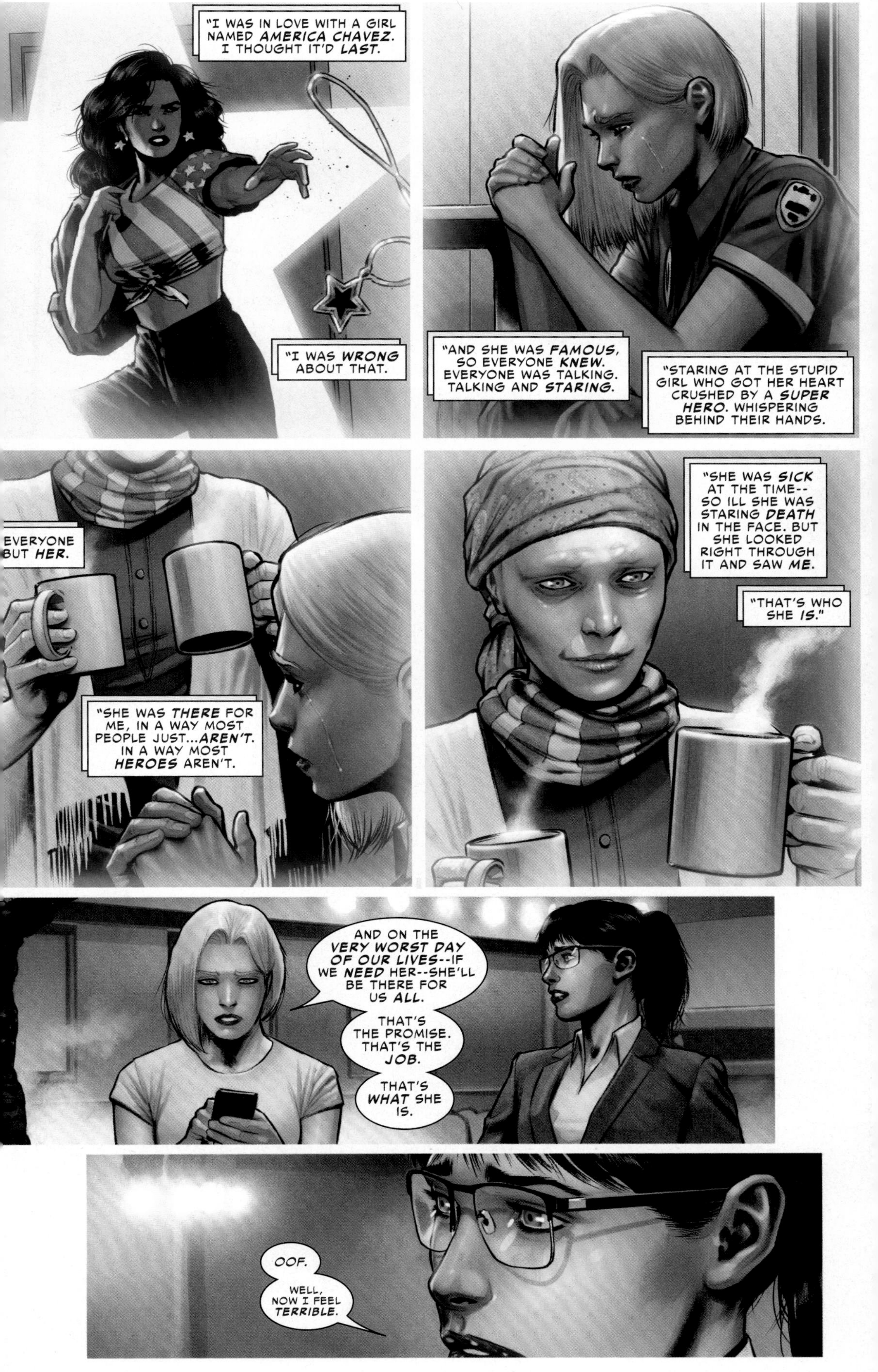
"I WAS IN LOVE WITH A GIRL NAMED AMERICA CHAVEZ. I THOUGHT IT'D LAST.
"I WAS WRONG ABOUT THAT.
"AND SHE WAS FAMOUS, SO EVERYONE KNEW. EVERYONE WAS TALKING. TALKING AND STARING.
"STARING AT THE STUPID GIRL WHO GOT HER HEART CRUSHED BY A SUPER HERO. WHISPERING BEHIND THEIR HANDS.
EVERYONE BUT HER.
"SHE WAS THERE FOR ME, IN A WAY MOST PEOPLE JUST...AREN'T. IN A WAY MOST HEROES AREN'T.
"SHE WAS SICK AT THE TIME--SO ILL SHE WAS STARING DEATH IN THE FACE. BUT SHE LOOKED RIGHT THROUGH IT AND SAW ME.
"THAT'S WHO SHE IS."
AND ON THE VERY WORST DAY OF OUR LIVES--IF WE NEED HER--SHE'LL BE THERE FOR US ALL.
THAT'S THE PROMISE. THAT'S THE JOB.
THAT'S WHAT SHE IS.
OOF.
WELL, NOW I FEEL TERRIBLE.

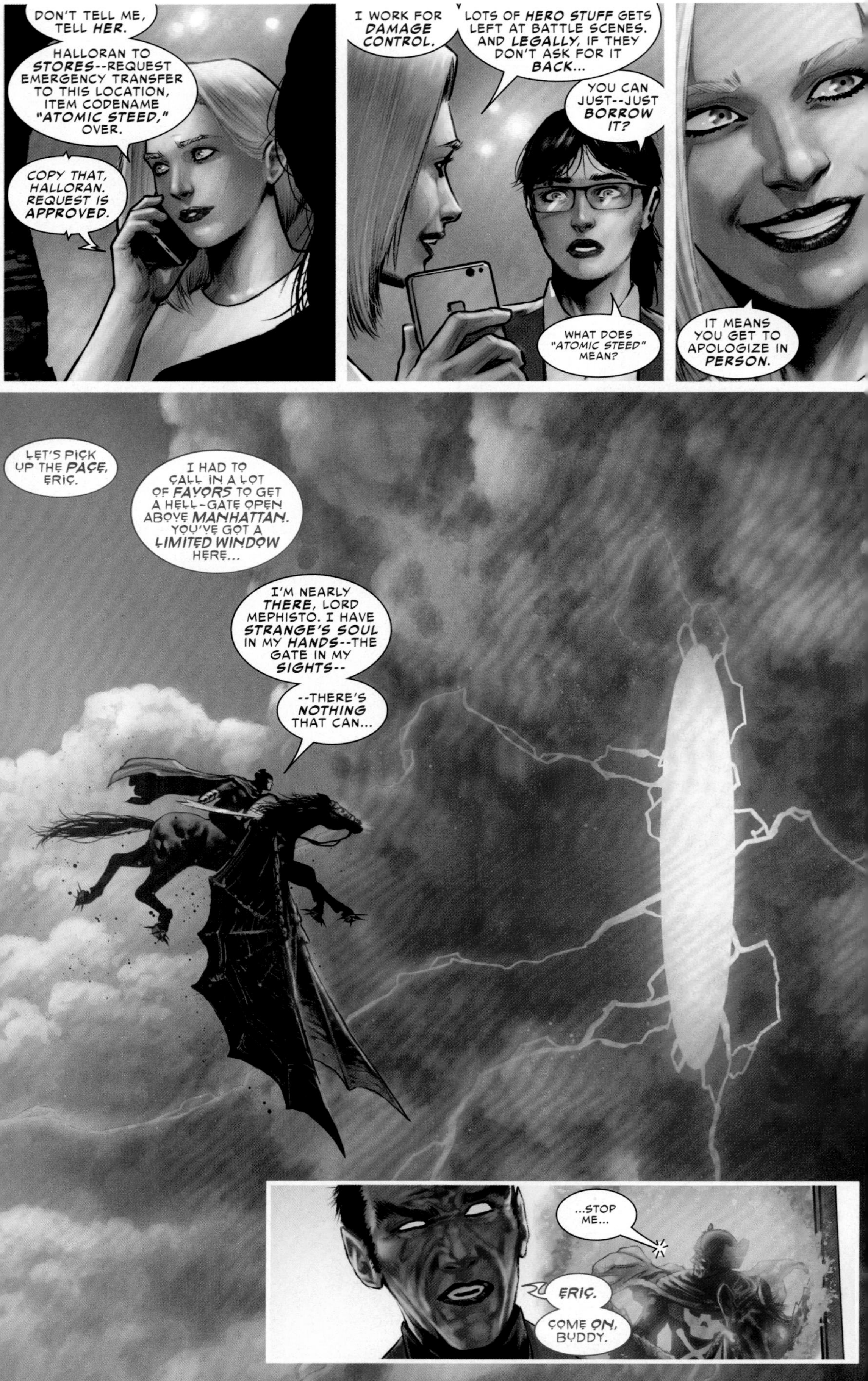
DON'T TELL ME, TELL HER.
HALLORAN TO STORES--REQUEST EMERGENCY TRANSFER TO THIS LOCATION, ITEM CODENAME "ATOMIC STEED," OVER.
COPY THAT, HALLORAN. REQUEST IS APPROVED.
I WORK FOR DAMAGE CONTROL.
LOTS OF HERO STUFF GETS LEFT AT BATTLE SCENES. AND LEGALLY, IF THEY DON'T ASK FOR IT BACK...
YOU CAN JUST--JUST BORROW IT?
WHAT DOES "ATOMIC STEED" MEAN?
IT MEANS YOU GET TO APOLOGIZE IN PERSON.
LET'S PICK UP THE PACE, ERIC.
I HAD TO CALL IN A LOT OF FAVORS TO GET A HELL-GATE OPEN ABOVE MANHATTAN. YOU'VE GOT A LIMITED WINDOW HERE...
I'M NEARLY THERE, LORD MEPHISTO. I HAVE STRANGE'S SOUL IN MY HANDS--THE GATE IN MY SIGHTS--
--THERE'S NOTHING THAT CAN...
...STOP ME...
ERIC.
COME ON, BUDDY.

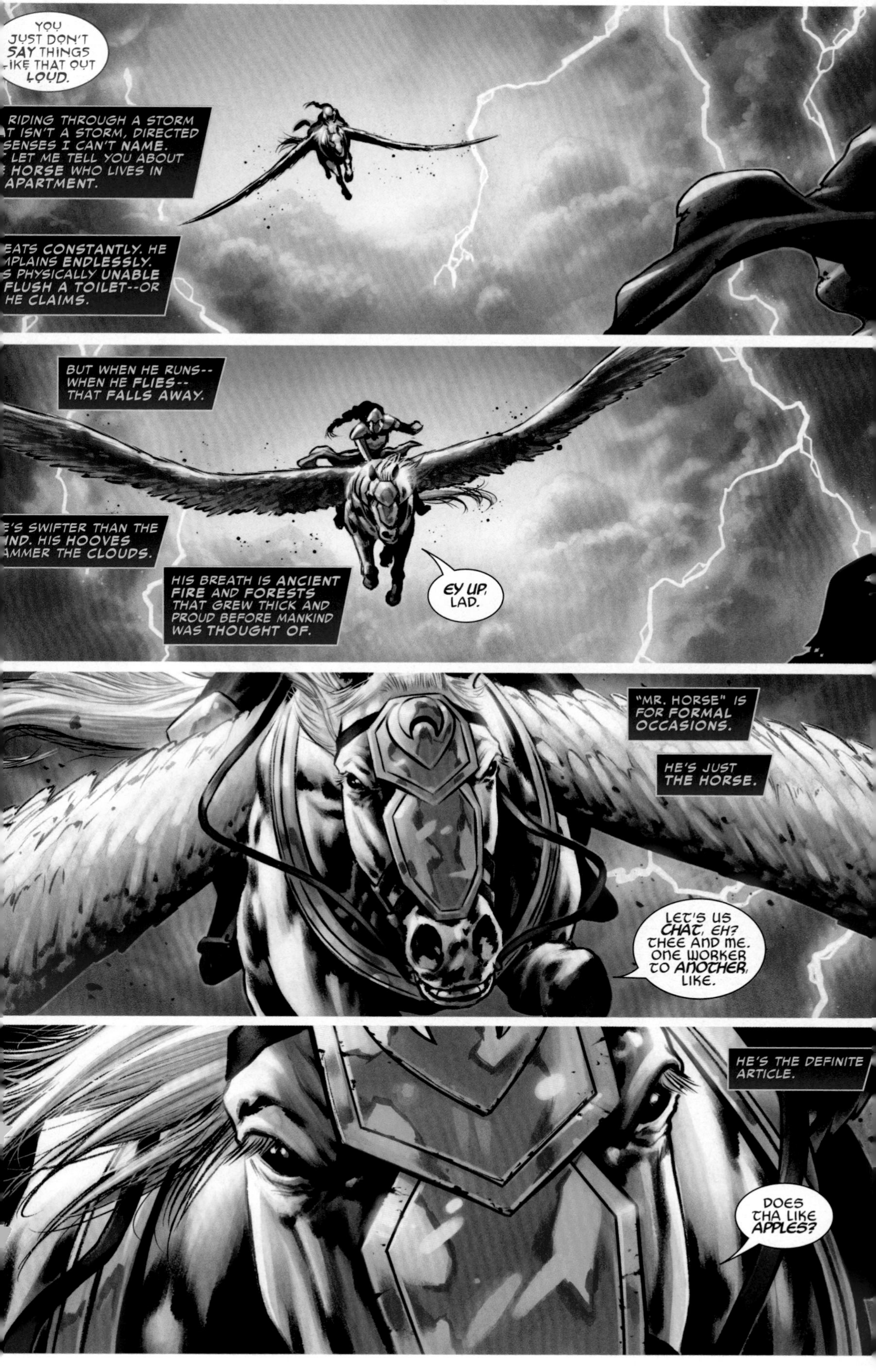
YOU JUST DON'T SAY THINGS -IKE THAT OUT LOUD.
RIDING THROUGH A STORM T ISN'T A STORM, DIRECTED SENSES I CAN'T NAME. LET ME TELL YOU ABOUT HORSE WHO LIVES IN APARTMENT.
EATS CONSTANTLY. HE MPLAINS ENDLESSLY. S PHYSICALLY UNABLE FLUSH A TOILET--OR HE CLAIMS.
BUT WHEN HE RUNS-- WHEN HE FLIES-- THAT FALLS AWAY.
E'S SWIFTER THAN THE IND. HIS HOOVES AMMER THE CLOUDS.
HIS BREATH IS ANCIENT FIRE AND FORESTS THAT GREW THICK AND PROUD BEFORE MANKIND WAS THOUGHT OF.
EY UP, LAD.
"MR. HORSE" IS FOR FORMAL OCCASIONS.
HE'S JUST THE HORSE.
LET'S US CHAT, EH? THEE AND ME. ONE WORKER TO ANOTHER, LIKE.
HE'S THE DEFINITE ARTICLE.
DOES THA LIKE APPLES?

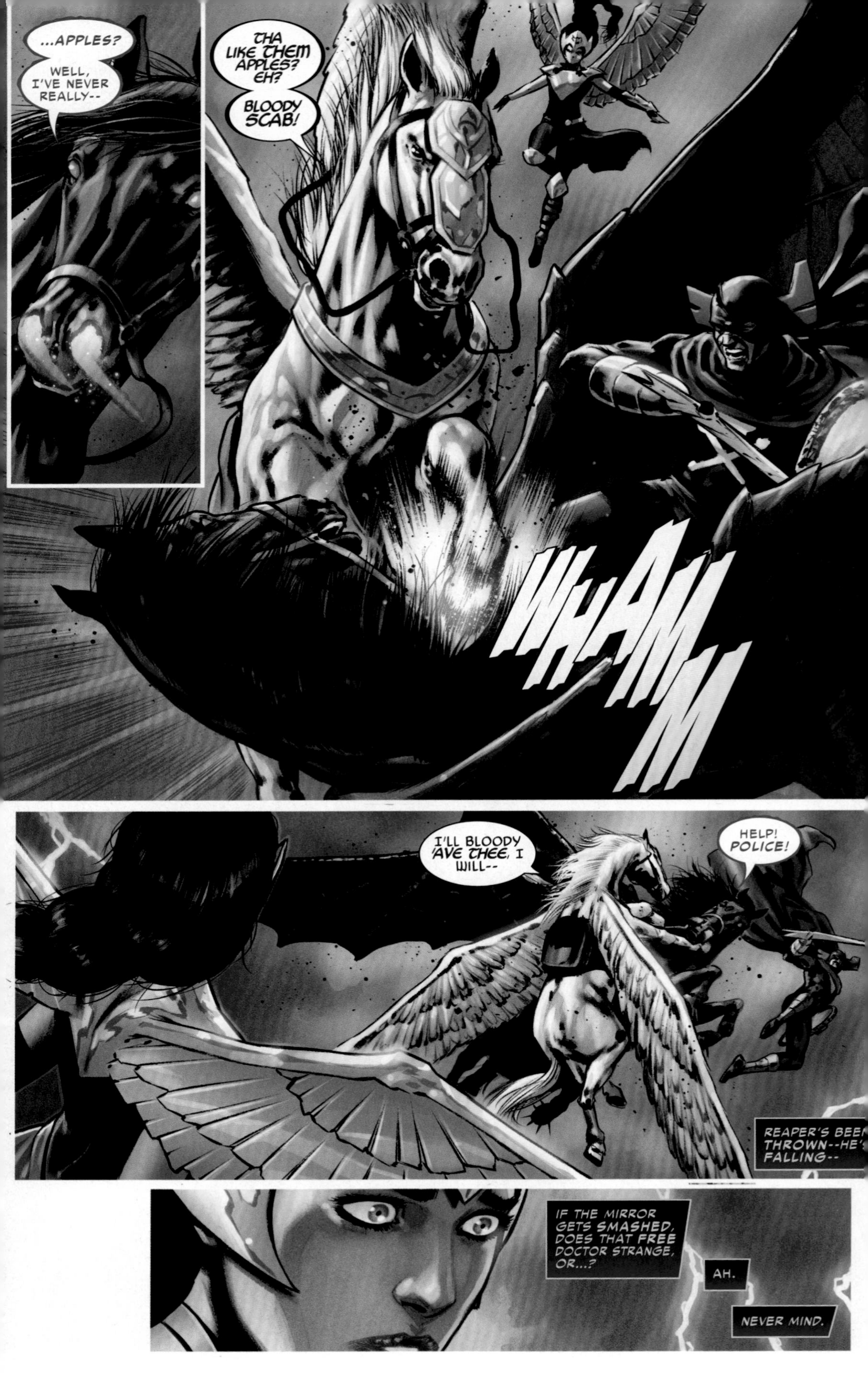
...APPLES?
WELL, I'VE NEVER REALLY--
THA LIKE THEM APPLES? EH?
BLOODY SCAB!
WHAMM
I'LL BLOODY 'AVE THEE, I WILL--
HELP! POLICE!
REAPER'S BEEN THROWN--HE'S FALLING--
IF THE MIRROR GETS SMASHED, DOES THAT FREE DOCTOR STRANGE, OR...?
AH.
NEVER MIND.

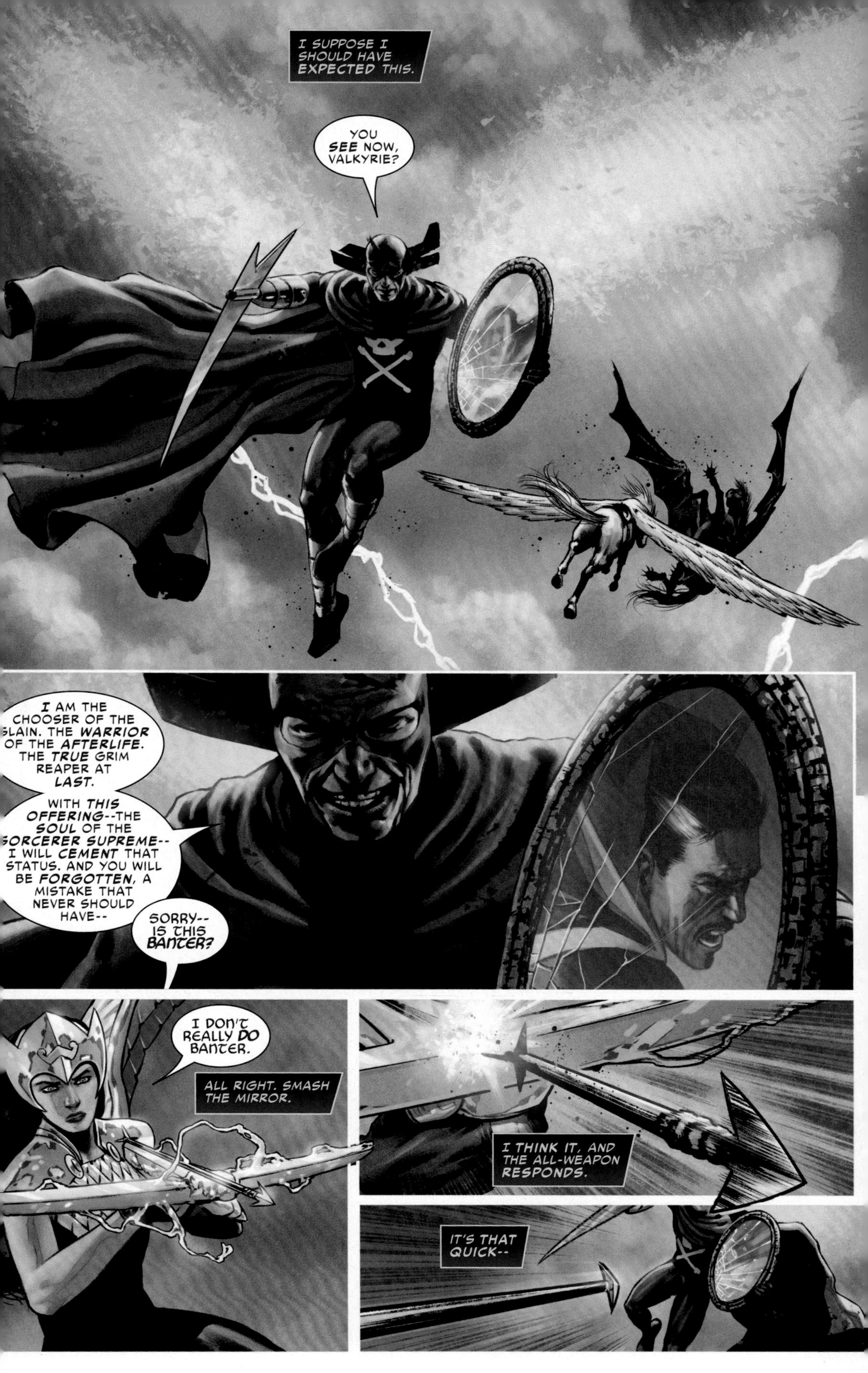
I SUPPOSE I SHOULD HAVE EXPECTED THIS.
YOU SEE NOW, VALKYRIE?
I AM THE CHOOSER OF THE SLAIN. THE WARRIOR OF THE AFTERLIFE. THE TRUE GRIM REAPER AT LAST.
WITH THIS OFFERING--THE SOUL OF THE SORCERER SUPREME--I WILL CEMENT THAT STATUS. AND YOU WILL BE FORGOTTEN, A MISTAKE THAT NEVER SHOULD HAVE--
SORRY-- IS THIS BANTER?
I DON'T REALLY DO BANTER.
ALL RIGHT. SMASH THE MIRROR.
I THINK IT, AND THE ALL-WEAPON RESPONDS.
IT'S THAT QUICK--

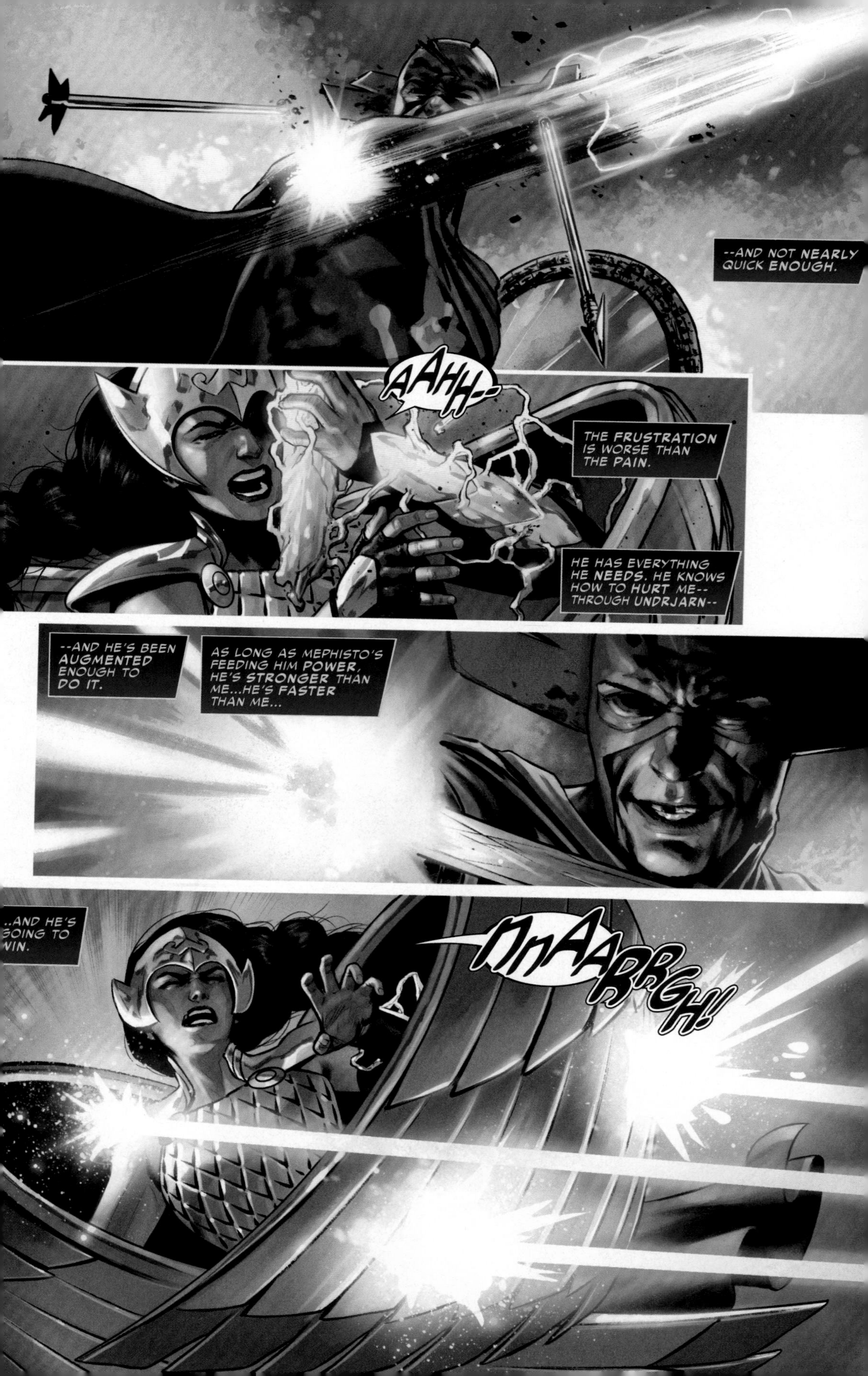
--AND NOT NEARLY QUICK ENOUGH.
AAHH--
THE FRUSTRATION IS WORSE THAN THE PAIN.
HE HAS EVERYTHING HE NEEDS. HE KNOWS HOW TO HURT ME--THROUGH UNDRJARN--
--AND HE'S BEEN AUGMENTED ENOUGH TO DO IT.
AS LONG AS MEPHISTO'S FEEDING HIM POWER, HE'S STRONGER THAN ME...HE'S FASTER THAN ME...
..AND HE'S GOING TO WIN.
NNAARRGH!

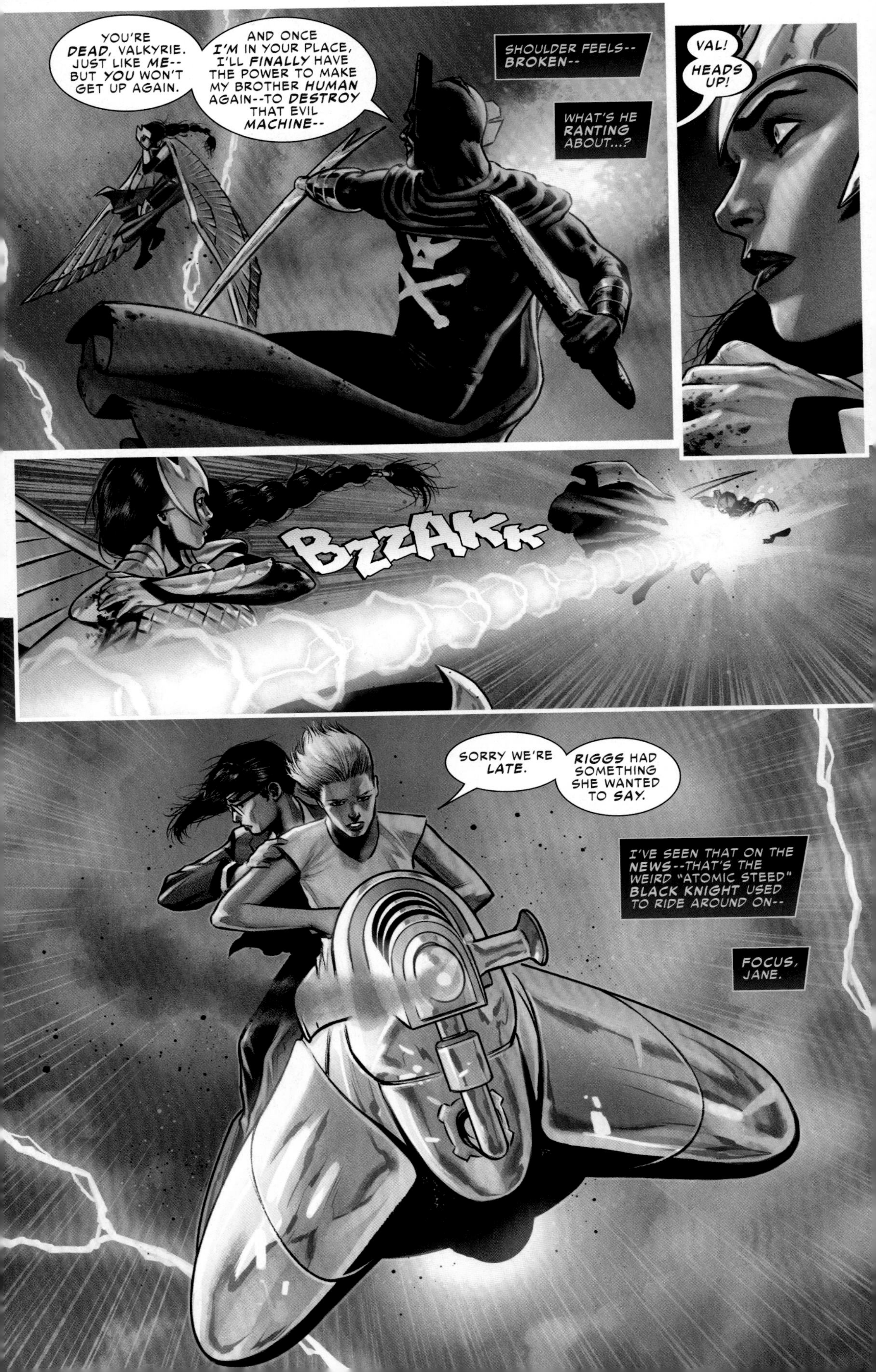
YOU'RE DEAD, VALKYRIE. JUST LIKE ME-- BUT YOU WON'T GET UP AGAIN.
AND ONCE I'M IN YOUR PLACE, I'LL FINALLY HAVE THE POWER TO MAKE MY BROTHER HUMAN AGAIN--TO DESTROY THAT EVIL MACHINE--
SHOULDER FEELS-- BROKEN--
WHAT'S HE RANTING ABOUT...?
VAL! HEADS UP!
BZZAKK
SORRY WE'RE LATE.
RIGGS HAD SOMETHING SHE WANTED TO SAY.
I'VE SEEN THAT ON THE NEWS--THAT'S THE WEIRD "ATOMIC STEED" BLACK KNIGHT USED TO RIDE AROUND ON--
FOCUS, JANE.

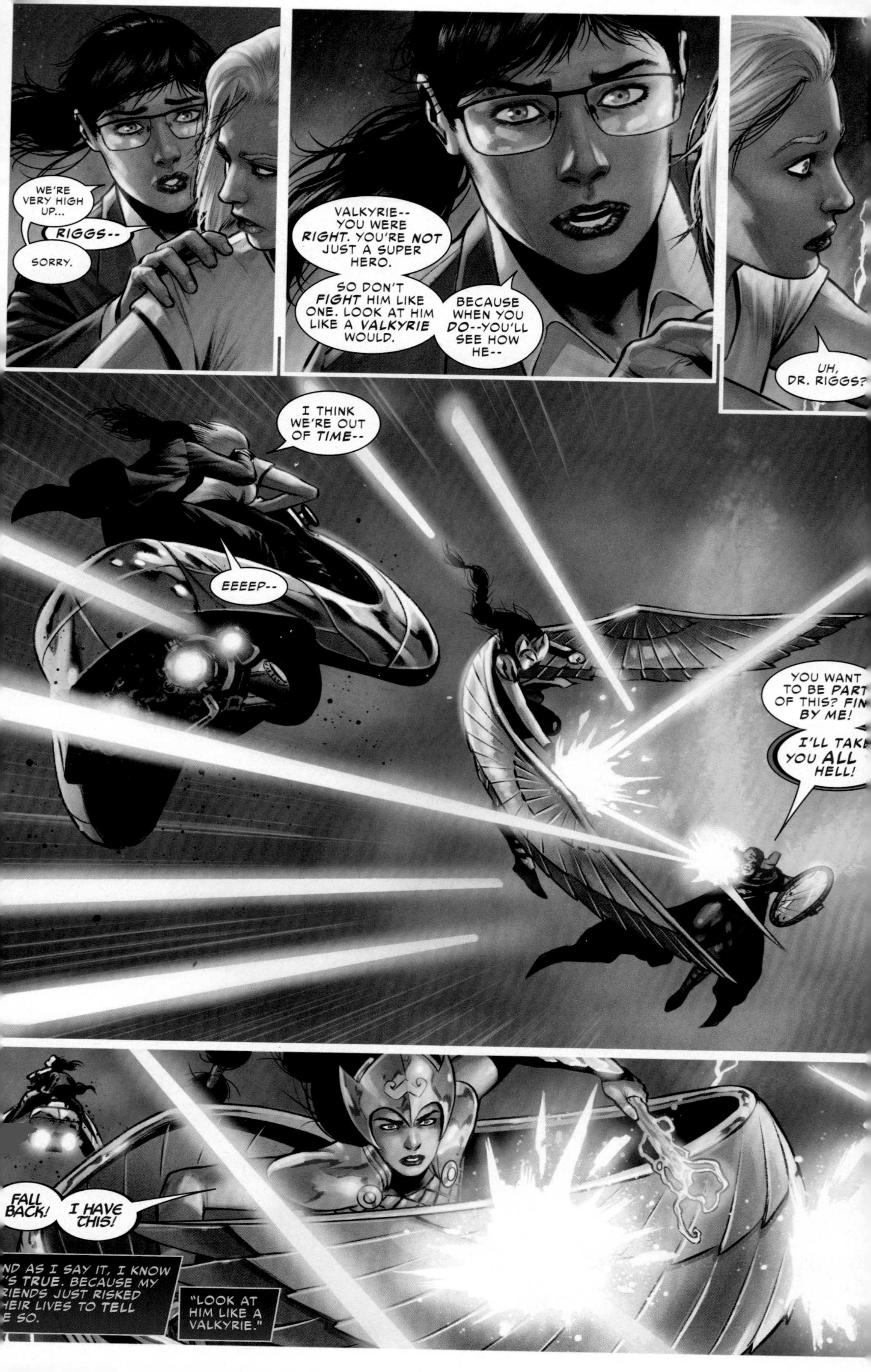
WE'RE VERY HIGH UP...
RIGGS--
SORRY.
VALKYRIE-- YOU WERE RIGHT. YOU'RE NOT JUST A SUPER HERO.
SO DON'T FIGHT HIM LIKE ONE. LOOK AT HIM LIKE A VALKYRIE WOULD.
BECAUSE WHEN YOU DO--YOU'LL SEE HOW HE--
UH, DR. RIGGS?
I THINK WE'RE OUT OF TIME--
EEEEP--
YOU WANT TO BE PART OF THIS? FIN BY ME!
I'LL TAK YOU ALL HELL!
FALL BACK!
I HAVE THIS!
ND AS I SAY IT, I KNOW 'S TRUE. BECAUSE MY RIENDS JUST RISKED HEIR LIVES TO TELL E SO.
"LOOK AT HIM LIKE A VALKYRIE."

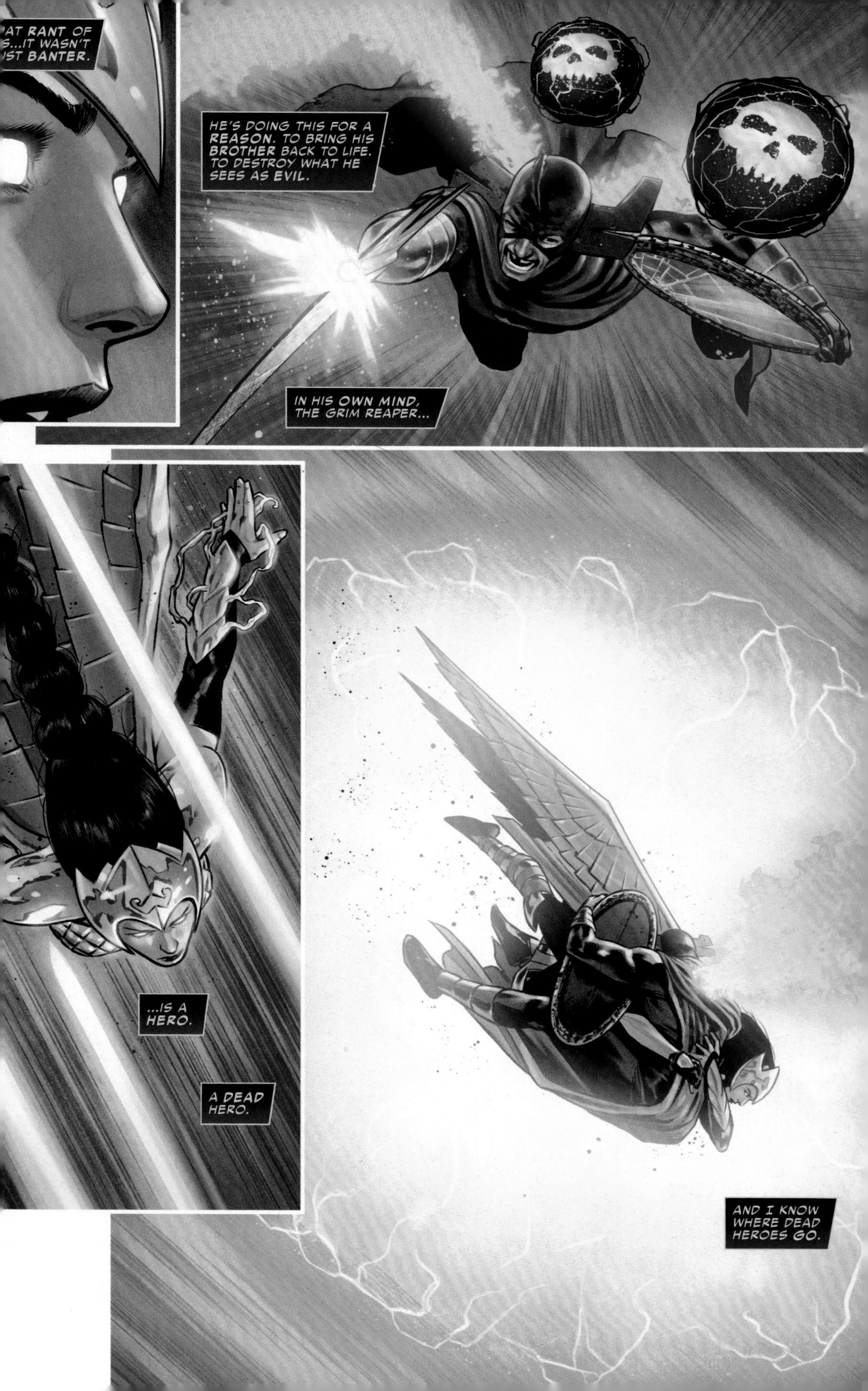
AT RANT OF
S...IT WASN'T
JST BANTER.
HE'S DOING THIS FOR A REASON. TO BRING HIS BROTHER BACK TO LIFE. TO DESTROY WHAT HE SEES AS EVIL.
IN HIS OWN MIND, THE GRIM REAPER...
...IS A HERO.
A DEAD HERO.
AND I KNOW WHERE DEAD HEROES GO.

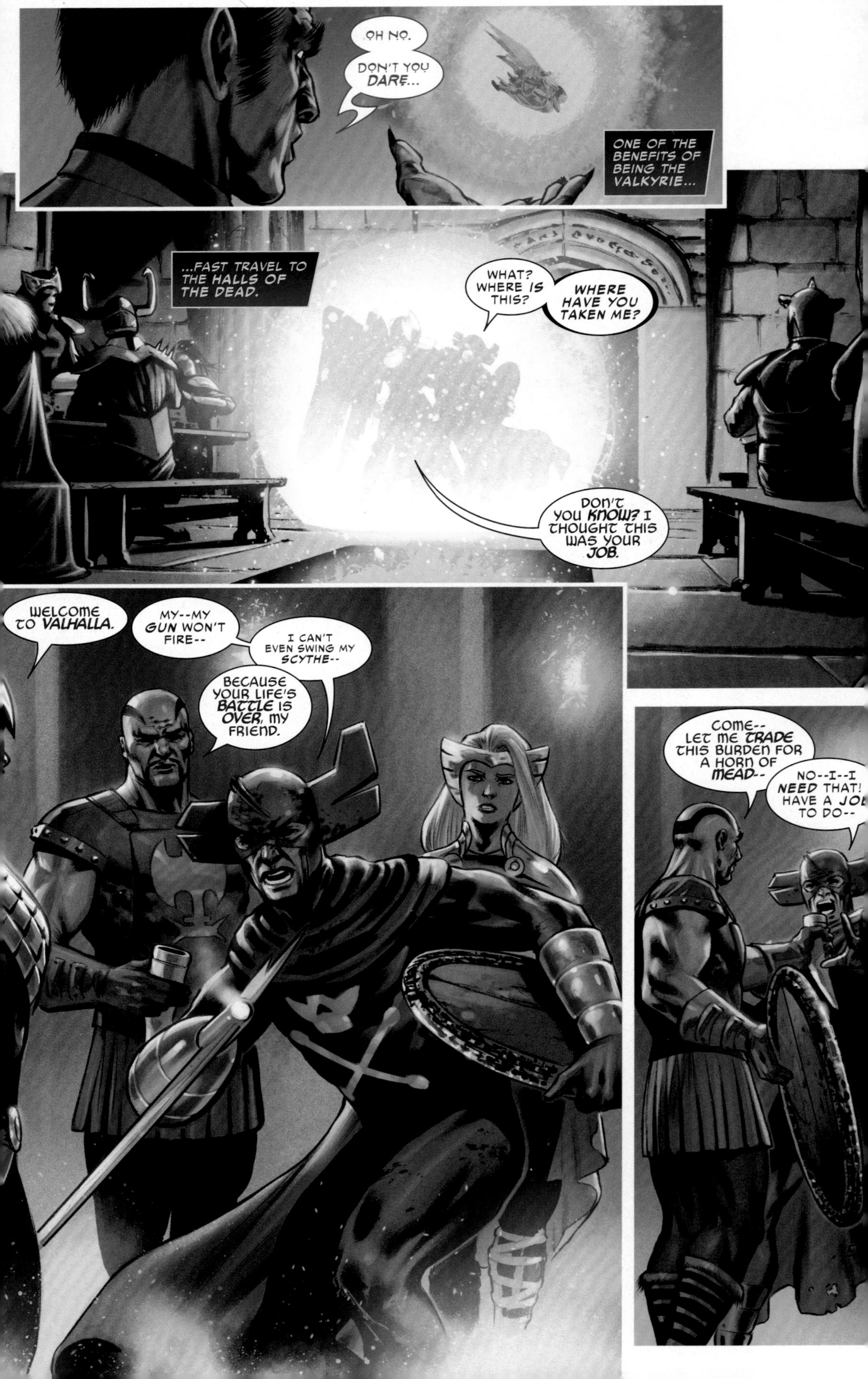
OH NO.
DON'T YOU DARE...
ONE OF THE BENEFITS OF BEING THE VALKYRIE...
...FAST TRAVEL TO THE HALLS OF THE DEAD.
WHAT? WHERE IS THIS?
WHERE HAVE YOU TAKEN ME?
DON'T YOU KNOW? I THOUGHT THIS WAS YOUR JOB.
WELCOME TO VALHALLA.
MY--MY GUN WON'T FIRE--
I CAN'T EVEN SWING MY SCYTHE--
BECAUSE YOUR LIFE'S BATTLE IS OVER, MY FRIEND.
COME-- LET ME TRADE THIS BURDEN FOR A HORN OF MEAD--
NO--I--I NEED THAT! HAVE A JO TO DO--

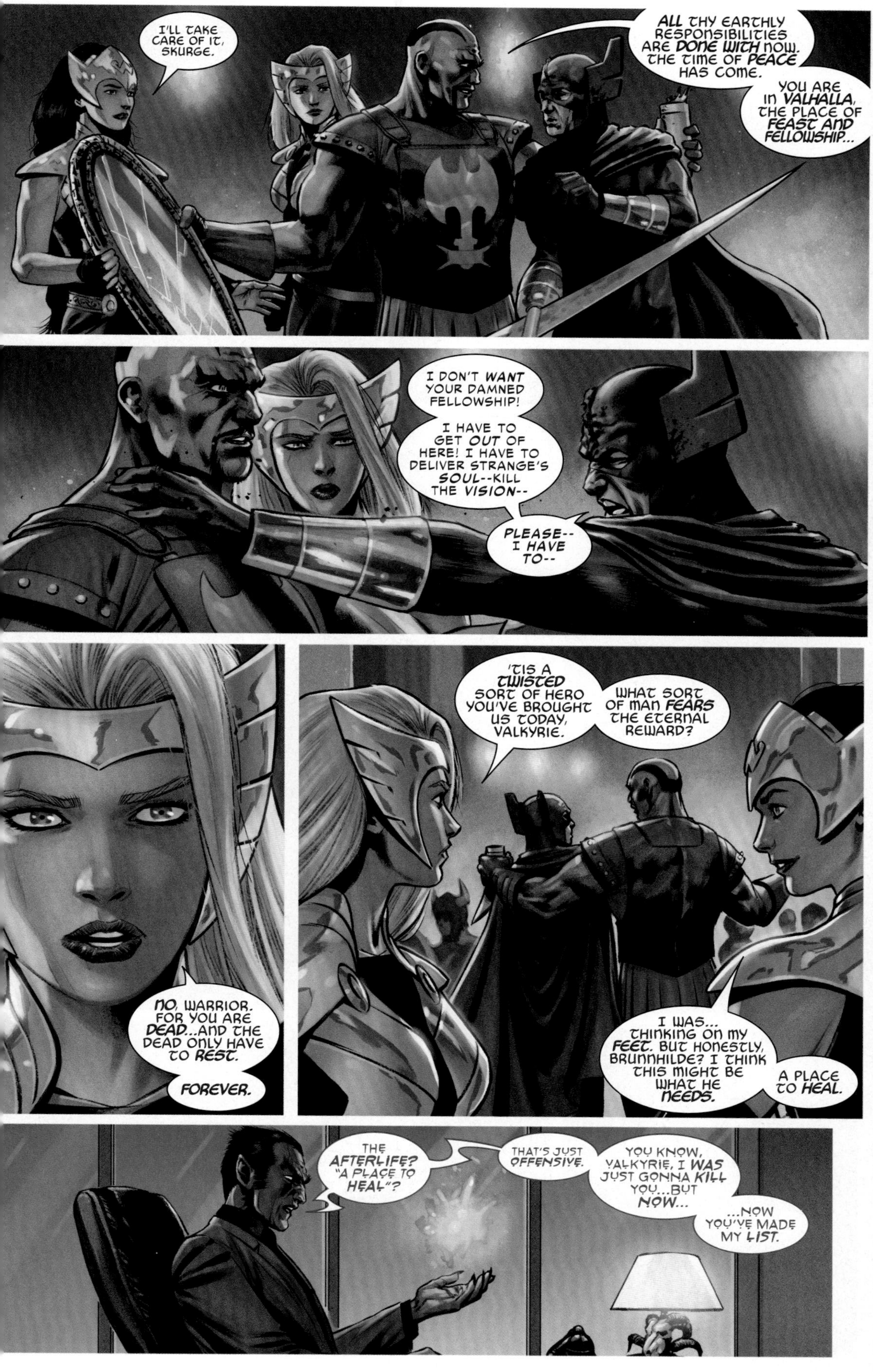
I'LL TAKE CARE OF IT, SKURGE.
ALL THY EARTHLY RESPONSIBILITIES ARE DONE WITH NOW. THE TIME OF PEACE HAS COME.
YOU ARE IN VALHALLA, THE PLACE OF FEAST AND FELLOWSHIP...
I DON'T WANT YOUR DAMNED FELLOWSHIP!
I HAVE TO GET OUT OF HERE! I HAVE TO DELIVER STRANGE'S SOUL--KILL THE VISION--
PLEASE-- I HAVE TO--
NO, WARRIOR. FOR YOU ARE DEAD...AND THE DEAD ONLY HAVE TO REST.
FOREVER.
'TIS A TWISTED SORT OF HERO YOU'VE BROUGHT US TODAY, VALKYRIE.
WHAT SORT OF MAN FEARS THE ETERNAL REWARD?
I WAS... THINKING ON MY FEET. BUT HONESTLY, BRUNNHILDE? I THINK THIS MIGHT BE WHAT HE NEEDS.
A PLACE TO HEAL.
THE AFTERLIFE? "A PLACE TO HEAL"?
THAT'S JUST OFFENSIVE.
YOU KNOW, VALKYRIE, I WAS JUST GONNA KILL YOU...BUT NOW...
...NOW YOU'VE MADE MY LIST.

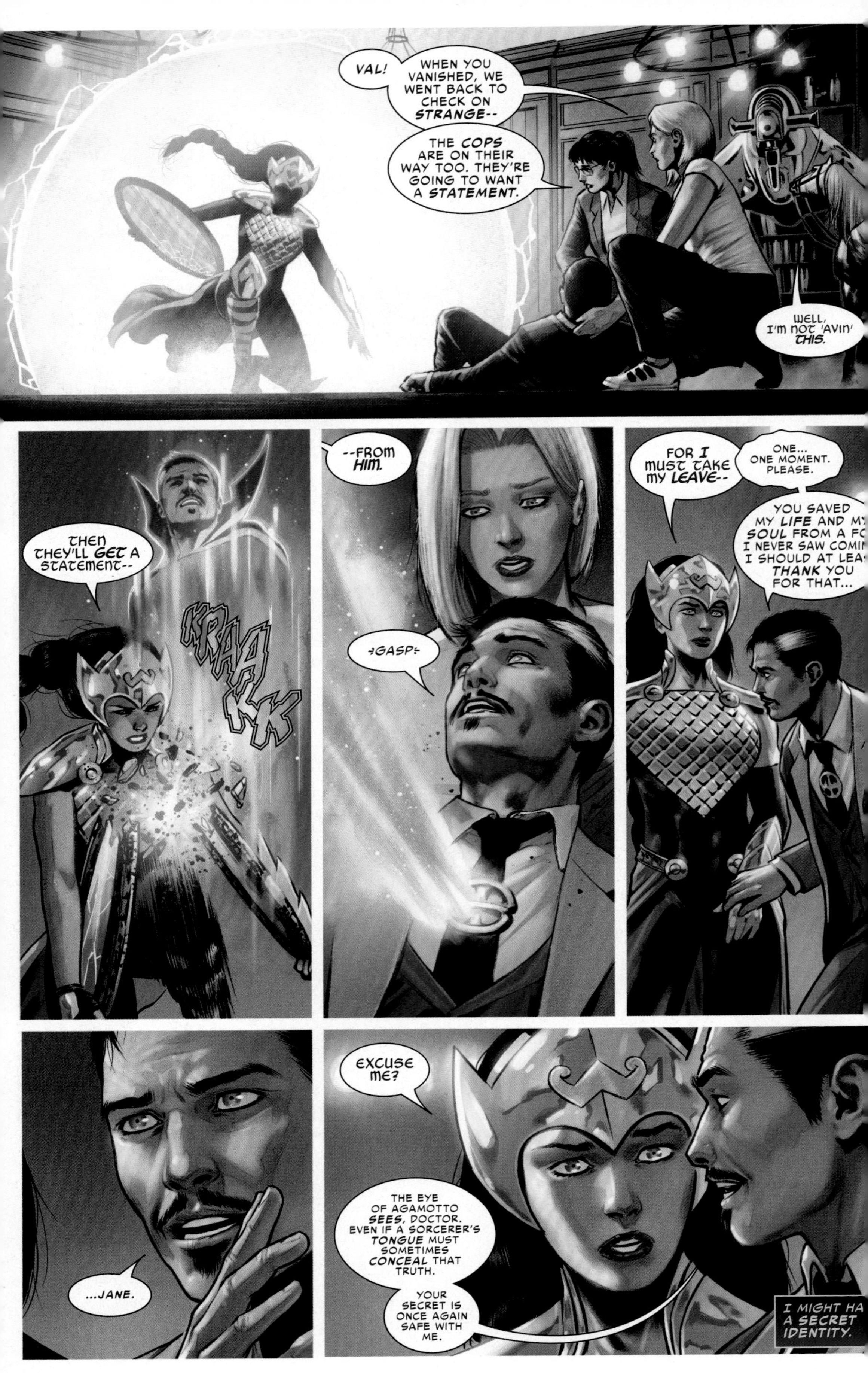
VAL!
WHEN YOU VANISHED, WE WENT BACK TO CHECK ON STRANGE--
THE COPS ARE ON THEIR WAY TOO. THEY'RE GOING TO WANT A STATEMENT.
WELL, I'M NOT 'AVIN' THIS.
THEN THEY'LL GET A STATEMENT--
KRAAKK
--FROM HIM.
GASP
FOR I MUST TAKE MY LEAVE--
ONE... ONE MOMENT. PLEASE.
YOU SAVED MY LIFE AND MY SOUL FROM A FO I NEVER SAW COMIN I SHOULD AT LEA THANK YOU FOR THAT...
...JANE.
EXCUSE ME?
THE EYE OF AGAMOTTO SEES, DOCTOR. EVEN IF A SORCERER'S TONGUE MUST SOMETIMES CONCEAL THAT TRUTH.
YOUR SECRET IS ONCE AGAIN SAFE WITH ME.
I MIGHT HA A SECRET IDENTITY.

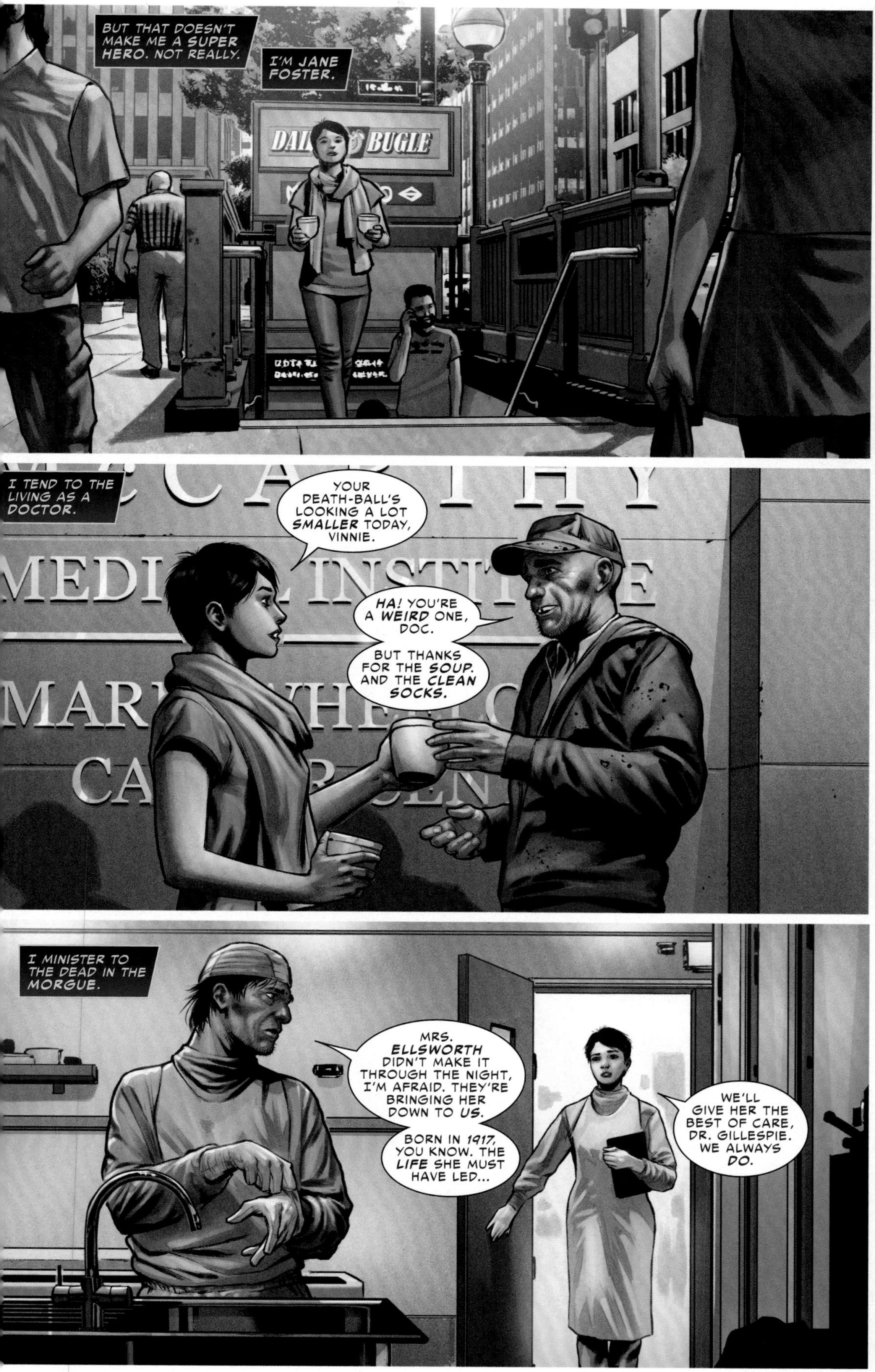
BUT THAT DOESN'T MAKE ME A SUPER HERO. NOT REALLY.
I'M JANE FOSTER.
DAILY BUGLE
I TEND TO THE LIVING AS A DOCTOR.
YOUR DEATH-BALL'S LOOKING A LOT SMALLER TODAY, VINNIE.
HA! YOU'RE A WEIRD ONE, DOC.
BUT THANKS FOR THE SOUP. AND THE CLEAN SOCKS.
I MINISTER TO THE DEAD IN THE MORGUE.
MRS. ELLSWORTH DIDN'T MAKE IT THROUGH THE NIGHT, I'M AFRAID. THEY'RE BRINGING HER DOWN TO US.
BORN IN 1917, YOU KNOW. THE LIFE SHE MUST HAVE LED...
WE'LL GIVE HER THE BEST OF CARE, DR. GILLESPIE. WE ALWAYS DO.

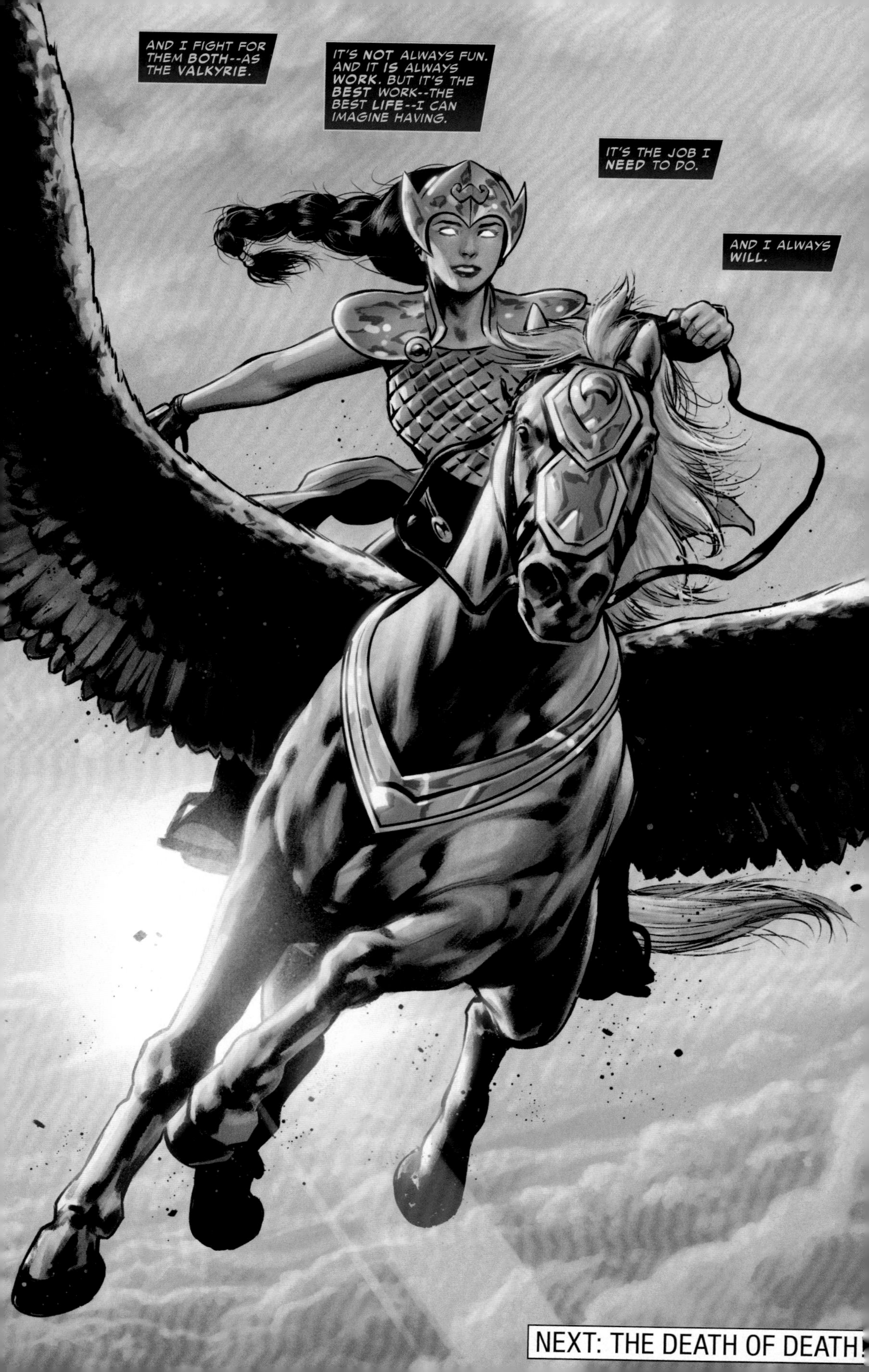
AND I FIGHT FOR THEM BOTH--AS THE VALKYRIE.
IT'S NOT ALWAYS FUN. AND IT IS ALWAYS WORK. BUT IT'S THE BEST WORK--THE BEST LIFE--I CAN IMAGINE HAVING.
IT'S THE JOB I NEED TO DO.
AND I ALWAYS WILL.
NEXT: THE DEATH OF DEATH!

Jane Foster refused to die.

I mean, I did straight up kill her back in THE MIGHTY THOR #705, which is definitely one of the issues I'm most proud of from my entire career. I cried writing that issue. Cried when Russell Dauterman's pages came in. Cried with fans after they read it. It was the culmination of a story I'd been working on for years. The story of Jane as cancer fighter/super hero.

That story ended, but Jane just wouldn't stay dead. I couldn't leave her dead. Even as she stood at the gates of Valhalla, poised to go on to the other side, to her well-earned eternal reward...she held back. Because she knew what I knew.

Jane Foster's story wasn't finished.

Her evolution into Valkyrie has been in the works ever since then. Since before then, really. Because I wanted Jane to fly again. To find a new place in the Marvel Universe. A new mission. New challenges.

And boy, does she have challenges coming her way. You ever tried to find a New York City apartment big enough for a winged horse?

Just like Jane's time as Thor, this will be a story set firmly in both the gritty mortal world and the ethereal, fantastical realms beyond this one. This is a story about life in New York City and death in Valhalla. About the cold slab of a hospital morgue and the golden throne of Asgard.

The Valkyries are dead, casualties of the greatest war the realms have ever known.

Who better to take up the mantle of the Choosers of the Slain...than the woman who refused to die?

Welcome back, Jane.

And as ever...stay worthy.

Jason Aaron
KC, June 2019

I've been thinking about death.

Partly for work. I write the IMMORTAL HULK book—death comes up. Partly... well, I'm not getting any younger, and the world isn't getting any safer. And even in the best possible circumstances, given a long enough time frame, the human body has a 100% failure rate.

The thing about death is what comes after. See, I'm more an agnostic than an atheist, but even so—I never quite got my head around that part.

Is it scary? Is it nirvanic? Am I missing the point?

Opinions differ.

It'd be nice if there were someone there for you, when the time came. Someone who could take your hand and show you what's next—maybe take you into it. Someone who was a little like a doctor. Someone who was a little like a super hero. Someone who would stand up for you and fight in your corner whether you were alive or dead or somewhere in between.

I mean, maybe this someone's learning the ropes a little. Maybe she's got a day job she has to keep and friends she has to look after, and maybe one of those friends is a horse. Maybe she's being targeted by the deadliest killer on the planet on the orders of a mysterious figure with an agenda of their own.

But still. It'd be nice.

Welcome to VALKYRIE, Jane Foster. Hope you survive the...

...hmmm.

Al Ewing

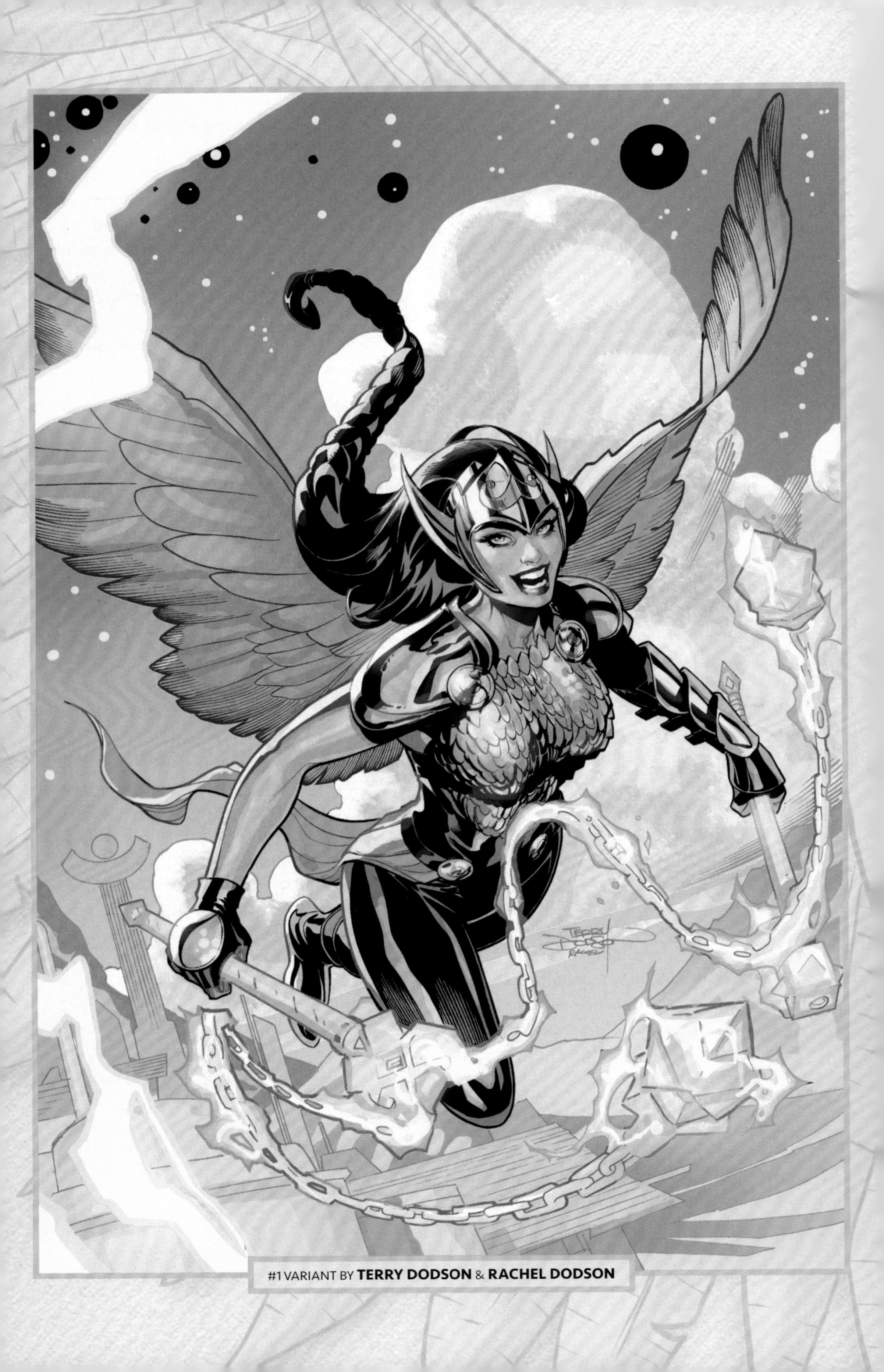

#1 VARIANT BY **TERRY DODSON** & **RACHEL DODSON**

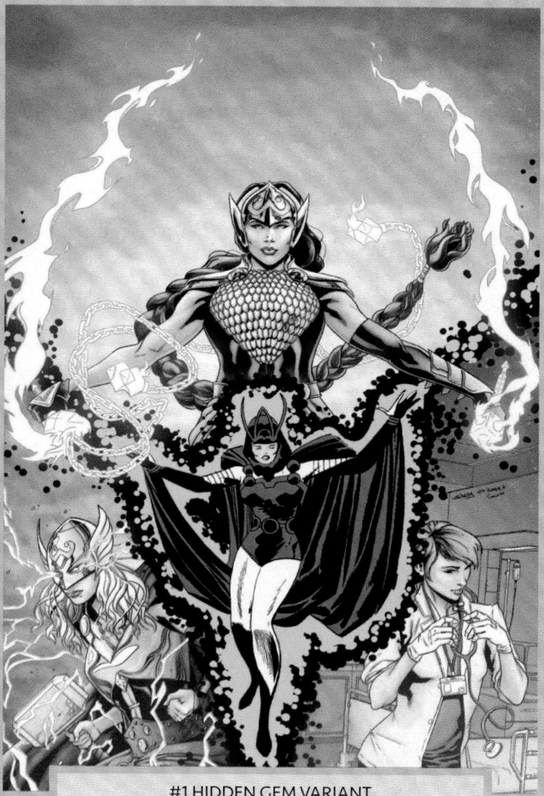

#1 HIDDEN GEM VARIANT
BY **WILL SLINEY**, **JACK KIRBY**,
VINCE COLLETTA & **MORRY HOLLOWELL**

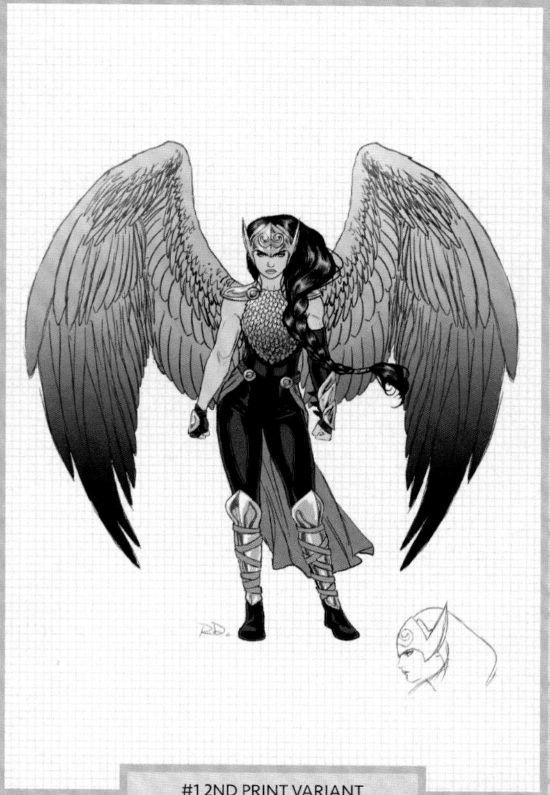

#1 2ND PRINT VARIANT
BY **RUSSELL DAUTERMAN**

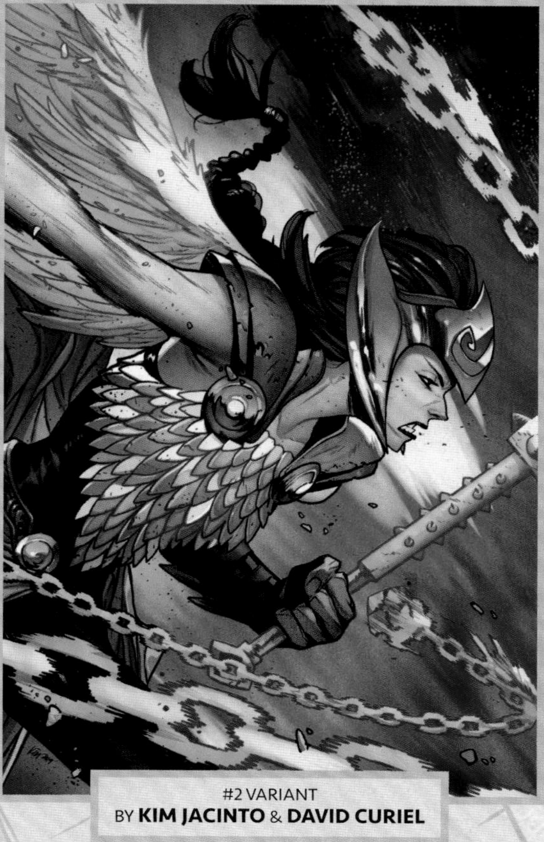

#2 VARIANT
BY **KIM JACINTO** & **DAVID CURIEL**

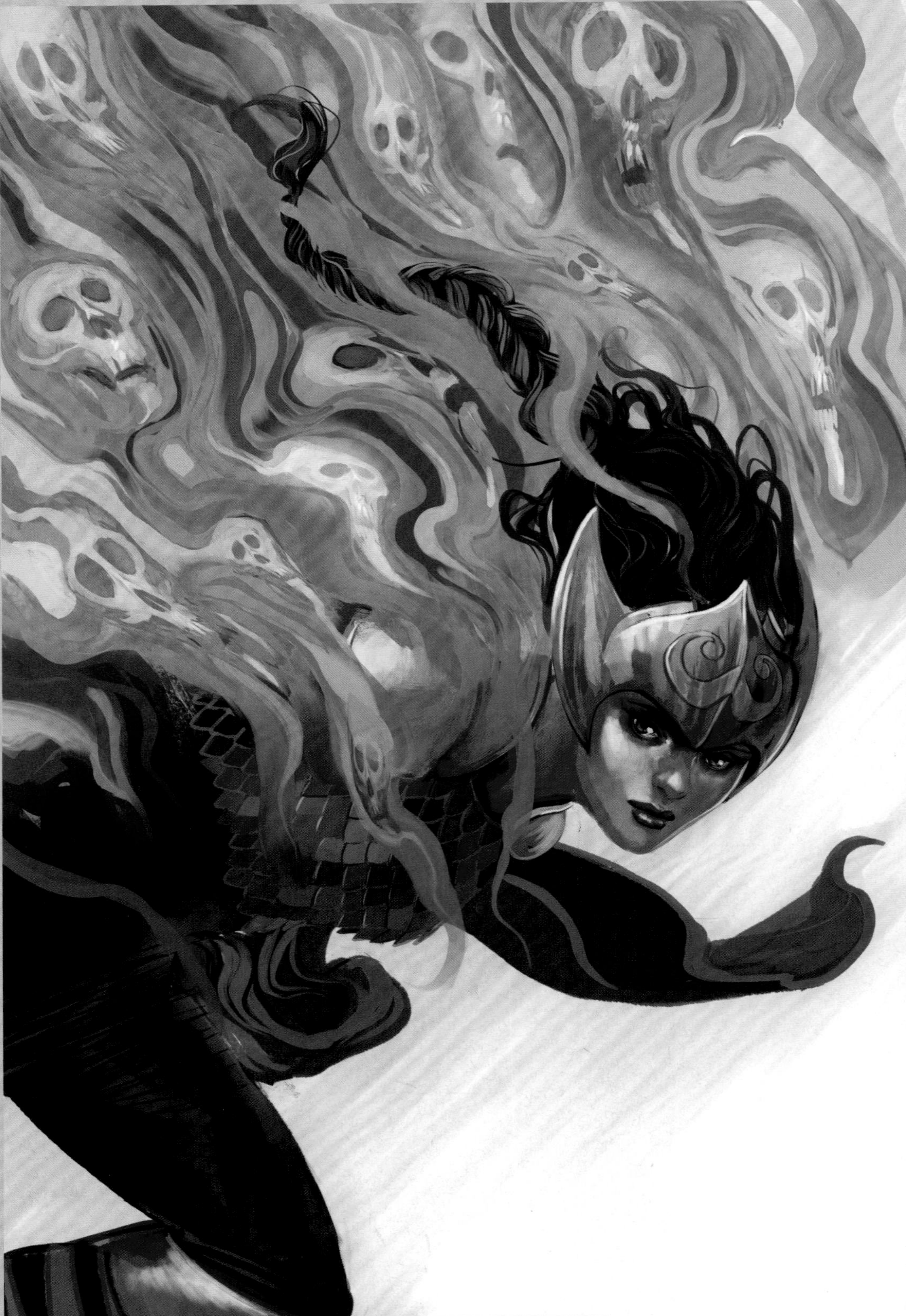

#3 VARIANT BY **STEPHANIE HANS**

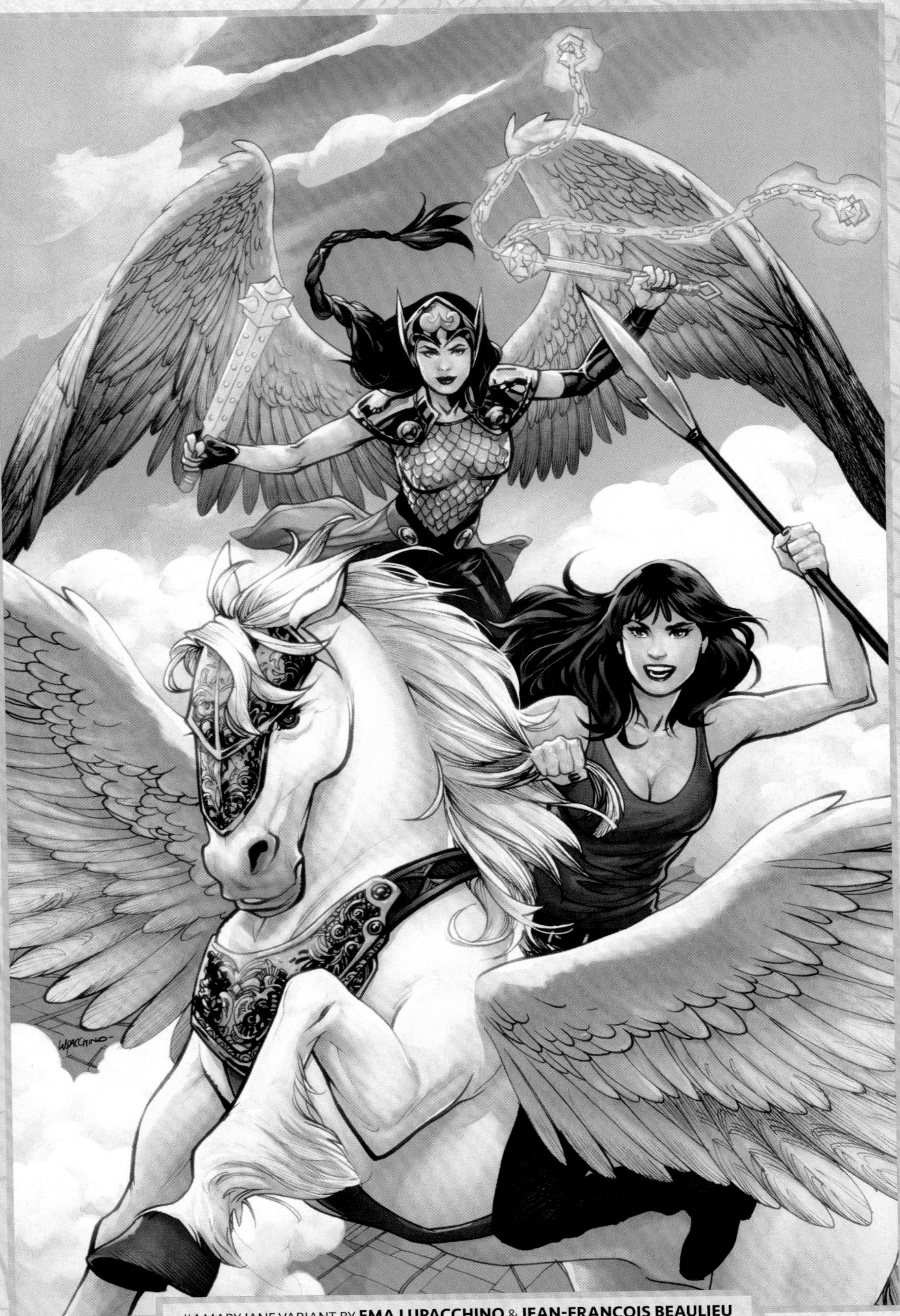

#4 MARY JANE VARIANT BY **EMA LUPACCHINO** & **JEAN-FRANÇOIS BEAULIEU**

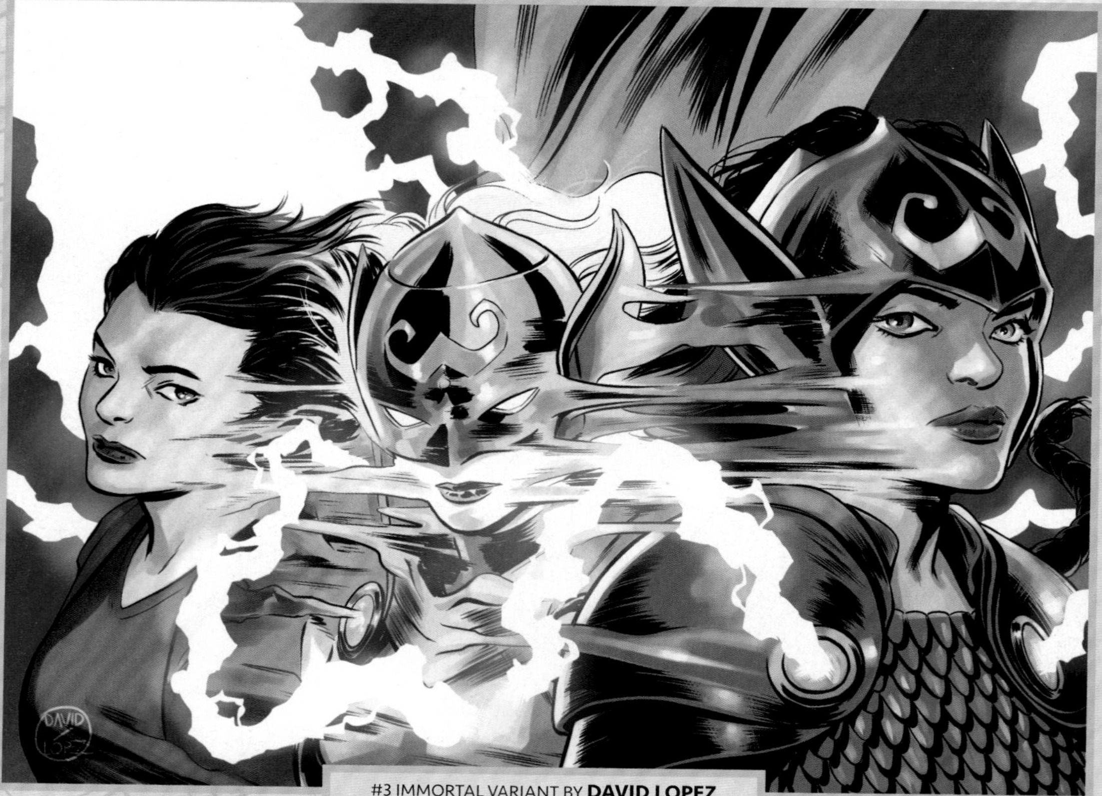

#3 IMMORTAL VARIANT BY **DAVID LOPEZ**

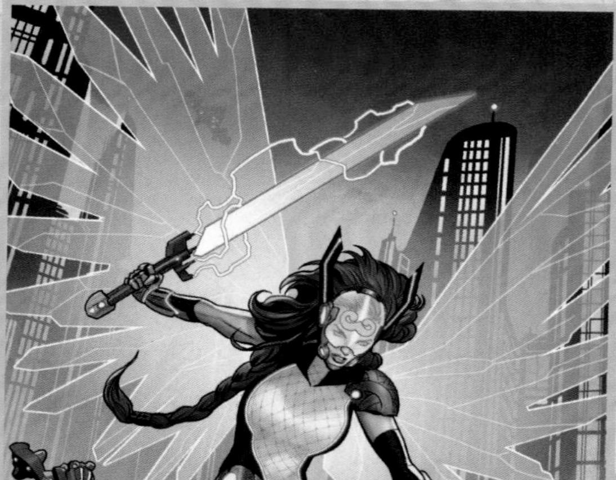

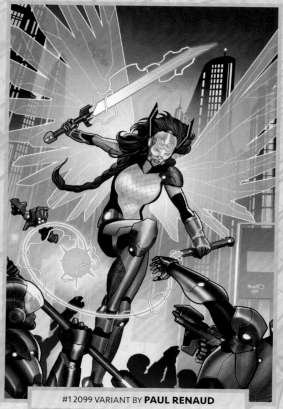

#1 2099 VARIANT BY **PAUL RENAUD**

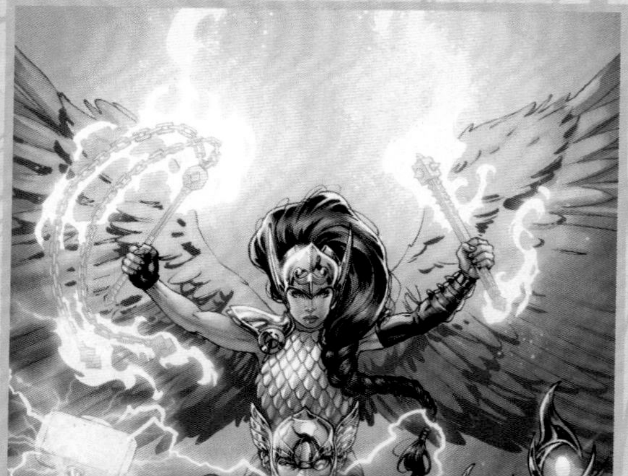

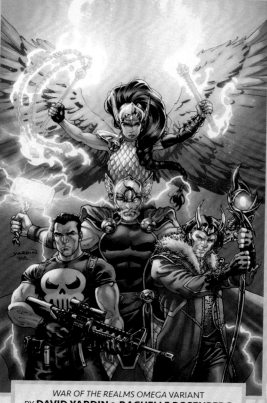

WAR OF THE REALMS OMEGA VARIANT
BY **DAVID YARDIN** & **RACHELLE ROSENBERG**